Globalization and Labor

GLOBALIZATION
Series Editors
Manfred B. Steger
Illinois State University, University of Hawai'i, Manoa,
and Royal Melbourne Institute of Technology
and
Terrell Carver
University of Bristol

"Globalization" has become *the* buzzword of our time. But what does it mean? Rather than forcing a complicated social phenomenon into a single analytical framework, this series seeks to present globalization as a multidimensional process constituted by complex, often contradictory interactions of global, regional, and local aspects of social life. Since conventional disciplinary borders and lines of demarcation are losing their old rationales in a globalizing world, authors in this series apply an interdisciplinary framework to the study of globalization. In short, the main purpose and objective of this series is to support subject-specific inquiries into the dynamics and effects of contemporary globalization and its varying impacts across, between, and within societies.

Globalization and War
Tarak Barkawi

Globalization and American
* Popular Culture*
Lane Crothers

Globalization and Militarism
Cynthia Enloe

Globalization and Law
Adam Gearey

Globalization and Feminist
* Activism*
Mary E. Hawkesworth

Globalization and Terrorism
Jamal R. Nassar

Globalization and Culture
Jan Nederveen Pieterse

Globalization and International
* Political Economy*
Mark Rupert and M. Scott Solomon

Globalism, Second Edition
Manfred B. Steger

Rethinking Globalism
Edited by
Manfred B. Steger

Globalization and Labor
Dimitris Stevis and Terry Boswell

Globaloney
Michael Veseth

 Supported by the Globalization Research Center at the University of Hawai'i, Manoa

GLOBALIZATION AND LABOR
Democratizing Global Governance

DIMITRIS STEVIS
AND TERRY BOSWELL

ROWMAN & LITTLEFIELD PUBLISHERS, INC.
Lanham • Boulder • New York • Toronto • Plymouth, UK

ROWMAN & LITTLEFIELD PUBLISHERS, INC.

Published in the United States of America
by Rowman & Littlefield Publishers, Inc.
A wholly owned subsidiary of The Rowman & Littlefield Publishing Group, Inc.
4501 Forbes Boulevard, Suite 200, Lanham, Maryland 20706
www.rowmanlittlefield.com

Estover Road, Plymouth PL6 7PY, United Kingdom

British Library Cataloguing in Publication Information Available

Library of Congress Cataloging-in-Publication Data

Stevis, Dimitris.
  Globalization and labor : democratizing global governance / Dimitris Stevis and
Terry Boswell.
      p. cm. — (Globalization)
  Includes bibliographical references and index.
  ISBN-13: 978-0-7425-3784-2 (cloth : alk. paper)
  ISBN-10: 0-7425-3784-6 (cloth : alk. paper)
  ISBN-13: 978-0-7425-3785-9 (pbk. : alk. paper)
  ISBN-10: 0-7425-3785-4 (pbk. : alk. paper)
  1. International labor activities. 2. Labor unions—Political activity. 3. Corporate
governance. 4. Labor policy. 5. Globalization—Economic aspects. 6. Social justice.
I. Boswell, Terry. II. Title.
  HD6475.A1S74 2008
  331.88091—dc22

                                                          2007002187

Printed in the United States of America

⊗™ The paper used in this publication meets the minimum requirements of
American National Standard for Information Sciences—Permanence of Paper
for Printed Library Materials, ANSI/NISO Z39.48-1992.

CONTENTS

In Memoriam: Terry Boswell, 1955–2006

Terry Boswell learned that he had ALS (amyotrophic lateral sclerosis, also known as Lou Gehrig's disease) in 1998. Once diagnosed, ALS patients usually die within two or three years, but Terry was a remarkable survivor—supported by his family, his institution, and his friends. He passed away on June 1, 2006, leaving behind an influential body of work in the areas of stratification and labor markets, revolutions and the political economy of the world system, and global labor politics. Born in 1955 in Yreka, California, Terry grew up in Kentucky and Arizona mining country—places that would leave a stamp on his sociological and political concerns. He attended the University of Arizona, in Tucson, where he stayed for his PhD in sociology, organizing a vibrant study group that brought together faculty and graduate students from various disciplines over many productive years.

As a student of societal stratification and labor markets, Terry worked, often with present and former graduate students, to understand the absolute and relative importance of race and class in labor markets and in labor movement politics. In a number of articles and books addressing these questions, Terry and his collaborators cast light on the parts played by paternalism, migration, union strength, minority strikebreaking, and institutionalized racial inclusion in worker and union fortunes. This work stretches from "A Split Labor Market Analysis of Discrimination against Chinese Immigrants, 1850–1880" (*American Sociological Review*, 1986) to *Racial Competition and Class Solidarity* (2007), with Cliff Brown, John Brueggemann, and Ralph

Peters. His interest in global democracy motivated a number of works, including *The Spiral of Capitalism and Socialism: Toward Global Democracy* (2000), with Christopher Chase-Dunn, and this volume. As a student of inequality and exploitation, labor organization, and revolution, Terry wrote important works with Linda Beer, William Dixon, Jeffrey Kentor, and Dimitris Stevis and founded a major work in progress on international clusters of revolutionary activity and social movements that have affected global history (with Joseph N. Cohen and April Linton).

Given Terry Boswell's extraordinary productivity and accomplishments, one might think that he spent all of his time working. Terry *was* amazingly committed to his work, and he was a public sociologist long before the term was common. He was a great colleague, leader, and example during his twenty-two years at Emory University. But he always found time for his family, friends, students, and hobbies. Terry was a sculptor, working mainly with metal and found objects. He loved baseball (American Sociological Association meetings always included a trip to the baseball stadium), modern art, Mexican food, cheap beer and expensive champagne, and travel (especially to Mexico, London, and the beach). He was loving father to Kate and Nick Boswell. He will be missed, and his presence will remain.

ACKNOWLEDGMENTS

Terry and I met while we were graduate students in sociology and political science, respectively, at the University of Arizona. Our friendship was shaped by various events. One of them was an effort to unionize graduate assistants. Another was our participation in a study group that brought together faculty and graduate students from anthropology, history, political science, and sociology, and that also provided the core for some extraordinarily fun social activities. After completing our degrees, we both pursued different aspects of our research agendas, but in the early 1990s we started talking about global labor politics, a long-standing interest for both of us. While at the beach in San Diego, Barry Gills invited us to contribute an article to an issue on globalization and the politics of resistance that he was editing for *New Political Economy*. Shortly thereafter, Daniel Cornfield and Christopher Chase-Dunn invited us to submit articles to thematic issues of *Work and Occupations* and the *Journal of Worlds-Systems Research*. We want to thank all of them for enabling us to put our thoughts on paper. Our collaboration continued until Terry's death, and his influence will shape much of my future work.

Over the years we have benefited from the generosity, advice, and comments of many people, some of whom prefer to remain anonymous. We would like to take the opportunity to thank them. They include Robin Alexander, Louise Amoore, Jim Baker, Peter Bakvis, Dick Blin, Ron Blum, Philip Bowyer, Jeremy Brecher, Kate Bronfenbrenner, Benedicte Bull, Joyce Campos Miranda, Jim Catterson, Julio Cesar

Guerrero, Christopher Chase-Dunn, Hyewon Chong, Lance Compa, Angela Cornell, Daniel Cornfield, Hermes Costa, Matt Davies, Michele Descolonges, Eduardo Diaz, Klaus Franz, Brian Fredricks, Dan Gallin, Paul Garver, Barry Gills, Reg Green, Eric Griego, Jeffrey Harrod, Pharis Harvey, Susan Hayter, Teresa Healy, Marion Hellmann, Andrew Herod, Owen Herrnstadt, Alex Hicks, Katherine Hochstetler, Christy Hoffman, Jenny Holdcroft, Jens Huhn, Tom Jenkins, Rob Johnston, Dwight Justice, Sheila Katz, Jerome Levinson, April Linton, Fernando Lopes, Benedicto Martinez, Thomas Metz, Sister Susan Mika, John Mondéjar, Eric Myers, Marsha Niemeijer, Veronica Nilsson, Tim Noonan, Robert O'Brien, Marta Ojeda, Kostas Papadakis, Marina Patriarka, Viviana Patroni, Paola Pinoargote, Duncan Pruett, Teofilo Reyes, Jorge Robles, Anabella Rosemberg, Lucien Royer, Magnus Ryner, Valter Sanches, Penny Schantz, Christoph Scherrer, Robert Steiert, Peter Unterweger, Fons Vannjeuwenhuyse, Peter Waterman, Don Wells, Lilli Wilcox-Poulsen, Ed Williams, and Gaye Yilmaz.

Many thanks to Susan McEachern, Sarah Wood, Jehanne Schweitzer, Renée Legatt, and Jennifer Knerr at Rowman & Littlefield for the professional work and their patience. They made it possible, as did Manfred Steger and Terrell Carver, the editors of the series, who invited us to contribute this volume.

Finally, our deepest appreciation to Toni Atkinson, Dan Gallin, and Jeff Harrod for their detailed and thoughtful comments on the whole volume.

ABBREVIATIONS

AFL	American Federation of Labor
AFL-CIO	American Federation of Labor–Congress of Industrial Organizations
BWI	Building and Wood Workers' International (former International Federation of Building and Wood Workers)
CIO	Congress of Industrial Organizations
EMF	European Metalworkers' Federation
ETUC	European Trade Union Confederation
EU	European Union
EWC	European Works Council
FTAA	Free Trade Area of the Americas
GATT	General Agreement on Tariffs and Trade
GUF	global union federation (former international trade secretariat)
ICEM	International Federation of Chemical, Energy, Mine, and General Workers' Unions
ICF	International Federation of Chemical, Energy, and General Workers' Unions
ICFTU	International Confederation of Free Trade Unions
IFA	International Framework Agreement
IFBWW	International Federation of Building and Wood Workers
IFC	International Finance Corporation (part of the World Bank)
IFJ	International Federation of Journalists

IFTU	International Federation of Trade Unions
ILO	International Labour Organization
IMF	International Metalworkers' Federation
IMF	International Monetary Fund
ITF	International Transport Workers' Federation
ITGLWF	International Textile, Garment, and Leather Workers' Federation
ITO	International Trade Organization
ITS	international trade secretariat (now global union federation)
ITUC	International Trade Union Confederation
IUF	International Union of Food, Agricultural, Hotel, Restaurant, Catering, Tobacco, and Allied Workers' Associations
Mercosur	Mercado Común del Sur, or Market of the South
NAALC	North American Agreement on Labor Cooperation
NAFTA	North American Free Trade Agreement
OECD	Organization for Economic Cooperation and Development
PSI	Public Services International
RILU	Red International of Labor Unions
SSI	Second Socialist International
TUAC	Trade Union Advisory Committee to the Organization for Economic Cooperation and Development
TUC	Trade Union Congress
UAW	United Automobile, Aerospace, and Agricultural Implement Workers of America
UNI	Union Network International
WCC	World Company Council
WCL	World Confederation of Labour
WFTU	World Federation of Trade Unions
WTO	World Trade Organization
WWC	World Works Council

INTRODUCTION

The formation of the World Trade Organization (WTO) in 1995 was heralded as evidence that liberal globalization that values growth over equity had emerged hegemonic and uncontested. Henceforth, the WTO would govern global integration by facilitating the negotiation of rules and the resolution of disputes. Those who called for more transparent and equitable governance were dismissed as radicals, utopians, or misinformed—until they burst upon the world stage at the WTO's 1999 Ministerial Conference in Seattle. To underscore that these objections were not temporary, the World Social Forum, which first met in Porto Alegre, Brazil, in 2001, has been motivated by the belief that "another world"—a more democratic world—"is possible."[1] Labor, increasingly represented by global union organizations, was present in Seattle and has been present at all subsequent forums calling for the democratization of the global political economy.[2]

In light of this renewed activism, some analysts and activists argue that unions are rising, however cautiously, to the challenges of global capitalism.[3] Others suggest that these efforts are too timid.[4] We find elements that we agree with in both accounts and want to highlight what is hopeful as well as the real obstacles faced by unions.[5] In order to do so, we examine global union politics as an important example of global societal politics whose rich history is matched by very few social movements. For this reason, we have chosen to take a historical approach because we think that the ways in which societal entities are responding to liberal globalization are as much affected by their historical trajectories as they are affected by more current developments.

We argue that the trend toward global integration, increasingly shaped by institutions of global governance that establish the rules of globalization, presents labor with both opportunities and challenges. While global integration forces unions to consider global collaboration, its uneven pace and its bias toward liberalization and away from social equity can well aggravate existing differences among workers and create new ones.

We explore these dynamics by focusing on global union organizations and globalization at two related levels. Our first central question is whether global union organizations are becoming stronger and more influential within the world of global union politics or, stated differently, whether there is evidence of global union governance. Evidence that these organizations are becoming more influential would mean that their various affiliates have found ways to bridge historical divisions and address emerging problems. Evidence that these organizations remain marginal would suggest the opposite. Of course, there are many variations within this range, variations that we plan to address in this volume.

Global union politics is characterized by one of the longest-standing networks of organizations in all societal politics. We know enough to avoid inferring that the presence of organizations implies collaboration. They may very well obstruct further collaboration by asserting the autonomy of the participants, as it happens with intergovernmental organizations like the United Nations. Yet, we do not think that there can be a strong global union politics without strong global organizations that will allow national unions to negotiate their differences and forge common programs of action or, as noted above, to govern global union politics. Our analysis would be incomplete and misleading, however, if we simply examined the architecture of global union governance without evaluating the world visions that global union organizations propose. More specifically, are global union organizations aiming at democratizing our world? Are they helping make another world possible? In short, this is an examination of both the form and the social purpose of global union governance.

Our second central question is whether global union organizations have had any influence on global public and private governance. The influence of global unions on global governance is important in its own right. It is well known, however, that global economic organizations and corporations have not been enthusiastic about labor rules and social regulation, in general. It is thus tempting to be very pessimistic about global union politics as a result of its limited influence on global governance, so far. Yet, evidence that unions have forged common agendas and strategies, and have held to them despite defeats, would be very encouraging. It would suggest not only that global union ties have become more profound but, also, that global union organizations will be better prepared for the next window of opportunity. The focus on global governance, therefore, also sheds light on self-governance.

We have chosen to focus on global union organizations, a choice that requires some justification because global union politics is manifested at various levels in various ways. Sometimes it involves heroic local struggles in support of distant workers, and sometimes it involves heroic local struggles whose intended aim or unintended result is to harm distant workers. Sometimes it involves well-coordinated global collaboration whose aim is to enhance global solidarity, and sometimes it involves militant global campaigns whose goal is to benefit particular groups of workers over others. In this volume we do not assume that the proliferation of local or uncoordinated struggles is evidence of global union collaboration or the potential for it. Quite often it is exactly the opposite. In short, we take seriously Marx's statement that people make history, even if it is not under circumstances of their own making. We recognize that our focus on global organizations does not pay enough tribute to those efforts that have kept and keep egalitarian internationalism alive in the midst of global wars and predatory capitalism. Yet, our work is motivated by and is a tribute to those efforts.

For us, global union organizations are the canary in the mine because they serve as indicators of the willingness of national unions to commit to global union politics rather than engage in foreign policies.

The volume consists of six chapters. In chapter 1 we argue that globalization and global governance are important tendencies in an unevenly integrating world and that global governance plays an increasingly central role in the politics of global integration. Based on this view, we submit that a number of key tensions involving globalization and global governance may well lead unions to choose any one of a number of alternatives, further fragmenting global union politics. Thus, in addition to clarifying our view on globalization and global governance, this chapter also provides the dynamic context for the rest of the volume.

In the second chapter, we situate our approach to global union politics within the debates on global societal politics. Responding to the liberal bias of global integration, many people have placed their hopes for a more just world in the emergence of a global civil society, as manifested in Seattle, Porto Alegre, and elsewhere. While we also recognize the promise of global societal politics, we do not think that it is uniformly inclusive and egalitarian. For these reasons, any meaningful discussion of societal politics must offer a way to differentiate among competing societal visions about our world. Stated differently, it must place societal entities within the global political economy, not outside of it. In particular, we outline different visions of global governance, ranging from inegalitarian ones to democratic ones, so that we may use them to evaluate the world visions of global union organizations over time and in the present.

Chapter 3 traces the trajectory of global union organizations from the formation of the First International, an organization of European unionists and radicals formed in 1864, to the creation of the most inclusive and largest global union organization—the International Trade Union Confederation—on November 1, 2006. We are very conscious of the fact that the major obstacles to global democracy are authoritarian and liberal states and societal forces and, of course, capital. Accordingly, we avoid the temptation of explaining labor's failures solely in terms of insufficient mobilization and solidarity. Yet, while global labor mobilization and solidarity are not sufficient conditions for bringing about a more democratic world, they are necessary. Thus, intra-union politics explains a great deal of the many tragedies and fewer triumphs of global union politics and, certainly, the unwillingness of national unions to create strong global union organizations. We ask, therefore, whether the trend toward unification at the global level, evident since the end of the Cold War, is profound enough. Does it reflect a willingness by national unions to transfer some authority and resources to global union organizations? What are the major gaps that must still be addressed? This, then, is a chapter about the self-governance of global union politics.

The fourth chapter examines the efforts of unions to democratize global public governance, focusing on the International Labour Organization and the global economic organizations. Recognizing the limited impacts of global unions so far, and the potentially divisive impacts of globalization on unions, we pay equal attention to whether unions have been able to formulate common policies and strategies vis-à-vis global governance and ask whether union proposals have gone beyond labor rights and toward a more comprehensive vision of how the global political economy ought to be organized. In light of past and current differences among unions, both across and within countries, evidence of a common agenda is an important accomplishment, although this does not preclude us from evaluating its potential and limitations in terms of democratizing global governance.

In the fifth chapter, we examine the attempts of unions to democratize global private governance. Recognizing that corporations have long resisted dealing with unions at the international level, we focus on the recent phenomenon of International Framework Agreements between global union organizations and multinational corporations. As with public governance, we ask whether unions have been able to formulate a common policy vis-à-vis private governance and whether they have had any success in moving the governance of global capital beyond corporate social responsibility.

In the conclusion, we comment on the major challenges and opportunities facing unions in their efforts to govern themselves and democratize the global state and global capital. We close by commenting on the relations between global union politics and the global justice movement.

GLOBALIZATION AND GLOBAL GOVERNANCE

The demonstrations in Seattle challenged the WTO's blindness to social equity and served notice that large numbers of people were not willing to accept global capitalism's challenge to social and environmental gains that many generations had fought for. The failure of the negotiations, however, also owed a great deal to deep divisions over the pace and content of liberalization among governments, many of which did not care about the organization's social deficit. The North, led by the United States, France, and Japan, wanted to liberalize information and services, while the South, led by Brazil, wanted to liberalize agriculture. In short, the debates over global governance during the past ten years or so have been about both its pace and its inequities across and within countries.

These debates are evident at all levels, causing grave concerns among the supporters of globalization and global governance. In late

November 2005, for instance, the Buenos Aires summit intended to move forward the creation of the Free Trade Area of the Americas (FTAA) was met with massive demonstrations. While unions proposed an alternative vision for the Americas, others, such as retired Argentinian soccer superstar Diego Maradona, employed a more nationalist language. While Brazil insisted on the liberalization of agriculture, the United States focused on services. The FTAA, originally planned to begin in January 2005, has fallen behind schedule for the same reasons that the World Trade Organization has failed to meet its own deadlines, as of May 1, 2007.

The demonstrations in Buenos Aires were not an isolated episode but, rather, evidence of the contested nature of regional integration. A few days after the events in Buenos Aires, Evo Morales was elected president of Bolivia, the first indigenous person to be elected president of a Latin American country and one of a handful of indigenous people to rise to authority by electoral or other means. One of his promises was to nationalize the natural gas of the country or, at the very least, to change the relations between Bolivia and foreign investors in the sector. Symbolically, he announced the nationalization on May 1, 2006, attracting more media attention in the *New York Times* than his election had a few months earlier.[1] This prompted a meeting between the presidents of Brazil, Argentina, Venezuela, and Bolivia to prevent problems in the continued flow of gas from Bolivia to Brazil or Argentina. Beyond the immediate reasons for the meeting, it was significant because it brought together a group of leaders who range from the leftist to the populist—reflecting an antiliberal trend in South America. Equally importantly, Brazil has staked out a regional hegemonic role for itself, while Venezuela is the loudest advocate of a hemispheric economic zone that does not include the United States. With Venezuela joining Mercosur in the summer of 2006, the possibility of deeper regional integration as a counter to U.S. influence has become even more likely.[2]

As these developments were unfolding, a company owned by the ruler of Dubai announced that it had purchased the operating rights to a number of U.S. ports. The announcement raised a furious reaction from many quarters. This placed them in direct disagreement with the Bush administration, which argued that this kind of protectionism endangered the liberalization of the global economy and made it that

much harder to make friends in West Asia. Coming from an administration that hardly used the term *globalization* during its first five years
in office and raised unilateralism in military and economic policies to
new heights, it is rather surprising.[3] Yet, this is an administration that
does want to liberalize the global economy, albeit in quasi-imperial
terms, and is very concerned that the delays in the WTO negotiations
may outlast the president's "trade promotion" authority. The results of
the 2006 congressional elections in the United States underscore this
possibility as many Democrats were elected on a populist and protectionist platform.

What do these stories tell us about our world? In broad terms, the
various views have been divided into ones that argue that our world is
globalized and ones that claim that it is internationalized.[4] Looking at
the United States' tentative courting of multilateralism, as it appears in
the 2006 National Security Strategy, the globalizers would see evidence
that cross-border interactions and rules are increasingly independent of
territorial boundaries and that not even the most powerful of countries
can resist their influence.[5] The internationalizers, on the other hand,
would see a world where states and regional blocs continue to play a
preponderant role in shaping global integration.[6] As we look at the
same picture, we agree with those who see a world that combines various tendencies, ranging from globalization to nationalization, in often
tense competition with each other.[7] More importantly, this is not simply the case of some countries consistently favoring one tendency
while others favor another, but rather, as the U.S. National Security
Strategy illustrates, of individual countries routinely advancing two or
more of them simultaneously. The disagreements about our world,
therefore, cut across and within countries.

Upon closer inspection, globalizers and internationalizers also see
the same picture but choose to accent a single color. Most works that
adopt globalization as their starting point spend even more time iden-
tifying exceptions, conditions, and modifications. For instance,
Kenichi Ohmae, whose *The Borderless World* (1990) made the model
case for globalization, followed that volume with *The End of the Nation
State: The Rise of Regional Economies* (1995), a volume that highlights
the significance of regionalization rather than globalization.[8] On the
other hand, even the strongest advocates of internationalization argue
that states and regions continue to thrive within a highly integrated and

competitive global political economy.[9] Globalizers and internationalizers alike find that the global political economy (i.e., the whole edifice of inter-related political, military, social, cultural, and economic interactions and rules that constitute our world) consists of various tendencies, globalization being very important among them. It is our view that an approach that employs this insight can produce more accurate descriptions and interpretations of contemporary developments, compared to the broad strokes of the globalization-internationalization dichotomy.

In the first and longer part of this chapter, we clarify our view on globalization and its governance and employ examples from the broader global political economy in order to underscore the general utility of our approach. After contrasting globalization with its competitors, we examine how it takes place and argue that governance, in general, has always been a key force behind globalization and that global governance has played a prominent role during the past two decades. Not surprisingly, global governance is also facing stiff competition. It would have been surprising if unions were not affected by these dynamics. In the second part, therefore, we argue that different union views on the pace and social impacts of globalization and global governance can well lead to the fragmentation of global union politics, thus providing a context for the chapters that follow.

The Fragile Hegemony of Globalization

The globalization-internationalization dichotomy covers such distinct and important tendencies that it is advisable to employ some additional concepts in order to highlight the contested nature of globalization—both as a concept and as reality. In our view, four major tendencies in the contemporary political economy are globalization,[10] internationalization, regionalization, and nationalization. Various sectors of human activity are characterized by one or the other, while some fuse two or more tendencies. How do these tendencies differ from each other, and what makes globalization a distinct and important trend? These are the questions that animate this section.

Globalization and Its Competitors

Analysts have used a variety of criteria to measure globalization. There is general agreement, however, that globalization is manifested by numerous cross-border interactions and connections, that these extend or can extend over the whole globe, have intense impacts on people, and, finally, that these interactions and connections are globalized because countries have "willingly" surrendered their right to control these crossings.[11] Yet, many human activities are global but not globalized, at least if the concept of globalization is to add something distinct to our understanding of world politics. World War II, for instance, was truly global, but most globalizers would have trouble thinking of it as globalized in the same sense that they think of finance as being globalized. Thus, what really distinguishes globalization from its competitors is that it involves all four criteria mentioned above, with the fourth criterion playing a central role in our view of things.[12] As will also become apparent, there are good reasons why we place "willingly" in quotation marks.

With these criteria in mind, we agree with most analysts who find that globalization is more profound in the economy and in infrastructure (communications and transportation) and least profound in political and military affairs.[13] Yet, many important aspects of the economy and of infrastructure are not globalized, while even the most globalized sectors contain elements that are exempted from or resist globalization, further challenging the globalization-internationalization dichotomy.

Finance is probably the most globalized sector of the global political economy and has been so for a number of centuries.[14] During the late nineteenth century, every major private and national bank in the world had to have a subsidiary or a representative in the city of London.[15] Without access to its enormous financial resources, they could not borrow or lend money, whether for infrastructure, industrialization, or trade. More than a hundred years later, banks may be able to choose between New York, London, Tokyo, or Frankfurt, but they must still be present in one or another financial center and must pay close attention to the operations of the global financial system.[16] Enormous amounts of monies cross boundaries every minute, their movement has intense and immediate implications for the domestic politics of countries, almost all countries in the world are integrated into the global financial system, and, finally, almost all countries in the world have committed to respecting their financial obligations and the rules of financial institutions. The strongest evidence of financial globalization is that no country has reneged on the repayment of its debt for decades, even when repayment involves high political and social costs.[17] Yet, after more than one hundred years of global financial integration, there is no global bank or currency, nor do the countries of the world agree on how to manage financial flows, making national and regional financial crises, such as the one that devastated the East Asian economies in the late 1990s, a threat to the whole global financial edifice.[18]

The successful laying of undersea cables connecting Europe and the United States around the time of the U.S. Civil War was heralded as an unprecedented event.[19] A few years later, all major cities, ports, and railway lines were connected through a global network of telegraphy, allowing real-time exchange of information.[20] Despite two world wars, global infrastructure continued to grow, with telephone lines increasingly replacing the telegraph. While in 1954 there were only thirty-two phone lines connecting the Americas and Europe, forty years later the system would handle billions of phone calls and Internet connections a day. Moreover, these connections could now use both undersea cables and satellites in space. Parallel to that, more efficient modes of sea and air transportation can carry people and products almost seamlessly from one end of the globe to the other. Yet, foreign vessels cannot navigate the coastal and internal waters of most countries, except to unload their cargo, and the Chinese government has forced Google, the dominant web search engine, to craft a program that limits access to non-Chinese sources of electronic information.

In fact, not only are there aspects of the most globalized sectors that are not globalized, but whole sectors of the economy and of infrastructure are largely internationalized. Internationalization refers to interactions and connections between two or more countries that reserve the right to control these interactions at the border.[21] As we noted earlier, the WTO has so far failed to globalize agriculture and services, both of which are currently internationalized. These and other sectors will become globalized if the WTO is successful. But important sectors, such as weapons, aeronautics, supercomputers, and space technology, the cutting-edge technologies of our era, are not on the agenda of the WTO. More interestingly, the WTO sometimes explicitly exempts sectors from globalization. An ideal example is air transportation, which is still regulated by intergovernmental agreements that recognize a country's right to decide which airlines can use

12

its airports and its right to reserve domestic air service for national airlines. Yet, all of the internationalized sectors that we have mentioned cover the whole globe, involve enormous amounts of interactions, and have intense impacts on people—just ask anyone who has been stranded in an airport.

While there are many sectors that are globalized or internationalized, regionalism has become an increasingly important tendency. Regionalism refers to interactions and connections among countries in the same geographic region, and its major difference from globalization is its geographic scope. During the past two decades, interactions within Western Europe, North America, and the Asia-Pacific area have increased enormously.[22] These regions are also involved in extensive interregional interactions with each other, underscoring the continuing significance of internationalization but now at the level of whole regions rather than individual states. On balance, most of the world's economic and infrastructural interactions take place within these three regions, with interactions among them following. Moreover, the regionalism evident in the North is now expanding into the South, particularly in South America and Southeast Asia.

Most significantly, for our purposes, regionalization also has global reach. Not only does the rest of the world depend on the United States, Western Europe, and Japan for finance and investment, but access to their markets is absolutely necessary, whether we are dealing with airplanes, oil, or roses. Colombia and Ecuador, for instance, specialize in the production of roses for the U.S. market.[23] U.S. health and safety standards allow minimal amounts of pesticide residue, while customers prefer the most beautiful and fresh-looking roses. In order to accomplish these ends, producers use very strong pesticides that can dissolve quickly and powerful fertilizers and preservatives that induce roses to grow fast and keep them looking vibrant in their long journey to the customer. There would be no Colombian or Ecuadorean rose industries without U.S. demand, but the rules of the U.S. market also lead to practices that have horrible impacts on workers thousands of miles away.

Finally, we think that nationalization continues to be a major tendency in the global political economy. We are not simply referring to the fact that the sectors that account for the largest share of most countries' national economy, such as the military, education, health, social security, and government employment, remain and are likely to remain largely nationalized.[24] The nationalization that we have in mind involves vast amounts of global interactions, which have intense impacts, and which cross boundaries with great ease—but which are under the control of a single country. More than 50 percent of the United States' battle-ready troops were overseas during the summer of 2003, and more than 95 percent of all troops stationed away from their country are U.S. troops. Just the communications involving these troops probably exceeds the cross-border communications of all countries but a few. The amount of information collected by the U.S. National Security Agency prior to September 11, 2001, was so immense that important intercepted items were not identified and translated until well after the tragedy. This from an agency that single-handedly employs most of the world's supercomputing capacity.

What we have argued is that globalization is dominant in only some aspects of the global political economy (especially finance and infrastructure), that it is incomplete even in those sectors, and that it is nearly absent in some other aspects of the global political economy (such as politics, security, and social welfare). If globalization referred to everything that is global, then the WTO's work would have been done. Take agriculture, for example. Whole countries depend on the export of particular products, whole countries have come to depend on the import of these products, and there is no country that does not import or export agricultural products. Even during the height of the Cold War, the Soviet Union imported grain from the United States. By the same token, the First and Second World Wars would have been evidence of globalization. Australians and New Zealanders fought and died in Southeast Europe during WWI and trace their nationhood to the bitter battlefields of Gallipoli. Uranium from the Congo fueled the production of nuclear weapons in the desert of New Mexico during WWII. It seems to us, therefore, that these are not the kinds of interactions and connections that globalists have in mind when they talk about globalization. The concept can bring something new to our understanding of world politics if it is used in the more narrow sense employed here and by various other analysts.[25] The concept must mean that countries the world over are "willingly" surrendering their power to control their borders. We turn to how this can happen and why the quotation marks serve a good purpose.

How Does Globalization Take Place?

Many analysts have argued that globalization is "a market-induced, not a policy-induced, process."[26] The implication is that globalization is the result of a multitude of uncoordinated corporate decisions with governments merely responding rather than initiating. We agree that this is one way in which globalization can take place but assert that states play a central role in facilitating and constraining corporate decisions. Underestimating the role of states, and the social alliances they represent, in engendering market dynamics is to build a wall between "politics" and "economics" and to further legitimate the liberal myth about the separation of the two. State choices, including inaction, shape the flow of global interactions. As we argue, international, regional, and national policies continue to play an important role. To this mix we can now add global governance, manifested primarily by the increasing role of global economic organizations.[27]

Since the mid-1990s, global governance—the adoption of global rules through organizations such as the World Trade Organization—has sought to take the driver's seat in globalizing the global political economy.[28] Even so, a closer look at global economic organizations shows that where some see global governance, others see another way to organize and legitimate the dominance of the North over the South and of capital over people and nature. The social deficits of global economic organizations have been the target of extensive criticism and global mobilizations, such as those in Seattle, Genoa, and Cancún.[29]

After WWII, the U.S. Senate rejected the formation of an International Trade Organization that would have taken into account the special circumstances of the South.[30] In its place, the capitalist countries of the North, led by the United States, adopted the General Agreement on Tariffs and Trade (GATT), whose aim was the liberalization of global trade without taking into account the needs of the less affluent countries. Not surprisingly, the South refused to participate, and from the 1950s until the early 1980s these countries sought, unsuccessfully, to reform the global trading system through alternative organizations. The GATT, in the meantime, facilitated the liberalization of trade among industrial capitalist countries. The process was slow because the Europeans and the Japanese, major prewar traders, were rebuilding their economies. During the 1960s, for instance, the reconstructing Western Europeans were railing against the "American Threat" as more and more U.S. corporations invested in Europe. By the early 1970s, however, global trade had two engines—the United States and Western Europe. By the late 1970s they were joined by Japan.[31] While during the 1960s the Europeans were afraid of the Americans, now both of them claimed to be afraid of the Japanese.

The resulting "trade wars" of the late 1970s and early 1980s threatened the further liberalization of the global political economy, which had taken place mostly through corporate decisions and uncoordinated national policies and less through the GATT.[32] In response, the key players agreed to explore changes in the governance of global trade, and over eight years—from 1986 to 1994—the GATT members negotiated the formation of the World Trade Organization.[33] The organization was given a broader mandate than GATT and, equally importantly, stronger dispute resolution power. Ever since, it has served as the forum where the countries of the world negotiate the rules of trade for sectors that are globalized, such as manufacturing, and for sectors that are not yet globalized, such as agriculture and services. Moreover, its agenda has expanded to include intellectual property rights and various aspects of finance and investment, rendering the term *trade* somewhat misleading.

With the WTO, global governance has become an important tendency in the global political economy. Yet, in addition to its social deficit, the WTO has some way to go in solving North-South tensions and forcing industrial countries to give up selective protectionism. But how did the South move from rejection by and opposition to the GATT to being such a central player in the WTO? This is a long and complicated story, but its general outline further demonstrates the move from globalization as the result of uncoordinated state and corporate choices, to globalization via global governance.

The International Monetary Fund (IMF) was an organization looking for a mission in the early 1980s. Then, the global debt crisis gave it one. During the 1970s, many countries in the South borrowed large amounts of money from Northern banks and governments. These were short-term loans that were spent on long-term projects that would not come to fruition for decades.[34] As a result, when their debts came due, the debtors were not able to make the payments, starting with Mexico in 1982. Rather than declare bankruptcy, the debtors asked for rescheduling of payments. The lenders would agree only if they were given some guarantees that they would get their money back, with interest.

That's where the IMF came in.[35] Instead of all creditors talking to all debtors, the IMF became the speaker for the lenders. After reviewing the economy of an indebted country, it would mandate a number of policies, collectively known as "structural adjustment," to get the indebted country's economy working again and to ensure repayment. As part of structural adjustment, the debtors were asked to produce more export commodities that would generate the income with which to repay their debt. At the same time, they were required to cut down on government hiring and subsidies, whether to national industries or the poor. Some of these policies had brutal impacts on people. When, in the 1980s, Venezuela interrupted its subsidies to public transportation, violent protests resulted in more than one hundred dead. When, in 1997, the Indonesian government ended subsidies to rice, a key staple for the country, violent riots resulted in thousands of deaths. Yet, the important thing is that none of the debtors has refused to repay its debt, despite the human costs. The governments that came to power during the 1980s and 1990s chose to abide by, and thus strengthen, the rules globalizing finance. Moreover, they decided that the main game in town was the global forums, such as the GATT/WTO and the IMF, that they had criticized in the past. By the end of the 1980s, then, more and more stalwarts of Southern politics, such as Mexico and Brazil, joined the GATT/WTO, with China joining them a few years later and Vietnam joining in early 2007. As soon as Russia and Iran also join, there will be no major country left outside.

In all cases, this integration into the world capitalist order took place against local opposition. That opposition continues, as the recent history of Bolivia demonstrates. In the fall of 2003, Bolivia's president, Gonzalo Sánchez de Lozada, called out the army to contain protests against policies that were largely dictated by global economic organizations. After more than sixty deaths, he had to resign and fly to the United States. His resignation is particularly poignant because as minister of planning during the mid-1980s, he implemented policies to stabilize and liberalize the Bolivian economy, policies that were considered to be the model for other countries.[36] In short, then, it is important to understand that when we say that countries choose liberal globalization "willingly," we are saying that particular domestic

17

interests choose globalization, often over strong opposition. So long as that opposition remains in existence, and there is evidence that it is growing, globalization's hegemony will be fragile.[37] Moreover, of course, in addition to opposition from national and regional groups bargaining for advantage within a more integrated global economy, there is increasing opposition coming from those who envision a more egalitarian globalization.

Global Governance and Its Competitors

Some analysts have used the term *global governance* to denote almost every human activity that exhibits some kind of a pattern or regularity.[38] We find this approach too general to be of use. For instance, countries routinely adopt each other's military innovations in order to fight with each other. Global governance, in our view, should refer to rules that extend or can extend over the whole globe, cover all relevant parties, and are supranational, that is, in which members give up some of their national authority to a global entity or process. What most distinguishes global governance from its alternatives—intergovernmental, regional, and national governance—is the relinquishing of some national autonomy.

We have noted that the icon of global economic governance is the WTO. The extent of its power is apparent when one contrasts it with the International Labour Organization (ILO), the oldest intergovernmental organization.[39] When the member countries of the WTO adopt a new agreement, they must integrate it into their domestic law and act accordingly. If a country does not adopt or implement a policy, another member can lodge a complaint with the WTO, which has been given supranational dispute resolution powers.[40] In contrast to the WTO, individual countries are not required to adopt the ILO conventions that they have helped negotiate. The United States, for instance, has ratified only 14 of the organization's 187 conventions (July 2006). Moreover, in contrast to the WTO's dispute resolution power, that of the ILO is largely symbolic.[41]

But the WTO itself is a combination of intergovernmental and supranational governance. The organization cannot adopt new policies on its own. These policies must be negotiated by member countries; small alliances of countries or even a single but determined country can keep an agreement from coming to be, as has been the case with the WTO's current round of negotiations. Contrast this to the European Union. It possesses organizations with significant supranational authority, its own budget and taxation powers, and a central bank. While the European Union has been around since the late 1950s (then called the European Economic Community), it was not until the late 1980s that it started moving away from regional intergovernmentalism to regional supragovernmentalism.[42] This intensification of European integration motivated South American, North American, and East Asian countries to initiate their own regional governance projects, largely ahead of actual economic integration, further underscoring the increasing role of governance at all levels.

Regional governance, the third tendency, routinely has global reach if not formal authority. After a series of financial scandals, such as those at Enron, WorldCom, and Parmalat, the United States and the European Union have been considering accounting standards that apply to any corporation operating in their territories. Outside Europe or the United States, these corporations could well employ different standards. Not only would their accounting systems become impossible to manage, but any statement by U.S. or EU authorities that a corporation's accounting is not transparent would directly affect its standing in stock markets. Given the fact that no company can afford to be excluded from these two regions, their rules have significant global influence.

National governance is the fourth tendency that is alive and well. Many countries adopt domestic policies intended to attract people and products. During the late 1990s, for instance, Canada was willing to extend citizenship to migrants fleeing Hong Kong before its reunification with China, if they could show that they were worth one million U.S. dollars or more. The United States relaxes its citizenship requirements for foreigners who serve in its armed forces. Most countries adopt various incentives to attract foreign investment, and many have set up special Export Processing Zones to do so.[43] These are regions where national environmental and labor laws are suspended, infrastructure is built at public cost, and taxes are minimized. In fact, whole countries may be thought of as Export Processing Zones.

While the above examples refer to incentives used to attract desirable people or activities, other forms of national governance are much

19

more aggressive and extraterritorial. The major source of such policies is the United States, but it is not the only one. A few years ago, for instance, Belgium adopted a law according to which it could prosecute people who are accused of violating internationally recognized human-rights laws regardless of the accused person's citizenship, place of crime, or relationship to Belgium. The law was so controversial that the United States threatened to have NATO's headquarters moved from Brussels lest one of its leaders be apprehended while in the country. Belgium has since been forced to water down this attempt at global governance through national means. The United States, on the other hand, has intensified its efforts. The National Security Strategy of the United States made public in September 2002 offered the most explicit unilateral and extraterritorial model of governance with global reach.[44] From beginning to end, this document asserted the right of the United States to influence, by force if necessary, the military, economic, political, and social map of the world. Brian Urquhart, a veteran observer of world politics and past undersecretary of the United Nations, in a review of various books on empires and imperialism, properly suggests that the adjective "imperialist" is well suited for this type of governance.[45]

We have shown in this section that intergovernmental, regional, and national governance continue to be important and growing tendencies and that each one of them can have global reach. This is necessary to underscore. We are not arguing that the various tendencies are evidence of countries or regions isolating themselves from the global political economy. Rather, we argue that there is contention and competition among these tendencies over the governance of the global political economy. What best distinguishes global governance from its alternatives, therefore, is the fact that the countries of the world have given their consent to global and supranational rules and organizations. In this sense, global governance is an emerging and still fragile tendency.

Its fragility keeps the most sophisticated supporters of globalization awake at night. They see very clearly that without global governance, there can be no globalization, a conclusion that is supported by the experience of the past few centuries. Without national governance, there could have been no national integration during the nineteenth century, and without the European Union or NAFTA, there could have been no regional integration in the late twentieth century. We turn, next, to the tensions of global integration.

Unions between Global Integration and Its Competitors

The concerns about the present and future of capitalist globalization and its governance come from various quarters. Supporters, such as the World Economic Forum, are more alarmed over the slow process of reaching agreement on the rules of globalization. Critics, such as the World Social Forum, emphasize that the social inequities of the ongoing processes justify resistance and renegotiation. We believe that both sets of tensions produce important challenges for all social entities, including unions. We have organized these tensions into two categories. The first category we call the challenges of pace. This refers to people and countries believing that, from their point of view, capitalist globalization and global governance are moving slower or faster than they would prefer. Yet, globalization and global governance can also be rejected by all those people and countries who are left behind by a process that, up to now, seems impervious to its human costs. The second category, therefore, we call the challenges of equity. One can envision how tensions due to pace or inequity can well lead whole countries and particular categories of people to choose nationalization, regionalization, or internationalization over globalization. Those interested in global democracy are naturally interested in questions of equity, but it is easy to see how disagreements over pace among them can create conflicts and inhibit collaboration. In what follows we choose examples that highlight these dynamics for global union politics. It takes little, however, to realize that they produce similar dilemmas for all social movements.

Challenges of Pace: Too Much Globalization

Important globalized sectors are not globally governed, and, in fact, they are resisting governance. Finance, perhaps the most and longest globalized sector in our world, is only partially governed at the same time that financial decisions can shape the fate of whole countries and classes of people. Since the late 1950s, investment has also become increasingly more globalized but remains largely ungoverned. More than the other economic activities, the globalization of investment has generated some important challenges for global labor. The migration of

21

labor-intensive work, for instance, has been a very controversial issue pitting unions from industrial countries against unions from less industrial countries.[46] Some of these labor-intensive products, such as soccer balls, are produced in sweatshops and family enterprises in South Asia by children.[47] Clothes are produced in sweatshops throughout the world, including major cities in the United States, by young women and men, many of them migrants with no rights. Still other products are produced in the hundreds of Export Processing Zones by people who have migrated to those locations, breaking any connections with their previous ways of making a living. In short, the impacts of these practices go beyond just the workplace and affect the whole social fabric.

As far back as the 1970s, U.S. unions railed against Mexican maquiladoras, a type of Export Processing Zone, accusing the U.S. and Mexican governments, U.S. corporations, and Mexican unions of colluding to move good jobs to Mexico's northern border region. The truth of the matter is that there was such collusion. "Official" Mexican unions did support the maquiladora program and opposed any collaboration with U.S. unions.[48] U.S. unions, on the other hand, responded in various ways.[49] Some were downright xenophobic, while others sought to establish connections with Mexican workers, even against the wishes of official Mexican unions. Some sought to get the U.S. government to solve the problem through national legislation. Others recognized the need for regional and multilateral arrangements. Then, during the past several years, hundreds of thousands of jobs have migrated from Mexico to China. China has the laws, the infrastructure, and the labor force to compete with Mexico. The official Chinese unions, like the official Mexican unions earlier, are supportive of their government's policies.

How should U.S. and Mexican unions respond? Should they call for national, regional, intergovernmental, or global rules? How should they pursue their goals? Through action at the national level or through collaboration with others, perhaps even Chinese unions? What kinds of rules should they call for? Only those that address their own concerns or broader rules that also address the concerns of Chinese workers? A close look at how U.S. unions have responded to the issue shows that all of these options have been raised and debated among and within unions. Societal entities, whether unions or environmental or human-rights organizations, are routinely confronted by these dilemmas, and they often find that common ground can be elusive.

Challenges of Pace: Too Much Global Governance

During the first term of the Bush administration, the United Steelworkers of America argued that the global governance of the steel industry, that is, the liberalization rules imposed by the WTO, had gone too far. In their view, which was based on some firm evidence, cheaper steel from South Korea, Brazil, and the European Union was threatening the U.S. steel industry and some measures were necessary to help the industry recover its competitiveness. Recognizing the critical role of this largely Democratic union in midwestern states, the Bush administration agreed to impose tariffs on certain categories of foreign steel. These were temporary measures because the Bush administration continued to promote global economic liberalization, even as it was promoting unilateralism in security affairs. Moreover, it had to take into consideration that steel consumers in the United States, such as the automobile industry, were against these protective measures because they would raise the price of the imported steel that they needed. On top of that, the affected countries took their case to the WTO, which decided against the United States in this case.

What should the Steelworkers, an often militant and internationalist union, do? Short-term protectionist measures are certainly not enough. The Steelworkers realize that the problem is larger and has to do with regional and global liberalization. Yet, the impacts of foreign competition, real or perceived, are immediate. Should they pursue protectionist policies even if these produce long-term divisions with unions in other countries, such as Brazil and South Korea, as well as with unions in the United States itself? Or should they seek common ground with them, even if this takes more time and may well aggravate nationalist elements within the union's own ranks? Unions must pay simultaneous attention to their membership, which may disagree about strategies, and the longer-term requirement of building strong collaborative ties with unions in other parts of the world. The Steelworkers have not abandoned their attempts at building global solidarity, but other unions have been more likely to adopt a nationalist approach.

Challenges of Equity: Liberalization versus Social Welfare

The most important issue for progressive unions and other egalitarian social forces is not that the global political economy is becoming globalized but that it does so without commensurate social provisions.[50] What we are observing is capitalist globalization, that is, globalization that values growth and profit, over egalitarian globalization, that is, globalization that values equity and social welfare. This is not an accident. The experience of the European Union, where economic integration and social regulation are more profound than anywhere else, highlights why liberalization and social regulation have not gone hand in hand.[51]

During the past twenty years, the European Union has moved toward more formal economic integration. Business has been very supportive, provided that there were no regional social policies. While not totally successful, they were largely successful in tilting the EU toward liberalization. The social provisions of the European Union are, on balance, much below the national social provisions of most member countries. Reacting to this situation, the unions of those countries with the strongest social welfare states have been vehemently against replacing strong national social regulation with weak European-level social regulation. These are the unions from Scandinavia, the Netherlands, and Belgium, unions that also happen to be at the forefront of union internationalism. Can these unions be simply labeled protectionist because they refuse to replace stronger national labor rules with weaker European rules? That would be too simplistic. What we are observing here are political struggles and choices that reflect the uneven pace of liberalization and social regulation even in a region like the European Union.[52] The situation is even worse in the case of the Free Trade Area of the Americas initiative, which, like the WTO, has refused to include labor issues on its agenda.

As we will discuss in some depth in chapter 4, global union organizations have long tried to insert a social clause into WTO agreements.[53] Accordingly, all agreements would stipulate that trade liberalization cannot take place at the expense of core labor standards and rights, especially the right to organize. This strategy came to a head at the 1999 WTO meeting in Seattle. Unions were not successful in inserting a social clause into the WTO, and subsequent meetings of the organization have underscored its unwillingness to address labor issues. Global union organizations were pursuing the social-clause strategy not as a proxy for protectionism but as a step toward a more socially regulated global economy.[54] In fact, these organizations have been among the strongest and most consistent supporters of free trade since the interwar period, often against strong protectionist affiliates. The liberal attitude of the WTO, however, is threatening the ability of global union organizations and other nonprotectionist unions to hold on to this commitment as important national unions are turning toward national or regional solutions.

How should unions respond in the absence of any global social regulation? Does it not make sense to hold on to national or regional social regulation? Why should they accept global liberalization that threatens to undo the social and political rights for which they have fought since the middle of the nineteenth century? Their choices, and those of other societal entities, are made even more complicated by the fact that a number of liberals also agree that social regulation is necessary.[55] Yet, most liberals prefer voluntary social regulation that deals with the worst impacts of globalization rather than social rules that have as much power as liberalization rules.[56] This trend toward private social regulation, known as corporate social responsibility, has certainly caught the attention of unions.[57] In chapter 5, we examine in more depth how unions have responded to this move toward private governance.

Challenges of Equity: Rich and Poor

For many analysts and activists, North-South inequities are the central division between rich and poor in the global political economy.[58] We agree with this assessment with two important modifications. First, wealth and poverty cut across countries; second, some of the policies advanced by Southern governments are not particularly egalitarian.

Let us continue with the social clause story. Most Southern political and economic leaders argued that the incorporation of labor (and environment) into the WTO was a thinly veiled form of protectionism from the industrial world. The truth is that some governments and even a number of unions and environmentalists from the North did promote them for protectionist reasons, while more of them had, and continue to have, a very paternalistic attitude toward the South.[59] The overwhelming number of Southern unions, however, were in support of the social clause.[60] The Southern leaders, therefore, did not speak for the unions of their own countries. Rather, their view was that more liberalization would bring more growth and more growth would lead to more domestic trickle-down effects. Social provisions, they argued, would simply slow down this process. Their logic, in short, was no different from that of Northern liberals who are also arguing that more growth will lead to better living standards, making social welfare policies unnecessary. It is not surprising, then, that Southern leaders found their strongest allies against incorporating environmental and labor provisions into the WTO among the more liberal business and political leaders from the industrial world.

Stated differently, then, the "rich-poor" gap is not only one between countries. It is equally, and more importantly in our view, a class divide that cuts across countries. Most of the developmentalist elites of the South who are objecting to the inequities of global liberalization are doing so not because it deprives workers and the poor of rights and benefits. Rather, they are objecting because they are concerned about the destabilizing effects of Northern-led liberalization on domestic class relations. It is for this reason that the reemergence of the democratic left in South America, tentative as it is, may undermine liberal hegemony by forcing institutions of global governance to address the social impacts of the liberalization that they are vigorously promoting.

Can global union organizations dismiss the argument of the political and economic leaders of the South? We do not think it is possible to disregard the major inequities between poor and rich countries and the biases of the rules that govern the global political economy. A more egalitarian and democratic world, however, is not possible if the agenda is shaped by developmentalist alliances with little concern for either domestic inequities or for the implications of their policies on the poor of other countries, South or North.

Conclusion

In the first part of this chapter, we clarify our view that globalization and global governance are important tendencies within the global political economy but, also, that they have strong competitors. We also argue that it is important to pay close attention to various forms of governance in order to avoid the myth that globalization is the result of inexorable and almost mystical "market forces." Wise capitalists know that without state rules, capitalism cannot establish any legitimacy. In the second part, we argue that the uneven pace and inequities of globalization and its governance can well lead national unions to choose any one of the competitors, further fragmenting global unions in the process.

One can easily see how the dilemmas facing unions, arguably one of the best organized and most experienced segments of civil society, can also confront any other civil societal entity, whether community, environment, human rights, public health, development, or gender based. Many societal entities, from corporations to sports organizations, can afford to adopt strategies that sacrifice some of their own on the altar of competition. Social egalitarian entities, however, cannot play by rules that sacrifice people in the name of economic efficiency or profit.

Many people emphasize the promise of "civil society" as our best hope for a more egalitarian and democratic politics.[61] We believe that there is much that is good and hopeful in societal politics but, also, much that is not.[62] Even the icons of global societal politics, such as Greenpeace, Friends of the Earth, and Oxfam, have been justifiably criticized for their Northern biases and their less-than-transparent internal processes. We are not ready to argue that unions have successfully solved all the challenges facing other societal entities, whether in their relations with the rest of the world or in terms of their internal operations. Global unions, however, have addressed these challenges over their long history and with increased urgency during this era of growing global governance, and their successes and failures can offer useful lessons to other social movements. Precisely because societal politics carries so much hope for so many people, it is important that we do not simply gaze at it, as we think is so frequently the case. In the next chapter, we offer our approach for interpreting and comparing societal politics in a manner that will help us answer the central question of this book: does this, the oldest of egalitarian social movements, have anything to add to those societal forces struggling to make a more democratic world possible?

SOCIETAL POLITICS AND GLOBAL GOVERNANCE

The demonstrations that shook Seattle in the late fall of 1999 have become iconic.[1] Thousands of people from various countries took to the streets to protest against the World Trade Organization's disregard for labor and environmental rights and the impacts of globalization on all aspects of life. The hostile view has held that these were a bunch of retrograde nationalists who could not understand the inevitability of liberal globalization and appreciate its benefits. The more sympathetic view has held that this was the turning point in the battle against neoliberal globalization. A more critical view recognizes that the people who took to the streets were all concerned about the impacts of globalization but differed a great deal in their tactical and political preferences. Some espoused militant tactics, while others did not. Some hoped for a more democratic global society, while others could not imagine how global organizations and rules would replace the state and its social provisions.

In the summer of 2005, Greeks (or some of them anyway) were distracted from the pleasures of summer vacations by a debate over whether the state should allow representatives from various fascist and national socialist parties to hold a festival in the southern town of Meligala. Most argued against allowing such a gathering, while fewer pointed out that a democratic system must allow freedom of speech, however obnoxious. All those who were planning to show up were strong nativists and racists, expressing openly their hostility toward non-European migrants and peoples. Even though they were participating in an international gathering, they made no secret of their belief that the nation was the primary unit for them. Yet, there were also important differences among them. Some emphasized the nation over race, others changed the order, and others combined the two equally. Some opposed the European Union as a threat to the nation, while others opposed it as an instrument of capitalism.

The moral of these stories is that societal politics is complex.[2] There has always been evidence that some societal entities aim at a more democratic world while others aim at a more authoritarian one. In the first part of this chapter, we clarify our view of societal politics, a central example of which is labor.[3] Looking at societal politics with a critical eye is particularly pressing because many people consider society as the primary or even exclusive locus of egalitarian and democratic politics,[4] while many analysts have found evidence of an autonomous global civil society. A more persuasive approach, in our view, asserts that societal politics, like all politics, must be placed within the political economy.[5] On this view, the priorities of societal entities may range from egalitarian to nonegalitarian and from nativist to cosmopolitan.[6] The role of the analyst, then, is to investigate rather than assume the worldviews of societal entities. Because societal politics and specifically global civil society are seen by some as the great hope for democratic global governance, we spend the second part of this chapter clarifying the concept of governance. We close by discussing how societal entities have confronted global governance and how we go about evaluating their impacts on it.

Societal Politics

There are various ways in which to analyze societal politics. For our purposes, we employ the distinction between the internal and external dimensions. Internal refers to what goes on inside societal organizations, movements, networks, or civil societies. Here we focus on organizational characteristics, constituency choices, and membership. External refers to the worldviews that societal entities have with respect to the world around them. This would include their views regarding equity and nationalism, dimensions that we emphasize.

Looking In

All societal politics are characterized by some mixture of local, national, and international organizations, networks, movements, or even civil societies. From our point of view, societal organizations are of paramount importance because networks, movements, and civil societies are based on and articulated around organizations, often called social movement organizations.[7] In short, we are very skeptical of claims that grassroots mobilizations can be sustained over the long term without the resources of some organizations behind them. Moreover, while international and global mobilizations can be and are often led by national organizations, we think that without long-term political commitments and more profound organizational ties, the end result is more likely to be societal foreign policy rather than sustained internationalism. In that vein, therefore, we ask whether a societal politics contains international or global organizations and whether these organizations have any authority above and beyond their affiliates.[8]

In terms of authority, we can distinguish between "weak" and "strong" organizations.[9] Weak organizations have no authority above and beyond that of the members, certainly the most powerful among those members. This is manifested in the absence of autonomous financial and human resources and in the need to consult the members for every consequential decision. Most global labor organizations fall into this category, mirroring intergovernmental organizations, such as the United Nations. Stronger organizations possess more autonomy in terms of resources and authority. The European Union is such an example, as are multinational corporations and many sports organizations and churches.[10]

The second important issue for analyzing the internal dimension of societal politics is that of constituencies. Every societal entity has certain constituencies.[11] Who makes up the constituency of an organization or movement? Why are some included and others excluded? At some level, constituency choices are commonsensical. Unions, for instance, focus on workers, women's organizations on women, naturalist organizations on nature. But as we look closer, we may find that unions focus on particular kinds of workers, women's organizations on particular kinds of women, and environmental organizations on particular aspects of the environment. In short, constituencies reflect important political choices, and these choices shape the internal and external politics of societal entities. An organization that excludes migrants, for instance, is not likely to speak in their favor as much as an organization that includes them.

It would not be prudent, however, to limit the reach of societal entities to their constituencies, because all societal politics are characterized by combinations of representative and advocacy organizations. Representative organizations aim to represent the interests of people who have chosen them in some identifiable, hopefully democratic, fashion. Unions are such organizations in the sense that they are speaking on behalf of their members rather than some other category of people. Of course, unions engage in advocacy work when they support the rights of nonunionized workers or the democratic rights of people subject to authoritarian regimes. Advocacy refers to particular groups or organizations arguing on behalf of categories of people or nature that have not chosen them, often because they are oppressed and voiceless. Amnesty International, for instance, advocates for the rights of people throughout the world who otherwise would have been totally forgotten. Greenpeace and other ecological organizations do the same for species and habitats. In looking at the constituency politics of global unions, therefore, we should pay close attention to both their representational and advocacy choices.[12]

The third issue brings together organizations and constituencies. How many doctors are members of the American Medical Association? How many steelworkers are members of the United Steelworkers of America? How many workers are members of unions? While degree of commitment and authority can sometimes compensate for low membership, negative trends will sooner or later result in declining resources and political influence. Equally important, we must ask whether large memberships may actually provide a false sense of inclusiveness while even larger numbers of people are excluded. Even during the 1970s, for instance, when union membership reached its highest level in the industrial world, the vast majority of the world's workers were not organized.

Looking Out

From a political economy perspective, one must also ask what kind of a world societal entities want. Two common ways for categorizing the external politics of societal politics are in terms of their approaches to cosmopolitanism and egalitarianism.[13] We employ these concepts below in order to distinguish the various approaches to the capitalist global political economy. The scheme can easily be applied to other anthropocentric societal politics, and with some modifications, it can also be applied to the environment.

From Particularism to Cosmopolitanism

Many analysts have sought to distinguish political preferences with respect to the role they assign to the nation. While useful, such an approach obscures a great deal. People can be particularistic in a variety of ways. In some instances they may be nationalistic, but in many instances they may be attached to other identities that cut within and across countries. Particularism, therefore, can be considered a general category. In addition to various kinds of extreme nationalists, it can also include those who engage in international politics with an eye toward shaping the world in a manner that serves them and punishes others. Imperialists, secure in the superiority of their own values and priorities and certain that others will benefit from them, fall into such a category. Predatory neoliberals, such as the Thatcher wing of the Conservative Party, can also be grouped here. Generally, people who privilege certain categories of nature or people at the expense of others are particularists without necessarily being nationalists.

The activists who wanted to meet in Meligala, Greece, were certainly nationalists (the meeting was finally prohibited). It would be unfair, however, to not distinguish them from other nationalists. Not only do fascists and national socialists consider the nation to be the desirable unit of organization, but they also privilege certain nations over others on the basis of racial characteristics. While not common today, there have been instances of national socialist and fascist workers' organizations. More frequently, there have been and continue to exist unions that exclude workers who do not possess certain characteristics not related to work.[14]

These aggressive particularists can be distinguished from those who advance the interests of particular categories of people using a multilateral or multistakeholder process.[15] Many analysts and activists who defend the significance of national politics, for instance, do not necessarily consider others to be inferior but, rather, may feel that the state offers more possibilities for democratic governance or protection from imperial domination.[16] Some among them may be considered internationalists in the sense that they aspire to an ever-integrating world, but others remain programmatically multilateralist and unwilling to compromise the relative autonomy of their state or group. Many human-rights advocates, for instance, value cultural differences and believe that the best way to preserve them is through global rules that raise cultural variability to a guiding principle.

At the other end of the spectrum, cosmopolitans challenge the primacy of territorial boundaries and nationality.[17] For them, human beings are global citizens and ought to behave as such. It is not the case that all cosmopolitans disregard cultural and other variations. Rather, they place these variations in a secondary position when compared to their ideals of universal citizenship. Yet, there are also important differences among cosmopolitans. Liberal cosmopolitans, for instance, emphasize the sameness of humans qua individuals but do not pay any attention to the inequities of power due to wealth. Socialist cosmopolitans, on the other hand, emphasize that global citizenship passes through the eradication of existing inequalities.

The recent debates over immigration into the United States and other countries illuminate the full spectrum of views from particularism to cosmopolitanism. At the particularist end of the spectrum, militias at the border between the United States and Mexico have taken the law into their own hands. Next to them, various factions of the Republican and Democratic parties want to manage migration through a combination of punishments and rewards, while many employers support a liberal cosmopolitan view that favors the free movement of labor across borders. Their cosmopolitanism, of course, differs a great deal from that of socialist cosmopolitans, who argue that migrant workers have rights, something that liberal cosmopolitans strongly oppose. This brings us to the question of equality.

From Inequality to Equality

Ever since its emergence, it has become apparent that capitalism can be organized in a variety of ways. At one extreme there have been totalitarian regimes that nurtured capitalism at the expense of social groups that stood in the way, whether peasants or workers. At the other extreme there have been proposals and attempts at overthrowing capitalism. Given that the global political economy of our day is characterized by capitalism, we outline the main perspectives competing for the hearts and minds of people and organizations, moving from the least to the most egalitarian visions.

The least egalitarian vision vying for primacy has been called hyperliberalism.[18] Hyperliberalism is based on institutional arrangements that allow full play of private property rights, and it is fundamentally "totalitarian" in the sense that it seeks to reduce every human activity to an economic transaction. Important dislocations, including the impacts of structural adjustments of the 1980s and 1990s and the financial crises in Mexico and East Asia during the 1990s, have led a number of liberals to advance alternatives to hyperliberalism. Some call for a more managed liberalism aiming, primarily, at maintaining the stability of the system by giving the IMF more surveillance and proactive powers. Managed liberalism may seek the selective input or collaboration of unions or other societal forces but only as a means to avoid destabilization.

Also concerned about the stability of global capitalism, a number of important global and national liberal leaders, such as the founder of the World Economic Forum, have gone a step further, asking that institutions of global governance take into account the social implications of their policies. For example, the Organization for Economic Cooperation and Development (OECD) has on occasion been at the forefront of promoting a more solidaristic social agenda, albeit one that is based on providing individuals with the skills to navigate the liberal global political economy rather than investing them with political and

35

social rights.[19] Even the IMF explored the social implications of its policies.[20] Many unions and other societal entities accept the logic of such limited social intervention, assuming, often correctly, that they will benefit from growth along capitalist lines. In their view, the regulatory role of societal forces should be limited to helping capitalism integrate social or ecological priorities in the most efficient manner, in the process commodifying them.

Social regulators find capitalism less desirable than do social managers but accept its inevitability and primacy. Thus, their goal is limited to taking certain aspects of human life out of capitalist competition and commodification. One route is that of compensatory policies. Programs that redistribute some wealth to particular groups of people, such as children, the aged, or the unemployed, as well as the paternalistic industrial relations systems of some East Asian countries, according to which workers were guaranteed lifelong employment by the corporation, would fall into this category. At the international level, most transfers of resources from the rich to the poor fall into this category to the degree that they are discretionary and are not based on rights and entitlements by the poor.

A second general route to social regulation may be called that of countervailing policies. Such policies extend the power of certain categories of stakeholders, enabling them to regulate the operation of capitalism. Laws that enforce the right to organize and bargain collectively across the whole working force are such policies, particularly when associated with the right to negotiate significant redistributions through collective bargaining. Laws that allow environmentalists to go beyond simply questioning the outcomes of economic activity and allow them to question investment choices, such as the building of new nuclear reactors, are such examples. In a number of European countries, these countervailing policies have become part of corporatist social welfare states, which require formalized relations between states, capital, and unions.[21]

Finally, social egalitarian policies go beyond the regulation of capitalism. While committed to the rights of the natural individual, they reject the liberal claim that corporations are also individuals entitled to operate in a private space independent of public authority. While committed to redistribution, they see it as a right and a programmatic choice, rather than a compensatory or countervailing mechanism. In short, social egalitarians aim at the structural reorganization of the global political economy.

Social democrats and syndicalists of the nineteenth and early twentieth centuries, and radical socialists and communists of the twentieth century, sought to transform capitalism, in the later case leading to significant redistribution but limited democracy.[22] As one looks at the failed efforts in Czechoslovakia (1968) and Chile (1973), however, one can imagine the potential of a political economy that is both open and redistributive.[23]

Scandinavian socialists have sought to reform capitalism by embedding it within more egalitarian and democratic rules that establish rights and entitlements, in addition to protections and corrections. The primary gathering of social egalitarians may be the World Social Forum, which has been taking place since 2001 and which brings together many parties, unions, and other societal organizations who share the view that "another world is possible," some seeking to reform it and some to transform it.

In our view, global democracy cannot simply be the expansion of participation to more and more stakeholders.[24] The market, for instance, does allow the majority of people to participate through buying and selling, but only within the parameters of their unequal resources. Liberal cosmopolitanism, in short, is not democratic in our view. Nor do we find ad hoc arrangements involving various stakeholders and more nongovernmental organizations sufficiently democratic. Sometimes they serve to marginalize weaker or less mainstream stakeholders while raising serious questions about representation and accountability. Nor are authoritarian or philanthropic redistributive arrangements democratic. Many authoritarian regimes, from Bismarck's Germany to Perón's Argentina, to the Soviet Union, engaged in various forms of redistribution but at the expense of democratic participation. Philanthropists like the Gates Foundation or CARE International are doing a great deal of positive work, but they can also discontinue a program at their own discretion. Democracy at any level must not only include broad participation or voice but must also allow the translation of that participation into policy choices that go against the grain of structural inequality.[25] This is the combined criterion against which we evaluate views on global governance.

CHAPTER TWO

Global Governance

Academics and activists have increasingly focused on global governance during the past fifteen years, largely due to the prominent role of global economic organizations, such as the IMF, the World Bank, and the WTO, but also due to the formation of the International Criminal Court.[26] These developments, combined with deeper regional integration in Europe, North America, and South America, the collapse of the Soviet Union, and the increasing internationalization of capital and communications, are the bases of two claims: first, that meaningful policy can only take place at the international and, indeed, the global level and, second, that this is actually happening.

We will not engage the questions in detail, but we do wish to situate ourselves in these debates. First, we ask whether more policy, specifically social policy, should take place at the global level. We think that there is enough evidence to suggest that this is necessary. Multinational corporations are present everywhere, particular states identify the globe or whole regions as relevant to their national interest, and infrastructure is increasingly globalized. Yet, we must keep in mind that for many countries and people, this has been the case for a long time. All of the South and much of the North have long been subject to external and, in fact, global policies. So, acting as if global governance is a recent phenomenon adds insult to the injury for those parts of the world that have been shaped by decisions to which they did not assent, whether the Treaty of Tordesillas that divided the New World between Portugal and Spain (1494), the Berlin Conference that divided Africa (1880s), or the Treaty of Versailles (1919) that shaped West Asia and much of the rest of the world.[27]

The second question is whether more and more governance is taking place at the global level. We think that more governance is taking place at the global level in the sense that some global organizations and processes do produce binding policies. As we note in the previous chapter, however, a great deal of governance is also taking place at the interstate level with key countries playing a dominant role without subjecting themselves to the same standards. Increasingly, policy is also taking place at the regional level, certainly in the European Union and NATO. Finally, most policies with international or global implications come from individual countries. The discourse of security against terrorism in the post–September 11 era has provided a wall behind which global decisions are hidden. Moreover, this discourse also provides cover for societal entities with nativist inclinations. It would be wrong for anyone to think that the rules of the WTO affect equally the trade of cars and the trade of weapons. Choosing to contest the trade of weapons in the United States, France, the United Kingdom, or Russia, therefore, may be prudent rather than nationalist. For European labor unions to act as if regional legislation is not important would be self-defeating. Acting as if the global context is inconsequential, however, can be equally shortsighted since Europe is very much a part of the global political economy.

Public and Private Governance

In recent years there has been a lot of attention focused on the rise of private governance at the expense of public governance.[28] What do the terms *public* and *private* mean? For much of recent history, the term *public* has been associated with the state. As the state has come to encompass more aspects of human life, from war to garbage collection, and because many states have violated their own rules against their citizens, it has become apparent that the term *public* cannot simply denote state participation. Quite often, a state's primary goal may be to strengthen the realm of the private. Thus, in order to argue that a policy is broadening and deepening the public sphere, we should not limit ourselves to state participation. Rather, we must ask whether the policy expands participation to include all stakeholders, in the process reorganizing the state itself in a more democratic direction.

For much of history, the term *private* has been associated with economic activities undertaken by corporations or other organizations with limited public supervision.[29] Clearly, the daily operations of large corporations have momentous implications for public policy and for the rights of natural individuals. Moreover, for various reasons that we examine in more depth in chapter 5, corporate social responsibility, manifested in the proliferation of codes of conduct and other instruments, has become very prominent over the past fifteen years. Can "private" policies be binding and effective? If one takes collective bargaining and contracts as examples, then, yes, they can. Even so, policies that enhance the discretion of private agents to negotiate among themselves agreements that have broader public impacts expand the realm of the private at the expense of the public sphere. A collective contract between a corporation and a union representing its formal workers, for instance, can very well work to the detriment of temporary and subcontracting workers. Policies that limit the discretion of private agencies and challenge inequalities, on the other hand, broaden and deepen a more egalitarian public sphere. On balance, arrangements that do not challenge existing power relations are only likely to legitimate them.

Society and Global Governance

Societal entities have become increasingly implicated in global governance politics.[30] In a few instances they have been able to gain a seat at the table, and in even more instances, a chair in the room of global negotiations. These developments have given rise to important debates over the preferable strategies and the effectiveness of global societal politics.

Strategies and Tactics

Where should societal entities place their energies? At the national, regional, international, or global levels? Should they aim at comprehensive policies or should they focus on particular species or practices? Should they lobby or should they demonstrate?

One is tempted to argue that the world visions of societal entities will also determine the arena or level at which they will contest governance. While such preferences are good predictors, they are not adequate. The nationalists of the nineteenth century, for instance, contested their nationality in various international forums, precisely because it was threatened from the outside. Human-rights advocates supporting cultural variability are very vocal at global conferences, as are unions that prefer protectionism over open trade. Multinational corporations employ global forums to promote global standards and mobility, and national forums to prevent social regulation.[31] The question, therefore, is not only the level that a societal entity chooses but, also, what it expects to accomplish. The fact that European unions expend a lot of energy on EU affairs is to be expected. Are they doing so, however, against the interests of extraregional unions, or are they trying to establish common ground with them?

Societal entities, and certainly unions, are often organized around particular groups of people or aspects of nature. It stands to reason that environmental groups that advocate for animals cannot agree to a comprehensive policy that does not include them. Yet, will they choose policies that protect specific animals at the expense of more comprehensive policies, or will they seek to bridge the two? It is often asserted that there is an inherent conflict between policies that focus on particular social or environmental issues and policies that take a more comprehensive approach. We find this dichotomy misleading precisely because there is some truth to it. Rather, we think that there is at least a third option: policies that focus on particular social or environmental issues can be integrated within more comprehensive policy visions. Preservationists, for instance, can set up nature preserves pretending that humans do not exist, or they can work to integrate them in a manner that is ecologically sound and socially equitable.[32]

How will societal entities go about influencing the forums that they have chosen to target? Will they adopt militant actions and outsider strategies or choose negotiations behind closed doors? It seems to us that the choice of tactics does depend on the access that an entity has as well as its own political preferences. Violent or militant tactics, however, are neither evidence of emancipatory politics nor of strong societal politics. Right-wing and religious fundamentalists use very militant tactics. They are certainly not evidence of an egalitarian order rising. Unions and other societal forces routinely engage in militant campaigns against governments and corporations not because they want to demonstrate their power but because they desperately want to modify the behavior of states and corporations. Militant tactics, such as strikes, may very well be evidence of a new movement rising or may be desperate acts by the disenfranchised.

Yet, it seems to us that an organization that wants profound change but only seeks the approval of the entities it wishes to change either is lying to itself or does not have another option. If the latter, it may be time to review the reasons why. Global union organizations, for instance, attend the meetings of both the World Economic Forum and the World Social Forum. An argument can be made that they must attend both. However, trying to please both may not be tenable without compromising their efforts to globalize social justice. In order to globalize social justice, moreover, egalitarian forces must bring along

41

constituencies that have been marginalized in the past, whether by the powers that be or the particularism of egalitarian forces themselves.

Effectiveness

The question of societal effectiveness over the institutions of global governance has given rise to profound debates over definition and measurement.[33] It seems to us that a thorough account of the effectiveness of societal entities must address two questions. First, are the institutions that societal entities are influencing consequential policy makers? Second, how profound is their influence?

Clearly, not all international institutions are equally important. As we discuss in more detail in chapter 4, the International Labour Organization (ILO) does not have the same powers as the WTO. Moreover, the locus of authority may not even be at the global level. The U.S. Department of the Treasury, for example, has more power over the world financial system than does the IMF. Unions may well be very successful in influencing powerless institutions but totally impotent in influencing powerful ones. Certainly, one can contrast the relative prominence of unions in the ILO to their exclusion from the WTO. This is not to say that unions and other societal entities should avoid engaging weak organizations, if that is their main or only choice. There is much to be said about using any forum for reframing the debate and, thus, the policy agenda. At some point, however, symbolic politics can well obscure where the power lies.

With that in mind, the second question that we must address is the depth of societal influence, particularly on powerful policy makers. At the most superficial level of influence, societal entities may be brought in as interlocutors but without any prospects for shaping policy. A bit more consequential is the ability of societal entities to shape the operations of a policymaking organization or forum. Environmental organizations, for instance, have influenced the operations of the World Bank over the years. Even more profound is the ability of societal entities to shape the constitution of policymaking entities. In that respect, the impact of environmentalists is limited. While they have forced the World Bank to create an environmental office, that office is auxiliary to the liberal growth bias of the organization. Finally, the more far-reaching influence is manifested in the ability of a societal entity to shape the broader rules of the global political economy. Corporations, for instance, have been much more influential in shaping the rules behind the WTO when compared to any other societal entity.

Engaging institutions of governance and power, whether public or private, is a two-way street. On one hand, societal entities exert their influence on these organizations; on the other, these organizations can reshape their interlocutors. Societal entities can be accepted at the table only if they modify their strategies and comportment, while policies may force them to reconsider their world visions. Stated differently, we must not only ask how effective societal entities are. We must also ask what the price of effectiveness, if any, may be.

ENGAGING EACH OTHER, 1864–2006: THE WEIGHT OF HISTORY

In January 2002, a number of global union organizations decided to abandon the name they had been using for more than a century, and instead of international trade secretariats (ITSs) they chose to be called global union federations (GUFs). This name change came at the end of a period during which a number of ITSs gave up their historical autonomy to unify with each other, eventually reducing their number to ten. In November 2006, after a century of separate existence, the International Confederation of Free Trade Unions (ICFTU), the largest union confederation in the world, and the World Confederation of Labour (WCL), the second largest, united into the International Trade Union Confederation (ITUC). Joining them were a number of unions that did not belong to a global federation.[1] The end result is the most inclusive global labor organization since the late 1940s. What is the history behind this unification, and how far is it moving unions toward

45

the globalization of solidarity, the theme of the ICFTU's 2004 conference during which it formally decided to seek unification?

While widely known among those interested in labor politics, the existence of such a comprehensive network of global and regional labor organizations has escaped the attention of almost all analysts who deal with global societal politics. As of March 1, 2007, there existed ten GUFs with a combined membership of more than 149 million people. Each of them had affiliates in more than one hundred countries, with Education International reaching 169. Most can claim lineages as far back as 1889, when the first ITSs were formed. One of the predecessors of the ITUC, the World Confederation of Labour, was formed in 1920, while the other, the ICFTU, can claim a lineage as far back as 1901 (see table 3.1). With the exception of sports organizations and some churches, there is probably no other global societal network with a history and geographic reach such as that of labor.

Some of the strongest acts of labor solidarity have not involved these organizations but have been the result of alliances of unions across borders.[2] Many analysts, in fact, have criticized these organizations for being too cautious, generally avoiding militant strategies and tactics when needed.[3] Yet, these organizations reflect a long-standing effort at institutionalizing collaboration and coordination—at establishing internal governance—while even the most heroic acts of solidarity have been episodic, precisely because of the absence of long-term connections. Our focus on global union organizations is predicated on the assumption that strong and democratic organizations, or some other type of permanent and strong connections that establish a degree of legitimacy and long-term global self-governance mechanisms, are a necessary component for a vibrant global union politics. In this chapter, therefore, we trace the history of global union organizations and identify the main reasons why national unions have not been able or willing to move toward stronger global self-governance, at the same time that they have formed such a comprehensive network. It is on that basis, we think, that one can best evaluate the promise and limitations of the unification that we started with. We are not among those who place all failures to achieve global solidarity at the feet of unions. Capital and nonegalitarian states have placed extraordinary obstacles in the way of this process. We do think, however, that unions have actively participated in their own triumphs

Table 3.1. Global Union Organizations, March 1, 2007

Name	Origins[a]	Current Status[b]	Membership (Millions)	Countries
International Trade Union Confederation (ITUC)	1901	2006	168	>153
World Federation of Trade Unions (WFTU)	1945	1949	?	?
Trade Union Advisory Committee to the OECD	1948	1962	66	30
Education International	1920	1993	30	169
International Federation of Chemical, Energy, Mine, and General Workers' Unions (ICEM)	1890	1995	20	125
International Federation of Journalists (IFJ)	1926	1985	<1	117
International Textile, Garment, and Leather Workers' Federation (ITGLWF)	1892	1970	10	110
Public Services International (PSI)	1907	1958	20	150
International Transport Workers' Federation (ITF)	1893	1900	4.5	148
Building and Wood Workers' International (BWI)	1883	2005	>12	135
International Metalworkers' Federation (IMF)	1893	1904	25	100
International Union of Food, Agricultural, Hotel, Restaurant, Catering, Tobacco, and Allied Workers' Associations (IUF)	1889	1994	12	120
Union Network International (UNI)	1892	2000	15.5	140

Sources: Origins and Current Status based on Rainer Gries, "Overview of the Development of International Trade Union Organizations," in *International Trade Union Organizations: Inventory of the Archive of Social Democracy and the Library of the Friedrich-Ebert-Stiftung,* ed. Peter Rütters, Michael Schneider, Erwin Schweißhelm, and Rüdiger Zimmerman (Bonn: Friedrich-Ebert-Stiftung, 2002), 85–94, updated by authors based on websites of organizations. Membership and countries with affiliates from websites of organizations or estimated by authors.

[a] *Origins* refers to the date of formation of the first organization that eventually joined the current organization. The date given by Gries for BWI would bring the first secretariat date to 1883 rather than 1889, which is commonly assumed.

[b] Current status refers to the date that the organization adopted its present status, usually as a result of mergers. In the case of IFJ, it refers to the year it became an international trade secretariat.

and tragedies. Nowhere is this more obvious than in the union politics associated with these organizations.

In order to accomplish these goals, we identify six periods articulated around key organizational developments that reflect the deeper dynamics of global labor politics. The first period is that of the First International (1864–1876). The second begins in 1889, when the Second Socialist International was formed, and ends with WWI, which brought with it the collapse of the Second International and deep divisions in world socialist and union politics. The emergence of the ITSs and the International Federation of Trade Unions (IFTU) were the major results of this period. The third period includes the interwar years. The efforts to move the IFTU from a confederation to a federation and the reasons behind its ultimate failure are central to this period. The fourth period covers the height of the Cold War, from 1945 to the late 1960s. The fifth period extends from the late 1960s to the early 1990s and is characterized by the rise of a multipolar global union politics that reflects the enhanced status of Europe, Japan, and the industrializing countries. The last period extends from the collapse of the Soviet Union and the global labor organizations that it supported, to the unification of the major union organizations mentioned above. In each case, we set the overall context of the era and then discuss the main organizational and ideological dynamics of global union politics.[4]

The subtitles we use for each period are grounded in our discussion of societal politics in the previous chapter and aim at capturing the organizational and ideological dynamics of each period. In chapters 4 and 5 we address more explicitly global union politics vis-à-vis states and capital. Here, references to the state do not simply refer to the state as a specific organization but also to the state as a territorial demarcation. Societal forces routinely participate in both the creation and disruption of the territorial divisions of the world. Unions have certainly played a very important role in shaping contemporary political geography. The references to capital cover both business and the capitalist organization of the global political economy as it has emerged since the nineteenth century. Combined, references to states and capital allow us to track the approaches of unions toward the organizational and ideological characteristics of the global political economy since the middle of the nineteenth century.

Table 3.2. Key Developments in Global Union Governance

Date	Event or organization
1864–1876	First International
1889	Formation of first international trade secretariats
1889–1914	Second (Socialist) International
1901–1914	International Secretariat of National Trade Union Centers (renamed International Federation of Trade Unions in 1913)
1919	Formation of International Labour Organization
1919–1945	International Federation of Trade Unions
1919–1941	Third (Communist) International
1919–1968	International Federation of Christian Trade Unions
1921–1936	"Red International of Labor Unions"
1934	German National Socialists outlaw autonomous trade unions
1937	American Federation of Labor joins International Federation of Trade Unions
1945–	World Federation of Trade Unions
1949	Split of World Federation of Trade Unions
1949–2006	International Confederation of Free Trade Unions
1951	Milan Agreement between International Confederations of Free Trade Unions and international trade secretariats (most recently revised in 1996)
1968–2006	International Federation of Christian Trade Unions renamed World Confederation of Labor
1968	World Federation of Trade Unions disciplined by Soviet Union for condemning invasion of Czechoslovakia
1966–1970s	World Company Councils period
1969–1982	American Federation of Labor–Congress of Industrial Organizations leaves International Confederation of Free Trade Unions
1973–	European Trade Union Confederation
1991–	Decline of World Federation of Trade Unions
1990s	Unification of various international trade secretariats
1990s	South African and Brazilian unions join International Confederation of Free Trade Unions
2002	International trade secretariats renamed global union federations
2006	International Confederation of Free Trade Unions, World Confederation of Labor, Trade Union Advisory Committee, and unaffiliated unions join to form the International Trade Union Confederation
2007	Council of Global Unions (ITUC, TUAC, most GUFs, and the International Arts and Entertainment Alliance)

The First International, 1864–1876: Challenging State and Capital

The First International was formed during a period of deepening global integration accompanied by state building, particularly in Europe. Global integration under the hegemony of British finance led to the creation of modern global infrastructure and the tying of the far reaches of the world to European and mainly British finance. While most of Africa, Asia, and South America could not resist British hegemony, continental Europe, the United States, and Japan adopted policies that would make them more competitive toward Britain and each other. These involved an active role of the state in both facilitating industrialization and protecting it from competition.

In this context the major direct incentive for international union collaboration was the importation of strikebreakers from the Continent into the United Kingdom, a strategy that aimed at stalling the growth of the British union movement. Responding to these challenges in "the summer of 1862, over 300 workmen from France and about a dozen from Germany came to the International Exhibition in London."[5] While there, they broached the possibility of an international workers' organization to help boost budding national unionization throughout Europe and address the importation of strikebreakers. On October 28, 1864, a mixture of British unionists, refugees from the radical and communist groups behind the 1848 revolutions in continental Europe, and representatives from political and workers' organizations from continental Europe formed the International Working Men's Association in London.[6]

The First International was formed during this formative period in the organization of national unions and parties. Existing unions or parties with national aspirations could join, but so could local associations of individuals. Although the rules of the International encouraged domestic coordination and unification, they did not allow any single organization to monopolize national membership. Its membership rules were motivated by the formative characteristics of the period as well as the cosmopolitanism of the more radical founders of the organization. Its leadership rested with its Governing Council, which reflected the national origins of the affiliates. Its responsibilities were to provide a forum for the exchange of information and shape an agenda for working-class politics and action. While more federal than confederal, the International was not a unitary organization like the Catholic Church or a corporation. Members belonged to affiliates more so than to the International. As a result, they could withdraw or become less involved, and resources were always a problem. In fact, efforts at giving the Governing Council more authority over sections were one of the reasons for the organization's eventual demise.

Despite the brevity of its existence and its limited resources, the International played more than a symbolic role. Even though it did not start the movement toward unionization, it played an active role by actually offering material and political support, particularly in the period from 1867 to 1870, and in some cases it played the key role in initiating and/or shaping the union movements of particular countries. Finally, it provided the forum for the negotiation of a labor agenda that, in its general parameters, has survived to our days.[7]

In terms of constituencies and membership, the First International both challenged and reflected the politics of the times. While not programmatically limited to Europe, it remained largely European—the only exception being some sections of individuals from the United States.[8] Since unionization was still in its infancy in Europe and the United States, and even more so in other parts of the world, it is fair to say that it did not actively exclude any countries where unions and related parties were emerging. As it became more radical, however, it lost the allegiance of the British trade unionists, and its efforts at attracting U.S. unions were not successful.[9]

In its General Rules, the International declared "that all societies and individuals adhering to it will acknowledge truth, justice, and morality as the basis of their conduct toward each other and toward all men, without regard to color, creed, or nationality." One can assume that "all men" included women; the organization, however, did not actively seek the participation of women workers, reflecting the active exclusion of women by many of the unions of the time.[10] Its attitude toward race emancipation was more positive. It did congratulate President Lincoln on his reelection and was clearly on the side of the northern states. In fact, British workers had stood resolutely against capital's desire to enter the war on the side of the southern states.

The world vision of the First International was contested through various political rounds, which have been the subject of debates that continued for decades.[11] During its early years, British trade unionists, whose goal was the regulation of capitalism and the building of unions, provided the backbone of the organization but increasingly withdrew, both because they had accomplished some of their goals and because they disagreed with the growing radicalism of the International. Without tracing the successive debates between cooperativists and communists or communists and anarchists, we can summarize the trend by saying that the International grew more critical of capitalism and the capitalist state—in short, it argued for a more egalitarian internationalism. Even among those who supported the organization in this direction, however, there were important tensions between discourse and practice. The difficulties of reconciling an internationalist-egalitarian discourse with an increasingly statist-reformist practice became more pronounced in the subsequent period, with disastrous implications for global labor and socialist politics as the nationalist component eventually overwhelmed the internationalist.[12]

From 1889 to World War I: Reforming State and Capital

The incentives for union collaboration during this period were very similar to those of the previous period. International migration—whether permanent or temporary—became an even more pronounced characteristic of the global political economy, now involving non-European countries as well. While in the previous period it was the British unions that objected to the importation of workers from the Continent, now it was the German and U.S. unions objecting to the importation of workers from throughout Europe or Asia, a result of the ascent of these two countries in the global political economy. To get a sense of the significance of migration during this era, it is worth noting that today's estimated 175 million migrants are a much lower proportion of the world's population than migrants were in the late nineteenth century. If migration can be the cause of so much debate in our days—when it is not even the main conduit of transnational flows—one can imagine how important it was then, when it was the most significant means of transnational flows, next to finance.

In addition to the direct impacts of migration on the maturing union movement of the industrializing world, workers also felt the competition with each other indirectly due to increasing international trade and finance. As a result, it was during this era that demands for "leveling the playing field" by establishing common labor rules first became an international issue (see chapter 4). Again, it is worth noting that global trade as a proportion of the global political economy did not reach pre-WWI levels until the 1970s.

The contradictory dynamics between globalization and national-ization became even more pronounced during the late nineteenth century as an increasingly predatory "nationalization" took place within an increasingly more integrated global political economy.[13] Many unions explicitly adopted this nationalist logic, siding with their state and capital against the rest of the world. This process was facilitated by domestic labor reforms whose aim was to contain the rising appeal of the socialist and labor movements. Union success in reforming the state, manifested in the increasing role of parliaments, raised additional opportunities for political action by or on behalf of workers.[14] These reforms led unions and parties to focus their ener-gies on further reforming domestic politics—not an unreasonable strategy.[15]

The difficulties of trying to build socialist and labor international-ism in the face of nationalization were very apparent in the history of the Second International and the emerging global union organizations. The "New [Second] Socialist International" (Second International) was timidly conceived in 1889.[16] So tentative was the process that the International did not have a permanent office until 1900.

The Second International was intended as an organization of social democratic parties.[17] Unions from countries that did not have socialist parties were allowed to join, but the goal was to help build such par-ties so that they could take their place in the organization. Moreover, by allowing only one entity per country to join, the Second International played a leading role in contributing to the territorializa-tion of global socialist politics. In the absence of supranational com-mitments, the national dynamic of the edifice overcame the interna-tional, resulting in most member parties supporting their own states during WWI.[18] A closer look shows that there were strong interna-tionalist tendencies within the Socialist International and that this out-come was anything but preordained.[19] These internationalists sought to establish a stronger organizational edifice even in the midst of the ruins of the war, efforts that eventually resulted in the formation of the Third International (1919).

The impacts of the Second International on unionism were both positive and negative. Politically, it encouraged the creation of unions, promoted international collaboration among them, and provided a powerful and comprehensive political program. Practically, its congresses offered union leaders an opportunity to meet and form their own organizations. On the negative side, it focused on the building of strong national units at the expense of suprasocietal ties. A second negative legacy was the division of labor between parties and unions, as promoted and required by the International. Accordingly, parties would be in charge of the political aspects of social change while unions would focus on economic and technical issues. While some division of labor made practical and political sense, the end result was the weakening of those unions that sought to combine political and economic action, whether syndicalist or radical socialist.[20] Moreover, the destruction of the Second International during WWI left social democratic unions unprepared for the political challenges that they had to face immediately after the war.

Global Union Politics: The Foundations of the Present

It was in this context that the contemporary architecture of the global union network came into existence (see table 3.2). First came the sectoral organizations bringing together unions from the same craft or line of work, called the international trade secretariats (until the recent name change—see table 3.1). Their primary concern was the impact of migrations on their members and their efforts to organize. The earliest ones were formed in 1889, and perhaps as early as 1882.[21] By 1914 there were thirty-two ITSs, twenty-four of them based in Germany, underscoring the country's preeminence in labor politics. The ITSs were wholly European until 1904, when a few U.S. unions joined. Almost all of them were programmatically weak and lacked permanent staff, depending on national union staff to play that role "in their spare time." As the case of one of the best organized among them suggests, that of the typographers, the members were hesitant to establish strong federal organizations.[22] Support activities were the exception, and there were no efforts at common organizing campaigns. Some of them—such as the International Transport Workers' Federation—were becoming more centralized and industrywide, but at no time in their early history did the ITSs see themselves as federal or transsocietal unions.[23]

54

The first ITSs were followed by an umbrella organization of national union federations, that is, national organizations of various sectoral unions. As unions became more prominent and because of their exclusion from the Second International, national union federations felt the need to establish an organization of national centers to also counterbalance the segmented nature of the ITSs.[24] The result was the formation of the International Secretariat of National Trade Union Centers (1901), renamed the International Federation of Trade Unions (IFTU) in 1913. Like the Second International and the ITSs, the International Secretariat of National Trade Union Centers (Secretariat) also adopted the one country–one union approach and used it to marginalize syndicalists and anarchists. Moreover, efforts at making the Secretariat more centralized and federal were resisted by the AFL and the British, who were afraid of German and social democratic hegemony.

Much of the work of the conferences of the Secretariat dealt with immediate organizational issues "and practical measures concerning labour were relatively neglected."[25] Yet, there was marginal evidence that international union politics was making slow progress in the direction of stronger organizational ties.[26] Early on, the Secretariat started collecting and disseminating national labor data in an annual publication, and in 1909 it launched a regular newsletter. In 1911 it also became a nodal point in coordinating strike support, adopting the responsibility for issuing appeals—on the basis of requests by national centers.[27]

The Secretariat also made progress in its relations with the ITSs, which were first invited to participate in its conference in 1913, supplanting the congresses of the Second International and demonstrating the growing influence and autonomy of labor unions even in the heart of the world's socialist movement. (The Secretariat and most ITSs were based in and depended on German national union support.) In many ways, the state of affairs between the Secretariat and the ITSs as it appeared in 1913 is quite similar to what is currently unfolding, an issue we discuss later in this chapter.

The global union network remained largely European with some U.S. participation (and brief participation by Australian unions), falling behind the Second International, which had some participation from Asia and South America. Not only did the global union organizations exclude syndicalists,[28] but they also did not establish connections with the emerging union movements of Latin America, nor did they express themselves on the plight of workers in the rest of the South, particularly the colonies.[29] Like national unions, they were also largely blind to gender issues, reflecting the often militantly sexist policies of their affiliates. Of the thirty-two ITSs before WWI, none of the organizations for which we have seen numbers had a majority of women members, and only one (that of the bookbinders) had almost as many women as men.[30] This is a major gap given the prominent role of women workers in the industrialization process and the prominent women's movements of the times.

The focus of international union politics on skilled workers was also underscored by the early ITSs, a tendency that ran against the emerging industrywide unionism of the day.[31] Most of the thirty-two ITSs in existence before WWI were organized along craft lines. Finally, the international union movement was not able to find a common policy with respect to migrants—a major labor constituency of the era.

By the end of this period, international union politics continued to exhibit a considerable ideological range, even though the Second International and the global union organizations had sought to marginalize anarchists and syndicalists. At one extreme were the liberal trade unionists associated with most of the AFL and parts of the British union movement. Their professed goal was to help national capitalism do better while ensuring that organized workers received their share. By demanding that capital recognize them and negotiate with them, however, they demanded a degree of regulation that even paternalistic capitalists, that is, those like Pullman and Carnegie who prided themselves on their social spirit, found hard to accept. These were also largely nationalists and preferred confederal, intersocietal arrangements. Christian unionists, who followed their own organizational route, were strongly opposed to the class-struggle approach of the socialists and advocated a protective approach to social policy. They managed to establish a strong foothold in a few European countries, primarily Belgium and the Netherlands, and were eventually to become a long-term tendency within global union politics.[32] Continental social democrats varied in their support of the contradictory internationalism of the Second International and its commitment to reforming capitalism. Finally, syndicalists[33] and radical social democrats advanced more radical views of capitalism and of the state system. Starting with opposition to WWI, these tendencies contributed to the radicalization of socialist and labor politics during the first years after WWI.

The Interwar Period: Global Civil War

The economic forces that had motivated unions to create international organizations before WWI continued to play an important role after the war. Migration remained a major direct incentive for European unions—though not for U.S. unions, as migration to the United States from outside North America was largely halted. Contrary to the common view of the interwar era as one of isolationism, moreover, the mid-to-late 1920s were characterized by growing international financial and trade integration.[34] The Great Depression put an end to that process but also led to the realization that the global political economy had to be managed.

More importantly, the interwar period was characterized by a fundamental struggle over the organization of the political economy—from the national to the global. Unions were active participants in this struggle—more directly now that the Second International had lost its hegemony. Two prominent analysts have sought to capture the dynamics of this era in their own ways.

According to Karl Polanyi, the misdirected effort of liberals to rebuild the nineteenth-century liberal order, in the absence of the pillars that had held it together in the past, deepened and prolonged the social devastation triggered by WWI. In the end, the liberal order "disintegrated as a result of . . . the measures which society adopted in order not to be, in turn, annihilated by the actions of the self-regulated market."[35] Yet, these measures, "the great transformation," were not all the same, either in form or in purpose. While in some instances society moved to the left, in others it moved to the right, always with dramatic implications for the losers. In short, Polanyi's concept of the "great transformation" obscures the complexity of interwar politics.[36] Thus, we prefer Eric Hobsbawm's suggestion that this was a period of a global civil war during which people fought to reshape the nature of the global political economy marching under ideologies that often directly challenged both state and capital.[37] Such an approach requires that we look at the world politics of the era more closely. While people were making history under circumstances not entirely of their own choice, choice seems to have played a much more important role than in the eras before and after.

Global Union Politics:
From the Shadow of Social Democracy into a World in Flames

The Second International was weakened irreparably by WWI, although it has continued to exist in one form or another to our day.[38] This left social democratic unions with international tasks for which the party-union policy of the Second International had not prepared them. Their weakness was all the more evident because the years immediately after the war were full of extensive and intensive mobilizations as well as important policy reforms, such as the formation of the International Labour Organization (discussed in chapter 4).

The IFTU was formally reconstituted at the Amsterdam congress of 1919, "the first international trade union congress ever held,"[39] an event that finalized the division between parties and unions that had started before WWI. Syndicalists and communists were excluded, and Christian unionists chose not to participate because of their opposition to the class politics of the social democratic unions. In 1920 they formed their own organization, whose successor joined the ITUC in November 2006.

In the first years after its reconstitution, the IFTU was active on many fronts, taking its position at the ILO as the representative of labor, advancing proposals for postwar reconstruction, and engaging in major actions in response to policies in Hungary and Poland. By 1923, the divisions within the world's labor movement broke down its prospects of becoming a hegemonic organization within global socialism. In addition to opposition from the left, the obstacles also came from within its own ranks.

From the very beginning, the AFL and its British allies were opposed to making the organization more federal and rejected a majoritarian decision-making process and the inclusion of political issues on its agenda.[40] Eventually, the AFL refused to join and focused on the Pan-American Federation of Labor in order to entrench its regional hegemony and deal with Mexican immigration into the United States. By the mid-1920s, a rapprochement resulted in a number of sectoral unions joining the ITSs, but the AFL did not return to the fold until 1937, when it did so in order to keep the Congress of Industrial

Organizations,[41] a rival federation formed in the 1930s, from taking its place in global labor politics.

During the 1920s a proposal intended to make the IFTU an organization of action came from Edo Fimmen, the leader of the International Transport Workers' Federation, who argued that the IFTU should be reorganized into an international of trade secretariats.[42] This reorganization, which would have given a primary role to the trade secretariats but at the expense of their autonomy, failed to attract serious consideration. Another proposal for closer organizational relations was floated during the 1930s. While Fimmen's proposal was intended to make the international union movement more dynamic, the new proposal was intended to generate more resources for the IFTU, whose continental members were being decimated by fascism. This proposal was also not adopted. In short, the debates about the relationship between the intersectoral and the sectoral global union organizations, which had started before WWI and which continue in our days, were very important during the interwar period.

While the historical divisions between social democrats and trade unionists continued to play an important role in global labor politics, it was the Russian Revolution of 1917 that truly divided national and global unionism. The formation of the communist Third International in the spring of 1919 is a significant event in interwar politics.[43] Not only did it bring together the most internationalist and radical elements in the global socialist movement—until its total subjugation to the Soviet state—but it also played a critical role in promoting radical unionism throughout the world.[44]

Originally, the communists did not wish to establish a separate international union organization nor break up existing national organizations; instead, they hoped to radicalize and lead existing organizations from the inside. Partly in response to the concerns of the syndicalists who were uncomfortable with the dominance of parties in the Third International[45] and partly in response to the IFTU's unwillingness to allow the operation of competing tendencies within unions, the communists formed the International Council of Trade and Industrial Unions during 1920 and 1921.[46] For much of the interwar period, the "Red International of Labor Unions" (RILU) competed with the IFTU over the Western European union movement, with limited success. During the mid-1920s, efforts by British and Soviet trade unionists to bridge the gap were unsuccessful, especially after the failure of the "general strike" of 1926 in Great Britain. The "social-fascism" strategy employed by the communists during the 1928–1934 period created lasting wounds between the communists and the socialists. After the ascent of Hitler, the "popular front" strategy against national socialism sought to heal these wounds.[47] As part of that strategy, RILU was dissolved in 1936, too late for the German unions, which had been destroyed by the national socialists a few years earlier, and, soon, for the Spanish unions, who were on the losing side of the Spanish civil war.

The divisions within international union and socialist/communist politics were disastrous because of the rise of the right. Their competition for members and influence, however, did help expand the political geography of unionism. Because of their inability to make major inroads in Western Europe, with the exception of France, the communists sought, with some success, to expand to the rest of the world. In the case of Asia, they made significant inroads into the nascent union movement,[48] while in a number of Latin American countries they enhanced their influence in existing union movements. This became apparent when, as part of the "popular front" strategy of the 1930s, they helped form a regional organization composed of socialist, nationalist, and communist unions.[49] The IFTU eventually responded to the challenge but was not particularly successful,[50] largely due to the imperial and often racist attitudes of British unionists, as the case of South Africa indicates.[51] In 1927 the IFTU admitted, for the first time, a "black" union from South Africa. Its representative, however, was not allowed to attend the annual meeting of the British Trade Union Congress in order not to offend "white" unions in South Africa.[52]

All major tendencies within international union politics advocated equal pay for equal work for women but also continued a paternalistic approach toward them. During the interwar period, the IFTU supported the Trade Union Women's Conferences, but no women reached positions of authority. The situation was quite similar with RILU.

In terms of broader world vision, the picture became as diverse as it had been before social democracy had emerged hegemonic.[53] On one extreme, some workers formed fascist and national socialist workers' organizations.[54] These organizations disappeared after WWII, but the legacy of fascist labor policies, largely intended to co-opt the working class and destroy democratic and socialist unions, continued to be felt in Latin America, where populist dictators, such as Getúlio Vargas in Brazil and Juan Perón in Argentina, built workers' organizations and adopted labor policies that were influenced by Italian fascism,[55] in the process destroying the more radical syndicalist unions that had been prominent in early Latin American union politics. To make the point here, it is ironic that one of the most radical unions of our day, the Brazilian Central Única dos Trabalhadores (CUT), has recently been defending the Brazilian labor code, tailored after fascist Italy's labor code.

Among democratic unions, some were strongly nationalist, with the AFL actively pursuing its regional hegemony at the expense of the IFTU. In response, some Latin American unions also used nationalism against U.S. domination. Important forces within the British Trade Union Congress continued to be multilateralist, while there were other elements both among British unions and on the European continent that were more identifiably internationalist. Finally, we must note that many of the unions that joined RILU were strong internationalists, as were the remaining syndicalists.

With respect to the organization of the political economy, the picture was also varied. At one extreme were the fascist and national socialist workers organizations that were thoroughly supportive of strongly managed national capitalism. Among democratic unions, the picture was more diverse. The AFL, as well as many British unions, favored the economistic regulation of capitalism. The Christian unionists also rejected class politics but were in favor of social protection and solidarity. The European social democrats continued to support the reform of the capitalist political economy with some socialist unions advancing more profound reforms. The communist unions and the declining syndicalists advocated a more revolutionary reorganization of the economy and of interstate politics. By the late 1920s, if not earlier, labor unions in the Soviet Union had lost their political and operational autonomy.

By the end of this period, the most internationalist and egalitarian unions had been decimated. On one hand, they had been physically exterminated by fascists, national socialists, and other right-wing totalitarians. On the other hand, they were also physically purged and politically disciplined by the Soviet communists. At the end of WWI, the largest unions still standing were the most nationalist and most liberal among democratic unions—those of the United States and the United Kingdom.

From World War II to the Late 1960s: Fighting Along with the State

Post-WWII union politics was very much affected by the institutionalization of the Cold War and the welfare state. No aspect of world politics was unaffected by the Cold War, including union politics. Moreover, the destruction of radical unions and socialists during the interwar period and the polarizing dynamics of the first part of the Cold War ensured that parties and unions would either have to take sides or be marginalized or crushed. By the late 1960s, however, it was also clear that the global economy was returning to pre-WWI levels of integration, exerting important pressures on the sharp divisions that the United States and the Soviet Union wanted to place upon the world.

The second major development, the precedents of which can also be found during the interwar period, was the deepening of domestic social welfare arrangements throughout Europe, the Americas, and parts of Asia. On balance, these post-WWII "settlements" aimed at social cohesion and were predicated on growth.[56] There were important differences among them, however, ranging from the more paternalistic Japanese model to the more reformist Scandinavian model. Continuing a process that had started before WWI, unions and associated political parties joined in domestic institutional arrangements of great significance for the decades to follow.[57] The reconstruction period came to an end by the late 1960s, and with it industrial peace. Throughout much of the North there was a great deal of unrest, increasingly involving unions.

Global Union Politics: The Cold War Inside

The event that closed the interwar period took place a few years after the end of WWII. The fitful rapprochement between communists and socialists that had started in the late 1930s as a result of the "popular front" strategy was strengthened during the war, resulting in the formation of the World Federation of Trade Unions (WFTU) in 1945.[58] The organization brought together the vast majority of unions in Europe, South America, and Asia, with the notable exceptions of the

AFL; the German national federations, which had been destroyed by the National Socialists and were now under the tutelage of the occupying countries; and the Christian unions.

The AFL was extremely hostile to the WFTU from the very beginning, partly as a result of its long-standing opposition to radical socialists and communists and partly because its domestic rival, the Congress of Industrial Organizations, had been a founding member of the organization. The WFTU also faced internal obstacles. One of its goals was to make the ITSs integral parts of the organization. This met with resistance by a number of ITSs, such as the International Transport Workers' Federation and the International Metalworkers' Federation. The ITSs' reaction was partly motivated by their opposition to communism.[59] It was also motivated, however, by the historical unwillingness to give up their sectoral identity, as we noted in the previous part. The end result was its split in 1949 into two federations— the International Confederation of Free Trade Unions (ICFTU) and the World Federation of Trade Unions.[60]

The period from the breakup of the WFTU to the late 1960s is a period of increasing polarization within international labor politics.[61] The two union camps became closely allied to state policies reflecting the priorities of the U.S. and Soviet labor-state alliances.[62] There is, therefore, much to support the "labor imperialism" critique.[63] One must also note, however, that there were significant pockets of resistance within almost all global union organizations. For example the IUF was successful at breaking the ties of its South American region with the Central Intelligence Agency.

The sheer existence of three federations—two of which were quite large—ensured that none of them would approach the inclusiveness of the pre-1949 WFTU. In some countries one or another federation had a practical monopoly. In the case of the ICFTU, this included the United States, the United Kingdom, West Germany, and a number of Western European countries, while in the case of the WFTU it included all the communist countries. In some cases, such as France and Italy, the national labor movements were divided mostly between the ICFTU and the WFTU, and in the case of Belgium and the Netherlands, between the ICFTU and the Christians.

Organizationally, the global union organizations remained weak. We focus here on the ICFTU. One important aspect of that weakness was the tenuous relations between the confederation and the ITSs. The Milan agreement of 1951 established a clear but not intimate relationship between them. Even though the agreement was revised a number of times since then, the relations between the ICFTU and the ITSs remained weak throughout this period and beyond.

There were also important differences within the ICFTU, the most important being the disagreement between the AFL and the British Trade Union Congress (TUC), the two leading unions in the organization. The AFL criticized the TUC's efforts to control unions in British colonies while it also felt that it was not doing enough to contain and reverse the communists both in the colonies and elsewhere in the world.[64] Even after the unification of the AFL and the CIO, the AFL leaders continued to handle their foreign relations through a shadowy organization led by an ex-communist leader and funded by the secret services. By the mid-1960s all major national federations, and some individual unions, had their own foreign-policy programs, thus lessening the resources and potential of the ICFTU.[65] Substantial resources for these foreign policies, moreover, came from governments, with strong conditions attached to them.

Decolonization and the sharp lines drawn in Europe increasingly displaced competition for new members to the South. In Latin America, the struggle was primarily between the AFL and the Confederation of Latin American Workers, the organization of socialists, communists, and nationalists formed in the late 1930s that had received some support from John Lewis, representing the United Mine Workers and the CIO. In 1948 the AFL set up the Inter-American Regional Workers' Organization (ORIT by its Spanish initials) as a means for limiting the influence of the left. The AFL's strategy was successful in containing communist influence,[66] largely at the expense of the vital and autonomous union movement that had been growing in South America since the late nineteenth century.[67]

Africa was another area of competition, and one that created the conflicts between the AFL and the British mentioned above. In the end, all three international federations became very active in the continent, the WFTU and the ICFTU in order to contain each other and the Christian federation as a result of a strategic move to the South.[68] By the late 1960s, the influence of the major federations was diminished because the emerging states of the region set up their own, state-controlled, regional union organization.[69] The superficiality of the move to the South by the international union federations was evident by the limited attention they paid to agricultural workers and occupations common to the South. The most prominent initiative of the ICFTU—the formation and support of the International Federation of Plantation, Agricultural and Allied Workers—was largely motivated by the threat of communism among Malaysian rubber workers and proved to be a sham. Finally, none of the federations paid particular attention to gender during this era, nor do we encounter any women in high positions.

The politics of this period further underscores the fact that "nationalist" societal forces can be extremely involved in world politics. The AFL, for instance, aggressively fought for the hearts and minds of global unionism, even though it recognized no rights of external involvement in its own affairs. On the other hand, there remained multilateralist and even internationalist forces within the ICFTU and the various ITSs, such as some of the Scandinavian unions. In neither case were those instances of strong internationalism similar to the First or Third International. In fact, they were even less so than the Second International, which had included substantial internationalist tendencies.

In terms of ideologies, the spectrum narrowed compared to the interwar period. Trade unionists, like the AFL-CIO and many of the British unions, continued to advance economistic regulation that aimed toward better wages and living conditions. Reflecting its greater ideological diversity, the British union movement did call for more profound reforms, some of which were institutionalized by the Labour Party government that came into power in 1945. The Christian unions continued to advocate social protection, but some of them moved in the direction of more class-based, reformist politics. The continental European members of the ICFTU ranged from those who supported compensatory social welfare policies, such as the Germans, to those who emphasized rights and redistribution, such as the Scandinavians. Finally, the WFTU unions in communist countries transferred political authority to the parties and largely supported their authoritarian redistributive policies. Communist unions outside of that sphere—particularly the French and Italian communists—followed a somewhat more autonomous approach.

1969–1991: Defending the Social Welfare State

With the completion of post-WWII reconstruction, trade and financial integration grew rapidly during this period while a new factor entered the mix, that is, multinational corporations and investment. The combination of integration and competition that was present during the late nineteenth and early twentieth centuries also characterized this era and beyond. The difference now was that neither Japan nor the Europeans were about to go to war against the United States, which remained the unchallenged hegemon. Yet, their reemergence challenged the simple geopolitical logic of the Cold War as they sought to build their own spheres of economic influence. In the case of Germany, for instance, this strategy involved Eastern Europe, leading to a challenge of the United States' doctrinaire anticommunism. Starting in the late 1960s, the Social Democratic Party adopted a carrot-and-stick strategy toward Eastern Europe, abandoning the more punitive approach of the Christian Democrats who had been in power since WWII. In addition to the emergence of Northern tripolarity, moreover, there was increasing evidence of a new international division of labor involving the newly industrializing countries of the world, such as Brazil, Mexico, South Korea, Taiwan, and others.

The new element in global economic integration was the multinational corporation. While multinationals have been around for a long time, it was not until the 1970s that they started becoming a generalized characteristic of the global economy. The multinationalization of national companies challenged the historical symmetry between national unions and national capital and was very much part of the attack on the welfare state and the rise of hyperliberalism.

As a result of union militancy, unions and their supporters were able to deepen the welfare state during the 1970s. Increasingly, however, it was becoming apparent that various hyperliberal elites were no longer willing to live with it. The first major manifestation of that was the election of Margaret Thatcher in 1979, followed shortly thereafter by the election of Ronald Reagan. Not only were those two leaders able to change the tenor of national and global policies, but they also used the power of the state to crush union resistance. While other factors have also contributed to the subsequent decline of union membership in many core countries, governmental policies played a key role.

During the early 1980s, for instance, Reagan fired all striking air traffic controllers, and Thatcher destroyed the miners' union through a combination of means.

Global Union Politics: Toward Multipolarity

The potential of European labor regionalism dates back to the formation of the European Steel and Coal Community in 1951. The unilateralism of the AFL-CIO, exemplified by its withdrawal from the ICFTU in 1969, coupled with incentives from the European Commission, led to the formation of the European Trade Union Confederation (ETUC) in 1973 as an organization separate from the ICFTU.[70] In addition to the European members of the ICFTU, the ETUC also included Christian unions and, before the end of the 1970s, communist unions.

Regionalism also affected sectoral union politics, leading to the formation of the European Industry Federations. Very few ITSs managed to keep their European members from forming an autonomous organization. Again, individual unions could belong to both the European federations and the ITSs, but Christian and communist unions found it easier to join the European Industry Federations.

One of the goals of the European unions was to bridge historical divisions. These were particularly acute in France and Italy—where communist unions were the largest ones—and in the Netherlands and Belgium—where Christian unions were very large or larger than social democratic unions. These ideological divisions made it difficult to confront multinational corporations, whose presence was increasingly felt in European politics, as well as formulate common policy vis-à-vis European integration.[71] Even so, communist unions met a great deal of opposition (the Italians did join the ETUC in 1974, but others had to wait much longer), while Christians found the doors more open.[72] On balance, then, the emergence of European-level organizations initiated a regional rapprochement across ideologies at the same time that it segmented global union organizations.

During this same period, the AFL-CIO (which had left the ICFTU from 1969 until 1982) continued its anticommunist policies in Central and South America, while also paying closer attention to Eastern Europe, where communist regimes, particularly that of Poland, were in crisis. The AFL-CIO, of course, was not the only major union with its own foreign policy. Its doctrinaire anticommunism, however, gave rise to significant discontent within American unions and among some of labor's historical allies, such as churches.[73] Lane Kirkland, the successor to George Meany as leader of the AFL-CIO and the person who brought the AFL-CIO back to the ICFTU, was criticized for paying more attention to foreign policy while working on the side of the Reagan administration, an administration bent upon destroying the U.S. labor movement. It is worth noting, however, that the more social democratic or less anticommunist forces within the ICFTU sought, with some success, to move its American regional arm (ORIT) out of the total tutelage of the AFL-CIO.[74] This is a development that, to some degree, balanced the regionalism of the Europeans.

A third development in the industrial world was the formation, out of various federations, of the Japanese Trade Union Confederation, RENGO, in 1989. With RENGO, Japanese unions started paying more attention to the global political economy, reflecting the rise of Japan and keeping in mind that Japanese foreign direct investment did not take off until the late 1970s. Second, its formation added a conservative federation whose domestic and international priorities center around collaboration with Japanese capital and the promotion of a paternalistic type of industrial relations.[75]

Finally, to these Northern poles we must add one of the most important union developments of the last quarter of the twentieth century, that is, the reemergence of radical unions in the South. Right-wing dictatorships and apartheid routinely resulted in the destruction or marginalization of union movements. In some instances, however, they also engendered militant unions, as was the case in Brazil, South Africa, the Philippines, and South Korea. These movements were heralded as the beginnings of a new labor internationalism and of social movement unionism.[76]

Their emergence in key industrializing countries was important for two additional reasons. First, these unions rejected the logic of the Cold War that divided Northern unions. It is not surprising, for example, that the South African and Brazilian unions did not join any of the global federations until well after the end of the Cold War. Second, these unions reflected the changing international division of labor and placed North-South issues on the agenda of global union politics.

The ICFTU remained a weak organization during the 1970s and 1980s. Its fragility was made evident as a result of the AFL-CIO's withdrawal and the unwillingness of the remaining members to close the door behind it. Yet, the return of the AFL-CIO also indicates that access to the ICFTU and other global union organizations is of significance even to the most powerful unions. One cannot say that this is due to the capacities of these organizations, which are largely weak. Rather, it is the legitimacy and access to various governmental forums that global union organizations provide that play the major role. Participating in them reinforces a union's jurisdiction and, in the case of regional hegemons, their regional hegemony. Additionally, participation in global union organizations can work as a tool against domestic competitors, who can be kept from joining.

A development toward stronger global union organizations that actually started toward the tail end of the previous period and whose impacts are unfolding today was the activation of the ITSs, largely in response to the growth of the multinationals. As we develop further in chapter 5, U.S. unions, especially the United Automobile Workers, were alarmed with the tendency of U.S. multinationals to invest in Europe and, in the process, break the post-WWI settlements between U.S. capital and unions.[77] As a result, they spearheaded efforts at forming World Company Councils to coordinate unions within the same corporation in order to formulate more effective global union responses. The key goal of the strategy was to negotiate with corporations from a position of "countervailing power"—or, stated differently, to shift the global balance between capital and labor in the direction of labor. The World Company Council strategy was not successful and had largely been abandoned by the mid-1970s. Yet, it is one of the few sustained efforts at building strong international ties since the First International. Moreover, elements of that strategy were kept alive, particularly by the IUF, and provide a very important link to more recent developments that we discuss in chapter 5. While only three ITSs were involved in this strategy, the longer-term impact was an opening of the practical horizons of these sectoral organizations, which had been largely inactive.

The expanding political geography of global union organizations, manifested in the moves to the South and the increased advocacy for gender and nonindustrial and nonservice workers, made a major and long-standing weakness of global union organizations even more pronounced. Specifically, even at the height of their membership, during the late 1970s, they represented but a small percentage of the world's workers—by some counts well below 10 percent.

While the constituencies for which global union organizations advocated expanded, the ideological range of world visions contracted further. Nationalism remained a considerable force in global union politics, particularly as the language of competition between the United States, the European Union, and Japan gained more currency. The deepening of European integration added regionalism to the mix. The multilateralism of the ICFTU, in short, came under a great deal of pressure. While internationalism remained weak, there were some encouraging developments, leading various analysts to identify the emergence of a "new internationalism" in labor politics. The major evidence came from the increasing role of the new social movement unions in the industrializing countries and the positive responses of workers and unions from the North. To this we must add the practical union internationalism associated with the strategy of the World Company Councils. While this strategy failed, it did reflect an important reservoir of internationalist commitment among traditional unions.

With respect to egalitarianism, the range narrowed as radical unions in the North became more reformist but broadened to the degree that North-South issues became as important as class issues. The AFL-CIO and the British continued to represent the more regulatory wing of the global labor movement, joined now by the Japanese. The continental Europeans continued to support the social welfare state, in its various forms. The most important changes were within the left. The WFTU's condemnation of the Soviet invasion of Czechoslovakia in 1968 demonstrated that there were still communist unions that envisioned a democratic and egalitarian political economy. The heavy-handed reaction by the Soviet Union led to the disciplining of the French, while the other major Western European affiliate, the Italian communist union, accelerated its withdrawal from the WFTU, formalized in 1978. Finally, the emergence of stronger, "social movement" unions in parts of the South placed North-South issues on the agenda—in the case of South Africa connected with questions of race. Combined with a number of radical unions and networks of workers in the North, they represent the more egalitarian wing of the global union movement. At the end of the period, however, most of them were formally outside of the ICFTU network.

1990s–2006: Beyond the National State?

The end of the Cold War has done away with a very divisive influence upon union politics even though the "war on terrorism" could well be used to discipline unions and hinder union collaboration.[78] Yet, as we have noted, the history of the global union movement has been shaped by differences not necessarily due to the Cold War since unions that were on the same side could not often find common ground. Union solidarity, in short, is not the mechanistic by-product of broad worldwide processes. The question then is whether the consolidation of the global union federations and the unification of the ICFTU and the WCL with which we open this chapter are moving us toward stronger global union connections that can resist the centrifugal tendencies that we have noted.

With this warning in mind, the aspect of globalization that we find particularly important for this period is the deepening of global governance—public and private. Public governance is manifested both in the decisions of various conferences and in the increasing influence of economic organizations. As we note in chapter 2, there are important questions to be raised as to whether more and more policy is taking place or should be taking place in global forums. The truth of the matter is that important policy is emanating from such forums and that unions can hardly pretend that they are irrelevant. In chapter 4, we discuss what has been called labor's "long march through the institutions" in its effort to engage and democratize them.

Private governance has also become more formalized and profound. On one hand, multinational corporations through their daily operations govern the lives of millions of people. They also affect public governance as municipalities, countries, and even regions compete to attract and keep investment. In addition, in response to public scrutiny, capital has sought to socially regulate itself, collectively known as corporate social responsibility, largely in order to avoid public regulation. As we discuss in chapter 5, unions have sought to engage and regulate capital at the global level and turn corporate social responsibility to their advantage.

Global Union Politics: Is Unification Enough?

After long negotiations, a meeting that took place on September 2 and 3, 2005, set the road map for the unification of the ICFTU, the WCL, the Trade Union Advisory Committee (TUAC), and various unaffiliated unions, as well as a mechanism for tempering European regionalism.[79] The new international, the International Trade Union Confederation, came into being during the first week of November 2006. While the new architecture of global union organizations envisions a more permanent form of cooperation between the ITUC and the global union federations in the form of the Council of Global Unions formed in January 2007, there is no plan for the unification of all global union organizations. In fact, some federations are strongly opposed even to the moderate reforms envisioned. On balance, however, the Council of Global Unions is likely to bring more cohesion and coordination to the global union network of organizations, a process facilitated by the consolidation that has taken place among sectoral organizations over the past ten years or so.

There is no evidence that the authority of the ITUC will grow. In fact, in order to accommodate personnel from both the ICFTU and the WCL, some personnel had to leave, albeit in a negotiated and humane fashion. In any event, the personnel and financial resources of global union organizations are glaringly small when compared to those of corporations or major national unions.[80] The decline of union membership in the North as well as the 2005 split of a number of unions from the AFL-CIO (a major supporter and contributor to the ICFTU, especially since the reorganization of the federation's foreign policy arm after the 1995 election of John Sweeney) have also had their impacts.

Slowly but surely the unions from the industrializing world have joined, including the Brazilians, the South Africans, and the South Koreans. In 2000, the successors to the Soviet-era unions also joined.[81] A development that we anticipated in the previous section has become a reality. Unions outside the North now account for a much higher percentage of organized workers than at any time in history. This has led to the broadening of the agenda of the global union organizations as well as to shifts in influence. Progress is still limited, exacerbated by the fact that the unions of the South do not have the financial resources necessary to sustain the global union organization edifice. Equally important is that key unions in South Africa and Brazil are facing the challenges of moving from being in opposition to their governments to being partners in power. These transitions have not always gone as expected, challenging both their domestic and international priorities.

The developments at the level of the ICFTU were actually anticipated at the sectoral level. During the 1990s there was a definite move toward consolidation, bringing the number of ITSs from seventeen to ten within a few years. In addition, with the end of the Cold War, more and more sectoral unions from the South and East also joined the ITSs. To some degree, these consolidations were motivated by practical needs, such as the pooling of limited resources. For some unionists they reflect the resurgence of activism by these sectoral organizations and their desire to be "more like unions," a desire that is exemplified by their change of name to global union federations. For others, the change in name is more of a public relations exercise.

Yet, while global union organizations are becoming more global, there remain some vexing problems and gaps. One problem that has significant long-term implications is that the ETUC will continue to be outside of the new international. The fact that the European Union is a policymaking body and that the ETUC is participating in some formal activities at the European level sets the organization apart from any other regional arrangement. The new edifice envisioned recognizes that and guarantees the autonomy of the ETUC. In the event of similar regional developments, however, this creates a precedent that could well change global union organizations into weak assemblages of regional unions as opposed to national unions.[82] In short, this is an issue that global unions will have to revisit in the future.[83]

A more controversial issue is that of China. Chinese unions continue to be part of the Chinese state-party-union structure and have been less than responsive to the major dislocations caused by China's directed liberalization. Because China is the major recipient of foreign direct investment going to the South and a rising force in its own right, there is hardly any union that is not affected. Unions in industrial countries are seeing capital-intensive industries migrating to China, while unions in industrializing and less industrial countries are seeing labor-intensive industries do the same. Yet, there are serious disagreements among ITUC and global union federation members on how to deal with Chinese unions. The Japanese, for instance, have close relations with them, while the U.S. unions are very hostile to them. Some global federations follow a policy of engagement, while others refuse to talk to their Chinese counterparts. The ITUC, specifically, is very hostile toward Chinese unions and the Chinese model.[84]

While China presents an explicit and controversial gap today, there are additional gaps that are likely to become equally important in the future. Most prominent is the case of India, where unionization is low and the labor movement is fragmented. There is strong evidence that India is attracting more and more foreign investment and is likely to compete with China as a source of both skilled and unskilled labor. Significantly, the Indian members of the ICFTU were the strongest critics of its social-clause strategy, an issue we discuss in chapter 4. Additionally, some of the more militant union federations are communist and have chosen not to join the ITUC.

In terms of social categories, global union organizations continue to represent organized workers, who are a minority of the world's workers, and they have not found ways to represent workers outside industry and services, even though they are more vocal in their advocacy for hitherto excluded categories. The ICFTU, for instance, has been at the forefront of gender and youth politics, while some global union federations, such as the IUF and the International Metalworkers' Federation, require that a percentage of the seats in their executive committees go to women. As one reads the documents of the ICFTU from the past two global congresses, one cannot help but notice the breadth of the categories of people that it seeks to include as well as advocate for, from HIV/AIDS victims to migrants to children and the aged.[85] Yet, so long as national unions persist with business as usual, global union organizations will remain organizations of the protected labor force. The IUF's decision to admit the Indian Self-Employed Women's Association (SEWA) in 1983 as well as its subsequent admission to the ICEM, the ITGLWF, and, in 2006, the ICFTU is a very positive step. Initiatives of some unions, such as the Central de los Trabajadores Argentinos, to redefine who constitutes a worker and to allow people to join directly may pick up steam and also have a catalytic effect on national unionism. Unions, whether national or global, need to rethink the nature of work and of workers and, thus, of their constituencies. In this sense, their critical stance on the question of the "informal sector" is encouraging to the degree that it rejects this fiction and recognizes that these are workers under very precarious circumstances in what is better called the "informal economy." The ILO's "decent work" agenda, discussed in chapter 4, opens additional possibilities for rethinking work and workers.

There is good evidence that increasing globalization does not necessarily lead to more unity among unions. Even though apartheid is a thing of the past, it is worth noting that the primarily Afrikaans union Solidarity is growing rapidly. The discourse on terrorism has also added impetus to possibly nativist views. During the recent debate over whether a company from Dubai could run some U.S. ports, there were pictures of Teamsters holding posters reading "Goodbye Dubai."[86] The same union had resisted liberalizing trucking in the Americas by playing to the common perception of Mexicans as dangerous and irresponsible drivers.[87] In addition to nativists, there are also many unions that take a very passive role when the impacts of the global political economy temporarily bypass them or work to their advantage. That certainly was the case with official Mexican unions during the NAFTA negotiations. The various global union organizations remain multilateralist and continue to support global rules, but there is good reason to be afraid that continued resistance to the social regulation of global economic organizations could well enhance the powers of the less multilateralist voices. Finally, there are some radical unions, both North and South, that hold to a more internationalist view of the world. Some of them, for instance, have been working on creating an alternative network within global union politics known as the Southern Initiative on Globalisation and Trade Union Rights (SIGTUR).[88]

The ideological narrowing that was evident in the previous period has continued, both within the ICFTU-GUF network and beyond. Much criticism can be placed at the doorsteps of statist communist unions that had become appendixes to the state.[89] On balance, the ICFTU aims at the regulation of the global political economy, as do most of the global union federations. Yet, as we discuss in the subsequent chapters, there is evidence of more reformist proposals becoming central to the global union agenda. The joining of the various communist unions, combined with the more radical unions of the South and various more militant socialist unions, promise the creation of a stronger left wing within global unionism. This gives us hope that there will be more profound debates about the organization of the global political economy. How far these debates will go remains to be seen. In light of our historical account, however, we would have to wait a while before they become transformative.

Conclusion

What can we conclude from the story so far? How far do the recent developments take us toward stronger global union organizations and connections and, thus, more legitimate and authoritative global labor self-governance? Global union politics has a long and contested history. Some of the legacies of that history cast their shadow upon the present, particularly the existence of weak global union organizations. While globalization and global governance are progressing, unions have yet to move toward forms of global self-governance that are significantly stronger than the historical ones. The recent developments that we outlined indicate that many unionists recognize both the need for stronger global organizations and the obstacles to strengthening them. Important breakthroughs will have to come from national unions and alliances of national unions that commit to strengthening global union organizations. As a result, we do not think that global union solidarity or any other global emancipatory vision can be the mechanistic product of overall developments in the global political economy, which, in any event, are contradictory, as they have always been. Rather, unions have to make history under historical circumstances that, in this case, are also of their making. We are optimistic that many unions have recognized the necessity of global union collaboration. Turning that recognition into reality remains a formidable task as national unions have to negotiate various incentives and punishments, some of which may lead them away from global internationalism and toward regionalism or national foreign policy.

The unification that has taken place is a positive step, not least because it does away with a historical division. It still does not address the governance capacities of global union organizations, however, and leaves other possibly divisive issues for the future. The new international is largely an important tactical step toward more profound global solidarity and self-governance.[90] Only when national unions agree to transfer significant resources and authority to global union organizations will global labor politics move beyond foreign policies and toward the globalization of solidarity.

It is not our argument that global organizations should or could replace the regional or the national. In the same way that local unions were forced to create national unions in order to address national governance, we believe that global governance will require stronger global unions, at the very least so as to prevent members unions from engaging in predatory behavior. In the next two chapters, we turn to the efforts by global union organizations to challenge global governance and forge a common program to influence both the governance of the global political economy and the governance of global union politics.

REGULATING THE GLOBAL STATE: BEYOND THE SOCIAL CLAUSE?

The efforts of national and global union organizations to include labor rules into the World Trade Organization were defeated in Seattle. In its subsequent meetings, the WTO did away with any hope that the issue would be put on the agenda. In early 2006, however, the ICFTU expressed its cautious satisfaction with the adoption "by the International Finance Corporation [IFC] (the private sector lending arm of the World Bank) of a new loan performance standard on labour rights and working conditions."[1] Over a number of years, in collaboration with the International Textile Workers and local unions, it had sought to influence the IFC's loan practices, focusing on Grupo M, a major employer in the Haitian and Dominican Republic Export Processing Zones. Even after the company had been forced to accept a union in Haiti, it refused to do so in the Dominican Republic. In January 2004, in response to pressures from the two global union organizations, the IFC decided to attach labor rights to a twenty-million-dollar loan to the company. During the following two years, the IFC initiated a process that resulted in its *Policy and Performance Standards for Social & Environmental Sustainability*, a document that they hailed as a major step.[2] Why would the ICFTU greet this initiative as a major step in the right direction at the same time that the ILO, over a period of almost ninety years, has produced 187 conventions (as of July 2006), many of which have been ratified by the Dominican Republic, where Grupo M is incorporated? In order to answer this question, we have to trace the history of global labor regulation since its origins in the nineteenth century (see table 4.1). We use the historical account that follows both to examine the impacts of global union organizations on global public governance and to see whether these efforts have or are contributing to stronger forms of global labor self-governance. As we have argued, global governance, like national governance, is likely to focus societal politics more so than diffuse and contradictory forms of globalization. Yet, the hegemony of global governance is rather tentative, and furthermore there is nothing that says that global governance will be good for labor.

We start with a discussion of developments before WWI because the approaches shaped during this era continue to the present. We then discuss the ILO and its promise and limitations. It is worth noting that no other societal movement has its "own" intergovernmental organization. Advocates of global environmental governance, for instance, look to the ILO as the model they aspire to. This is followed by an examination and evaluation of the efforts of unions to introduce core labor standards and rights into global economic organizations, focusing on the social-clause strategy associated with the World Trade Organization.[3] In the last part, we situate global policies among the main current alternatives and identify the tensions and complementarities between them. We close by evaluating the ability of unions to formulate common global policy and their impacts on global labor governance.

Before the ILO But Very Close to the Present

One of the central legacies of the First International was the elaboration of a specific agenda of labor rights and standards that has survived to our days. Starting early on, it identified specific proposals and called

Table 4.1. Key Dates in Global Public Labor Governance

Date	Event or organization
1866	First International proposes international labor policy agenda
1890	Berlin Conference on international labor legislation
1900	International Association for Labor Legislation
1901	International Labor Office
1904	First bilateral labor treaty between France and Italy
1906	First multilateral treaties on night work by women and use of white phosphorous
1919–	International Labour Organization
1950	International Trade Organization shelved, replaced by GATT
1976	OECD Guidelines on Multinational Enterprises
1977	ILO Declaration on Multinational Enterprises
1984	U.S. Generalized System of Preferences
1992	European Social Charter
1994	European Union Generalised System of Preferences
1994	European Works Councils Directive
1994	North American Agreement on Labor Cooperation
1995	World Trade Organization
1996	First WTO Ministerial Meeting—Singapore
1998	ILO Declaration on Fundamental Principles and Rights at Work
1998	Social and Labor Declaration of Mercosur
1999	Third WTO Ministerial Meeting—Seattle
2000	Revised OECD Guidelines on Multinational Enterprises
2000	Revised ILO Declaration on Multinational Enterprises
2001	U.S.-Jordan bilateral agreement with labor provisions
2006	International Financial Corporation includes labor rights
2006	Global Reporting Initiative includes labor rights

for international labor legislation, building on various voices to that effect going back to the early nineteenth century.[4] While the British trade unionists were satisfied with these proposals, the more radical elements within the International envisioned a more profound transformation of the national and world political economies. Proposals for labor regulation were but one aspect of a broader strategy toward that end.

The social democratic movement—as well as other social egalitarians—continued this prioritization into the period of the Second International. Consistent with the developments outlined in the previous chapter, social democrats adopted increasingly narrower labor policies, responding to their own successes at the national level and the labor reforms that were put in place in Germany starting as far back as the 1870s. Accordingly, one of the most thorough reviews of the early history of global labor regulation concluded that by 1910, when the last regular meeting of the Second International took place, social democrats placed "less reliance . . . on the control of industry through the political subversion of the present order and more on its control through factory and social insurance legislation, coupled with trade union action."[5]

This shift was forced and facilitated by the emergence of two additional players in global labor regulation—states and professionals. The role of states became eminently apparent when the new German kaiser, or rather his advisers, took over the initiative for an international meeting on labor regulation from the Swiss, who had been leaders during the 1870s and 1880s.[6] This meeting took place in Berlin during March 1890, the year after the Second International was formed. The kaiser was very much motivated by the rising social democracy and found in this initiative a way to seem like a champion of workers while at the same time dividing them by emphasizing the implications of labor rules for international competitiveness. The competition rationale for labor rules remains central to our days.[7]

Nothing was decided at the Berlin conference, and it took fourteen years for the first international policy to be adopted. This was the 1904 bilateral treaty between France and Italy that dealt primarily with workers' insurance or pensions. It also had provisions for raising Italian standards to avoid unfair competition between France and Italy. Another twenty-six bilateral treaties were signed up to 1915, almost all among Western European countries. Questions of transferability of pensions and social insurance were central issues, as these treaties usually involved a country of emigration and a country of immigration.[8]

Two years after the first bilateral treaty and as a result of the 1905 and 1906 Bern conferences, the European countries adopted the first two multilateral treaties on night work by women and the use of white (yellow) phosphorus in the manufacturing of matches, the latter making an explicit connection to the importation of white phosphorous and, thus, international trade. Conferences in The Hague (1907) and Bern (1913) did the preparatory work for additional treaties on the prohibition of night work by minors (under sixteen) and the working hours for minors and women, but WWI did not allow their completion.[9] Thus, fifty years after the formation of the First International, interstate labor policy was limited to a few bilateral and only two multilateral treaties.

A central role behind the drafting and promotion of international labor legislation must be attributed to the growing international movement of labor professionals who formed the International Association for Labor Legislation (1900), which, in turn, formed the International Labor Office in 1901. The association was a hybrid entity of government and private members and met on a regular basis until 1912. Governmental participation rose from four governments in 1901 to twenty-two in 1912, while nongovernmental participation rose from seven sections to twenty-four. In this hybrid arrangement we see the beginnings of the tripartite nature of the ILO. The motivations of these specialists varied, depending on whether they worked for governments, business organizations, churches or other philanthropic organizations, or unions. Overall, however, they converged toward policies whose aim was to protect rather than empower workers. As a result, the role of unions in international policymaking diminished.[10]

By the end of this period we can clearly identify the three sets of goals and the major strategies that characterize the politics of global labor governance to our days. Some advocates of global labor policy, mostly unions and egalitarians, aimed primarily at empowering labor while also making the workplace safer and creating a more level playing field by raising lower standards. States and business, as well as a number of unions, aimed primarily at reducing the competitive advantage of countries with lower labor policies rather than empowering or protecting workers. Finally, professionals and philanthropists focused on protecting workers through workplace standards and regulations. While it is often difficult to disentangle these three sets of goals, it is generally easy to differentiate among various proposals in terms of their relative emphasis.[11]

In addition to these three sets of goals, there also emerged various strategies for their accomplishment. One way to differentiate among these strategies is in terms of the number of countries participating, ranging from unilateral to multilateral, or multipartite policies, as they were known then. As we will see, the same range still exists today. The second way to differentiate among strategies is in terms of whether they were attached to trade or other world processes—as was the case with phosphorous—or whether they were promulgated as freestanding policies.

Regulating the State Directly:
The Promise and Limitations of the ILO

The debates about the nature of an international labor organization started before WWI, but the final result was shaped by two developments catalyzed by the war. One was the radicalization of European politics, starting in the midst of the war, accelerating with the Russian Revolution of 1917, and receiving further impetus with the Hungarian and German revolutions of 1919. The other was the decision of the United States to get involved in the war and claim its hegemonic role in world politics.[12]

The radicalization of the working class and the appeal of communism led trade unionists and social democrats to agree on the need for some concrete steps toward a global labor organization in order to contain further radicalization. However, there was clear disagreement among them over the powers of such an organization. Social democrats envisioned an organization whose decisions would be directly binding upon the member states.[13] AFL leader Samuel Gompers and his allies wanted to lessen the influence of social democrats on the global union movement and to prevent the creation of a strong intergovernmental organization that would limit the discretion of their own states, especially the United States.[14] In a preemptive move they struck a deal with the U.S. government and elements of the British government that produced the ILO. Even though the IFTU was disappointed by the end result, it moved quickly to establish its hegemony within the organization, a task made easier by the decision of the United States not to join (it did in 1934) and by the exclusion of the Soviet Union. Moreover, the first convention, as ILO treaties are called, was on an eight-hour day in industry (six-day week), giving skeptics a reason to hope that the organization would address issues central to unions.

Even so, the ILO was and is different from all major global intergovernmental organizations in that it provides for a tripartite system of representation,[15] a factor that also accounts for the more collaborative nature of its policymaking. Accordingly, each country has four seats in the organization—two held by the state and one each by workers and business organizations.[16] There is no requirement that the representative of the workers be from a union, and, in fact, the ILO does not use the term officially.[17] The power to join or leave the ILO rests with governments, as does the decision of who will represent workers and business. The All China Federation of Trade Unions, for instance, represents the Chinese workers even though it is ostracized by the global union network.

The partners negotiate the various conventions (187 as of July 2006 and recommendations (198 as of July 2006), both of which apply to states.[18] The conventions must then be ratified by the member states and follow the conventional route to enter into force. The slow and uneven rate of ratifications has been an issue throughout the ILO's whole existence. It is not only the pace of ratifications that is worrisome. It is also the implementation of conventions once ratified and in force. Compared to economic organizations, the ILO lacks the implementation authority, such as the dispute resolution power of the World Trade Organization (WTO), or the financial resources of the World Bank and the International Monetary Fund. For instance, every country that joins the WTO must accept and apply all of the associated agreements, an enforceable requirement. On the other hand, while the ILO's Declaration on Fundamental Principles and Rights at Work is binding on all member countries, its enforcement is based largely on shaming and suasion.[19] Those conventions not covered by the declaration, moreover, can be accepted at the discretion of the member countries.

Structurally, then, the ILO presents global union organizations with a dual challenge: first, how to employ the institutionalized but constrained presence of workers' representatives in order to shape international union politics and international labor policy; second, how to turn the ILO into a stronger organization that represents the interests of workers among increasingly stronger economic organizations.

Workers and the ILO

For much of the ILO's existence, the organization as a whole and the Workers' Group within it were the arenas of Cold War competition.

The IFTU emerged as the stronger element within the Workers' Group soon after the organization's creation, but there were clear limits on what it could do since a number of very important countries, such as the United States and the Soviet Union, did not join the ILO, while others, such as Germany, left after a while. The Cold War exercised an even more important influence after WWII when communist countries also joined. The ICFTU, however, established its hegemony within the Workers' Group of the ILO, with the director of its Geneva office serving as the group's secretary. As a result, the ICFTU, and now the ITUC, has been able to shape the positions of the Workers' Group and, by extension, influence the activities of the ILO.

While the global union network has long consolidated its hegemony within the Workers' Group, it has not been successful in enhancing the powers of the organization. The weakness of the ILO has been felt more strongly during transitional periods in global governance, such as the years immediately after WWII and the early 1990s. During the WWII negotiations that led to the formation of the global economic organizations, it became apparent that the new hegemon, the United States, was not feeling the pressures of destruction and radicalization experienced by the Europeans during and after WWII and was determined to create liberal institutions. Its task was made easier since important elements of the global labor and socialist movements had been decimated by the fascists, the national socialists, the Francoists, and the Stalinists. Even so, as Wilkinson argues, there were some connections between the economic organizations and the ILO, particularly in the ill-fated International Trade Organization (ITO),[20] which also included an explicit reference to fair labor rules in what some see as an example of a social clause.[21] The ITO, however, never came into existence as a result of U.S. Senate opposition.

The weakness of the ILO has become more evident during the past thirty years as neoliberalism has started undoing the social welfare state in the North and the developmental state in the South.[22] The formation of the WTO brought things to a point of crisis as a number of governments and most unions, led by the ICFTU, sought to include a social clause in trade agreements. This raised the important question of the role of the ILO at the interface of the world's trading and labor regimes. The ICFTU's proposal would have given the ILO a prominent role in conjunction with the WTO. The provisions that have given the

ILO its inclusiveness stood yet again in the way of its meaningful reform as most governments and all business (and some unions) lined up against the ILO's enhanced role. Here, we must also highlight the very tentative approach of the organization's leaders, who felt that such a role would detract from its tradition of persuasion rather than coercion.[23]

A number of analysts have noted that the ILO has become more active and labor friendly in recent years under the leadership of Juan Somavia, a Chilean diplomat. We have no reason to dispute this claim. What this means, however, is that the organization is deploying its resources in a different way; it does not mean that the organization has more authority or resources. With that clarification in mind, we turn to some of the labor priorities that the ILO has spearheaded over the years.

Over its long existence, the ILO has produced an impressive body of legislative work and agenda-setting initiatives that do establish the parameters of international labor legislation and have shaped international labor policy debates. As we have noted, the organization has produced 187 conventions and a vast body of interpretations and related investigations.[24] With the exception of five or six of them, these conventions deal with standards protecting workers rather than rights empowering them. This is not to say that conventions that prohibit discrimination, limit working hours, allow for the transferability of pensions, and protect migrants and other categories of workers are not important and cannot empower workers. Such laws, however, can and often have been implemented without union participation and as a result of initiatives by states, professionals, and others (including corporations).

The ILO has also generated an enormous amount of research as well as training. It is easy to dismiss these contributions, particularly since they are also colored by the organization's overall collaborative spirit. Yet, in the hands of unions such information and training can become another tool in their global struggles. The global union network is well served by the Bureau for Workers' Activities for research and networking activities that it would be hard-pressed to do on its own.[25] One of the most interesting results has been the Global Union Research Network (GURN) launched in 2004 by the bureau, the global union network, and the ILO's International Institute for Labour Studies. The network seeks to connect the resources of researchers throughout the world with the political priorities of global unions. Another important innovation involving the Bureau for Workers' Activities is the Global Labour University, set up with various German labor advocacy and research entities.[26]

One could stop here and simply evaluate the ILO in terms of its practical outputs. Yet, it would be unfair to not recognize its agenda-setting function. One of the organization's contributions was its attention to the impact of multinationals on social policy, a concern that was placed on the organization's agenda in the late 1960s. As we discuss further in the subsequent chapter, the end result was the 1977 Tripartite Declaration of Principles Concerning Multinational Enterprises and Social Policy, revised in 2000 to include the language of the 1998 Declaration on Fundamental Principles and Rights at Work (discussed in the next part of this chapter). The ILO's work put the social dimension of the multinationals on the agenda and, with union influence, it has provided for a global document that unions have used to influence policy toward multinationals (as discussed in chapter 5). It is worth noting that while multinationals have been criticized by various social forces, these criticisms are not always demands for more equity. Southern developmentalists in the 1970s were mostly concerned about the power of multinationals over domestic politics. More recently, critics of corporate governance often focus on corruption and responsibility toward shareholders rather than the impacts of corporations on the broader universe of stakeholders, such as workers and communities.

The ILO has also played an important, if often ambivalent, role in defining the nature of work more broadly.[27] Starting in the 1970s, it has been the forum where the "informal sector" has been discussed, forcing unions and other activists to address the issue. Global union organizations have been active participants in the debates over the nature of the "informal sector" and have attacked the term for normalizing work practices that are precarious and exploitative. The end result has been a discursive move to the "informal economy" that has satisfied both unions and representatives of organizations from the informal economy.[28] The ILO's move toward the "decent work" agenda during the past decade is a positive step toward a more holistic delineation of what constitutes acceptable work practices.[29]

Finally, the ILO has also served as the springboard for a more socially informed approach to globalization, as indicated by its 2004 report entitled *A Fair Globalization*, the product of the tripartite Commission on the Social Dimension of Globalization.[30] The report's call for a more equitable globalization, coupled with the ILO's decent work agenda, exemplifies the view of the ILO vis-à-vis the overall structure of the global political economy and the ways in which things can be improved.

Do the practical and symbolic contributions of the ILO cancel out its organizational and political weaknesses? This, we think, is an important question with broader implications as unions and other societal entities are encountering more opportunities to participate in public or private governance, albeit not as principal policy makers. When is the acceptance and legitimation of a weak policy or organization a necessary step toward something more profound, and when is it an obstacle? We will return to this question in the conclusion to this chapter and the conclusion to the volume.

Scaling the Commanding Heights: Unions and Global Economic Organizations

It may seem surprising, but it should not. Global economic governance picked up steam during the 1980s, exactly at a time when hyperliberalism was attacking the role of the state. Evidently, the issue was not just any state but, rather, the Northern social welfare state with its redistributive policies and the Southern developmentalist state, also often predicated on redistribution.[31] Starting with the debt crises of the early 1980s, the IMF found a new mission in reorganizing the South in the direction of liberalism through financial discipline, while the World Bank did so through loans and programs that aimed at the liberalization of the domestic economies. Soon, the World Trade Organization emerged as a largely liberal organization, certainly compared to the International Trade Organization.[32] By the time the WTO formally came into operation, these three organizations, along with the regional banks, exercised a very profound if uneven governance on the global political economy. The IMF and the World Bank (as well as the regional banks) exercised governance on the South and the post-Soviet countries. Their influence over the North remains less profound or negligible. On the other hand, the World Trade Organization has the potential to affect the North—whether with respect to intra-North issues or by allowing the South to call the bluff of the North's selective liberalization. That this is an important issue is evidenced by the interminable debates over the liberalization of services, which the North wants, and the liberalization of agriculture, which parts of the South want.[33]

The global union organizations have taken and continue to take detailed positions on the various aspects of global economic governance, going back to 1959 when the ICFTU called the World Economic Conference of Free Trade Unions.[34] During the 1970s they responded to the South's developmental agenda, during the 1980s to the impacts of structural adjustment, during the 1990s to the proliferation of Export Processing Zones, and currently to development, poverty, and health issues.[35] In this part we focus on the social-clause strategy for two reasons. First, it is not possible to do justice to the full range of global union views on global economic governance; second, the social-clause strategy is qualitatively different.[36] Most global union interventions regarding global governance in the pre-1990s era could be seen as lobbying exercises since the financial organizations were already in place and labor did not have the power to revise their constitutional provisions (other social forces could and did). The social-clause strategy, however, reached its height at a time when new global (WTO) and regional (NAFTA) policies and organizations were coming into existence. We first focus on the most famous case—the efforts of global unions to insert a social clause into the WTO. We then discuss how this strategy, somewhat modified, has been applied to the global financial organizations. Once these tasks are completed, we offer an evaluation of the strategy and identify developments that both reflect the broader agenda of global unions and are also promising in terms of preserving the key accomplishment of the strategy, that is, the formation of a global union agenda.

The WTO and the Social Clause

Proposals for the inclusion of labor rights and standards in international economic agreements go back to the mid-nineteenth century. At the time, they were considered inferior to other alternatives and dismissed as not worthy of closer attention. The German kaiser, and more likely his early chancellor Bismarck, was explicitly concerned with competitiveness, while various unions in more industrial countries were already complaining about unfair competition from workers in countries with weaker labor rules. The issue continued to be of concern during the interwar period. The ILO's approach was to enact free-standing treaties that would be applicable regardless of their impact on trade. It was clear, however, that a key aim of these treaties was to do away with egregious labor practices that provided an unfair advantage to some countries. During the 1940s the Havana Charter of the failed ITO did include something akin to the social clause, essentially ensuring that labor rules would not be sacrificed to liberalization nor be used to gain competitive advantage. Organizationally, it also reserved a role for the ILO. The resurgence of integration and liberalization in the 1970s raised, once again, the demand for some form of binding international labor provisions integrated into economic agreements.[37]

The search for such a connection received a great deal of support from the AFL-CIO, which as early as 1962 had abandoned its support of "free trade" in favor of "fair trade."[38] By the 1970s, the "fair trade" argument gained even more urgency.[39] During the 1970s, the AFL-CIO, under pressure by member unions more exposed to international competition, such as textiles and automobiles, pursued a unilateral policy of attaching labor provisions to U.S. foreign trade policies. Beginning in 1974, the strategy produced results; ever since, various U.S. foreign trade and investment policies, the most important among them being the Generalized System of Preferences of 1984, have contained provisions whereby trading partners would be punished for not respecting certain labor rules.[40] What is surprising, on the surface, is the support of the hyperliberal Reagan administration for such a coupling. There are good reasons for it, however. First, it was a low price to pay in order to get free-trade agreements accepted; second, these rules could and were used selectively against unfriendly governments; third, they allowed the U.S. to protect less competitive sectors, particularly textiles, in politically important southern states.

During the 1970s, the ILO and global union organizations, such as the International Metalworkers' Federation, started considering the multilateral connection between trade and labor rules, partly concerned about the implications of U.S. unilateralism.[41] In the late 1980s and early 1990s, the possibility that the General Agreement on Tariffs and Trade would be replaced by a stronger global trade organization added urgency to the deliberations of global union organizations. Yet, according to our background interviews, unions did not adequately insert themselves into the Uruguay Round negotiations (1986–1994) that produced the WTO. As a result, their strongest efforts were reserved for the period after the 1995 inaugural meeting of the WTO, especially from 1996 to 1999.

By the mid-1990s, the major issue was whether and how trade and labor rules would be connected. A second, intimately related issue was who would enforce the relationship and how it would be enforced. A lesser controversy—but the one that often loomed as the most important—was the delineation of the labor rights and standards that would be included. The two primary forums where these controversies were played out were the ILO and the WTO.

The strongest supporters of the inclusion of a social clause in the WTO, the first issue, were the United States and the global union organizations. The strongest opponents were capital and all liberal states in the North, with the notable exception of the United States, and developmentalist states in the South—especially Asia, with notable exceptions. The views of social welfare states varied.[42] An issue over which many of the supporters of the linkage parted ways was the United States' evident willingness to make sanctions a prominent component of the implementation process.

With respect to enforcement, the ICFTU's approach to the social clause was one that would be antiprotectionist and would be implemented by a joint ILO-WTO body in a series of steps. The first steps, involving the identification of the violation of labor rules and efforts at rectifying them through suasion and assistance, would be in the hands of the ILO. Only after these steps had been exhausted would the case be referred to the WTO for "possible trade measures."[43] At the WTO, the process would include various options with a gradual move to sanctions as the last option.[44]

The European Union was moving in the same direction. Shortly before the Singapore Ministerial Conference, however, at a meeting of EU trade ministers, the United Kingdom, Germany, and Ireland came out resolutely against such a policy, forcing the EU to adopt the position "that the International Labor Organization is the appropriate forum for labor standards."[45] The remaining twelve members continued to be supportive of WTO involvement, but the EU could not present a unified position in favor of a trade-labor linkage.

Most Southern governments were against any WTO involvement. They supported the view that the ILO is the proper forum but opposed giving the ILO the requisite powers to play a consequential role. There were good reasons why the South was suspicious of those who supported the linkage. After WWII the North had espoused liberalization where it had an advantage—manufactures—and had imposed protectionism where the South had an advantage—textiles.[46] Yet, after years of trying to change the architecture of the global economy, the South had "decided" to join—thanks to the disciplinary measures of the global economic institutions, the rise of domestic neoliberalism, and the aggressive developmentalism of many Southern states. Their arguments were not informed by the impacts of world trade on domestic equity or labor. Rather, they adopted what van Roozendaal calls the "neo-liberal" discourse, largely predicated on social improvements as a side effect of growth.[47] That these views did not reflect the whole South is evident by the fact that most Southern unions supported the linkage, despite serious concerns. Moreover, those Southern countries with stronger union movements were those most supportive, as was the case with South Africa and Brazil.

The WTO's First Ministerial Conference in Singapore adopted a declaration that did not commit the WTO other than to state that "the WTO and the ILO secretariats will continue their existing collaboration." Both sides greeted the compromise as a victory. The opponents had managed to avoid a commitment by the WTO while the supporters argued that the issue was still on the table.

During the subsequent years, the ICFTU undertook a concerted effort to inform and persuade its members to rally around the social-clause strategy.[48] The campaign involved multiple regional meetings, a dedicated system of communications, and efforts at forming societal alliances. The end result of this process was that most unions, including key Southern unions, consented to the strategy even though many had reservations. This is important to note and must be considered as evidence of the growing programmatic influence of the ICFTU but, also, of the willingness of key Southern unions to break ranks with their states, their capital, and parts of their domestic societies.

The target of this strategy was the Third Ministerial Conference of the WTO, which was to take place in Seattle from November 30 to December 3, 1999. The story of Seattle has been the subject of many accounts by participants, reporters, and analysts. The ICFTU was present, and many local labor officials were clearly familiar with the fact that they were participating in a broader campaign emanating from the ICFTU.[49] In this sense, the ICFTU reached to the grass roots of the U.S. labor movement. Yet, if the AFL-CIO and some of its member unions, such as the Steelworkers, were not in favor of the strategy, the ICFTU could not have reached below the top echelons of the U.S. union movement. In short, the case of Seattle is not evidence of a stronger global union movement that finally manages to assert itself vis-à-vis a major member, but the product of programmatic convergence between the AFL-CIO and the ICFTU, albeit with a clear imprint of the ICFTU's multilateralism. In short, Seattle is evidence both of the policy limitations of the global union network and of its ability, however tenuous, to converge around a common strategy.

The Fourth Ministerial Conference of the WTO (Doha, November 2001) practically severed the linkage of trade and labor rights within the WTO.[50] This uncoupling was greatly facilitated by the Bush administration's unwillingness to support the linkage any longer.[51] The current director of the WTO, Pascal Lamy, made no mention of labor rules in a recent speech entitled "The WTO in the Archipelago of Global Governance."[52] Moreover, his answers to relevant questions during an Internet chat leave no doubt that there is no room for labor rules in the WTO at this time because he feels "that the solution lies in strengthening other organizations and not weakening the WTO on the pretext that it has a particularly sophisticated mechanism for implementing the rules it negotiates."[53] As a result, there are no labor provisions within the WTO at a time when the organization is increasingly affecting the backbone of the social welfare state through the General Agreement on Trade in Services. This agreement will clearly affect the public sector, which also happens to be one of the strongholds of unionization in much of the world.[54]

As we have noted, the debate over the social clause confronted the ILO with a major dilemma: should it support the connection, and what should its role be? The first meetings of the ILO's Working Party on the Social Dimensions of Liberalization of International Trade, established in 1994, "were given over to a general discussion of two complementary aspects of its initial mandate, namely, whether to introduce a specific social dimension into the multilateral trade system, and the impact of the liberalization of trade on the attainment of the ILO's social objectives."[55] As a result of broad opposition from the same alliance that had been opposed to any linkage at the WTO, the Working Party soon decided that there should be no linkage between labor and trade. This left open only the second question of how the ILO would attain its goals in the context of trade liberalization.

The possibility that a labor-trade linkage would be accepted at the 1996 Singapore Ministerial Conference of the WTO motivated opponents to continue these intra-ILO negotiations. Once the Singapore Declaration reaffirmed the traditional role of the ILO without committing the WTO, the opposition was under much less pressure to compromise. In order to foreclose further attempts at strengthening the ILO, moreover, the Employers' Group proposed a declaration that would not be binding and would encourage incentives.

The end result of the debate was the 1998 Declaration on Fundamental Principles and Rights at Work.[56] The most significant contribution of the declaration was its formal delineation of core labor rights and its application of these rights to all member countries. Before the declaration, neither the ILO nor any other intergovernmental organization had formally identified a list of core labor rights and all ILO conventions were adopted at the discretion of the member countries. While not enforceable in any binding fashion, the 1998 declaration gives these rights a special status through its follow-up mechanism, which can evaluate their application by all ILO members regardless of whether they have ratified the relevant conventions.

The delimitation of core labor standards and rights had been the subject of profound debates since the 1970s.[57] Van Liemt's review of eight social-clause proposals found that occupational safety and health were included in six of them, as were freedom from discrimination and forced labor.[58] Other versions of the social clause have also included "an acceptable minimum wage, based on the level of economic development of a particular country."[59] During the NAFTA debates, for instance, the AFL-CIO called for occupational safety and health, while in some earlier pronunciations it also made references to wage standards.

According to the ICFTU, a social clause should include "freedom of association; the right to collective bargaining; the minimum age for employment; non-discrimination and equal remuneration; and prohibition of forced labour."[60] It should not include wages or occupational health and safety, since both would impose substantial economic demands on poorer countries, and sanctions should be used only after incentives were exhausted. In short, the core labor rights identified in the declaration were consistent with the ICFTU's program. Ever since, arguments against the social clause that are based on the inclusion of standards for wages and occupational health and safety can only be a misrepresentation of the position of global union organizations, if not all national unions.

Employers and their allies were and are more opposed to labor rights, such as the right to unionize and bargain, but often accept occupational safety and health standards. Their opposition stems from the fact that labor rights empower workers while labor standards can be used to preempt organizing by co-opting workers. Southern governments, which have been largely opposed to any rights or standards, have specifically rejected occupational health and safety provisions as too costly. Moreover, even though the wage issue had long dropped off the global union agenda, opponents continued to use it as an argument against the social clause. Such misrepresentations, however, can be very easily supported by the fact that the U.S. Trade Act of 2002 includes conditions of work with respect to minimum wages, hours of work, and occupational health and safety.[61]

Engaging the Global Financial Organizations

While global unions have become more sanguine about a social clause in the WTO, and have in fact abandoned the use of the term, they have not abandoned their commitment to integrating core labor rights, or standards in their terminology, into global governance. Efforts at promoting these rights have become particularly prominent at the International Monetary Fund and the World Bank. The global union organizations have long sought to influence the actions of these organizations.[62] For much of the post-WWII era, however, these efforts were made at an arm's length, consisting of participation in various conferences and of the submission of position papers on the various issues that these organizations were dealing with. Their efforts took a more formal and permanent tone in 1994 when they decided to open a Washington office dedicated to monitoring and engaging the financial organizations. Combined with the developments vis-à-vis the WTO, then, the mid-1990s can be considered as a turning point in the interactions between global unions and organizations of global governance. Ever since, the global union network, in close collaboration with the World Confederation of Labor, has submitted its views to the annual meetings of the World Bank and the IMF.

As a result of sustained lobbying, in February 2002, the global unions and the financial organizations signed an understanding on regular meetings and contacts, formalizing the ad hoc pattern that was emerging. These meetings and contacts have been taking place on a regular basis ever since. Global union leaders believe that they have been more successful with respect to the World Bank, actually parts of the bank, but much less so with the IMF.

The Asian crisis and the significant criticisms that were launched against the IMF, even from the World Bank, raised hopes within the global union network that the IMF would incorporate a modicum of social accounting into its policies and that such social accounting would take into consideration core labor rights. To date, nothing consequential has come out of that opportunity. It is worth noting, however, that members of the ICFTU's Asian regional organization envisioned an Asian Monetary Fund with formal representation by unions—consistent with the model of paternalistic corporatist arrangements common in the region.[63] Central behind this idea was the Japanese RENGO in collaboration with the Japanese Finance Ministry. This proposal was strongly criticized by a variety of societal entities, including other unions. While nothing has come out of this initiative, it is strong evidence of the cleavages within the regional and global union movements.

The World Bank has been somewhat more open to unions. A major reason for that, we believe, has been the bank's general, if selective, "move to civil society." The global union network, for instance, contributed its views to the bank's 1995 World Development Report, *Workers in an Intergrating World*, as well as subsequent reports, such as the 2006 *Development and Equity*.[64] Some consider the preparation of the 1995 report a symbolic turning point in the relations between global unions and the World Bank. Yet, while the report has recognized

97

the role of workers in development, it sees workers as a factor of production rather than an organized force with an alternative world vision.[65] More recently, the global union organizations have expressed their dismay at the World Bank's active promotion of weaker labor rules and, in fact, its advocacy of their elimination.[66] Perhaps reflecting the serious tensions within the bank on the subject of labor rights,[67] a few months later it announced that it would now start respecting core labor rights in its infrastructural projects.

Following the approval of the ILO Declaration on Fundamental Principles and Rights at Work, global unions increased their pressure on the IMF and the World Bank. In January 1999 and October 2000, large delegations of union leaders from global and national unions visited the organizations. The obstacles that they had to overcome were formidable. In 1999 the World Bank informed unions that it had no problem supporting the core labor standards with respect to forced labor, child labor, and nondiscrimination, but they could not do the same with the right to organize and bargain. These, they argued, were "too political." That, from an organization that was rewriting the internal organization of much of the South. The distinction they made, however, does show that it is easier for global economic organizations, like the German kaiser in the late nineteenth century, to live with labor protections and standards that they choose to implement but not with labor rights that empower workers—or any other subaltern social constituency.

The IFC's decision to attach labor rights to its loan to Grupo M and to integrate these rights into its social and environmental sustainability guidelines, with which we opened the chapter, has to be evaluated in the above context. The question, therefore, is whether this opening is intended to co-opt unions into a weak consultative role or whether it is the beginning of a new approach to global social regulation by global organizations. Compared to the historical record, the IFC's policy and the World Bank's more recent commitment do stand out as important concessions to global union organizations. Specifically, one of the IFC's Labor and Working Conditions Objectives is "to establish, maintain and improve the worker-management relationship" and explicitly includes all of the core labor conventions.[68] It is worth noting, however, that the IFC's rationale is consistent with the overall rationale of the World Bank and other enlightened employers and organizations. Accordingly, "for any business, the workforce is a valuable asset, and a sound worker-management relationship is a key ingredient to the sustainability of the enterprise."[69] The rationale, in short, is that of any sensible human resources manager rather than an endorsement of labor rights as a prelude to strengthening unions in their own right. In this regard, it is encouraging that the global union network has a much broader agenda with respect to these organizations that touches upon questions of poverty, development, privatization, and the role of unions.[70]

Evaluating the Social-Clause Strategy

The debates over the social-clause strategy have been voluminous and can be divided into two positions.[71] One position is that they do not go far enough; the other is that they go too far. In some instances the two positions overlap, but it is still possible to distinguish those who argue that the core labor rights and standards are too limiting from those whose primary goal is to prevent any labor rights or standards from being adopted. In the first category fall some unions, most radical socialists and egalitarians, and some faith-based organizations. In the second category fall business, developmentalist elites in the South, and most liberal governments in the North. Of course, the stance of countries such as the United States is enough to make one think twice about the real reasons behind the social-clause strategy. We cannot do justice to the breadth of the debate over the social clause, but we do want to address both categories, as well as the role of the United States.

The broadest criticism of the social-clause approach is that it does not address the overall structure of the global political economy. It essentially accepts the nature of the current governance apparatus as well as capitalism and seeks to regulate their operations. In this regard, union opposition to privatization and broader agendas about the systemic inequities of capitalism can be considered as necessary steps toward challenging the capitalist global political economy rather than containing its worst impacts. While the push for core labor rights may be a necessary strategy, that strategy will not build a strong counter-hegemonic movement unless it is part of a broader politics that questions the capitalist order itself.

Another very compelling criticism of the trade-labor linkage is that it is limited to traded items rather than the whole economy.[72] As a result, it produces two problems. First, it omits the majority of the world's workers who are not directly employed in trading industries. Second, it can and has pushed some of the categories of workers employed in substandard export production, such as children and young people, into even worse areas of work, such as the informal economy and prostitution. The problem here is practically the same as the one faced by environmentalists. Accordingly, most environmentalists are also opposed to the emphasis on products rather than process and production methods.[73] It is very possible, for example, to produce tomatoes, flowers, or computers that satisfy the most stringent environmental standards at the border but that have been produced using substances that are devastating to both nature and workers during the production process.

Recognizing the limitations and the discursive baggage of the strategy, labor unions have abandoned the term "social clause" in favor of the freestanding "core labor standards" terminology. To the degree that the quest for core labor rights and standards is not limited to trade, it is a broader strategy. To the degree that rights and standards are triggered only as a result of specific economic practices, the strategy is very similar to the social clause. The ICFTU has long advocated for the protection of labor rights throughout whole countries, as its annual report on the violation of trade union rights demonstrates. It is not fair, therefore, to accuse it of having a programmatically narrow view. The challenge that global unions are confronting is that it is very difficult and often impossible to distinguish between sectors that are affected by the global economy and sectors that are not. The impacts of the Export Processing Zones, for instance, are not limited to the workers in those zones. As people migrate to them, abandoning their land or other occupations, the impacts spread throughout the economy. As governments offer incentives to corporations to invest in those zones, the shift in budgetary priorities is felt throughout the economy and the society.

As we have noted, Southern unions have both supported and criticized the trade-labor connection.[74] More radical unions from Brazil and South Africa see the merits of a binding type of linkage but have disagreed with the implementation of the strategy. Most importantly, they feel that the social-clause strategy was a policy from the North supported by the South rather than a policy derived by the changing global union movement. Southern unions, as we have noted, stuck by the strategy, and this is an important accomplishment. Unless Northern unions appreciate this and genuinely enter into more open and less paternalistic relations with the unions of the South, this will be a golden opportunity lost. Moreover, it will have grave implications because, as we noted in the previous chapter, the new international division of labor has made unions in the newly industrialized world an important pole within the global union movement. Without support from unions in Brazil, Mexico, South Africa, Turkey, South Korea, and other countries like them, the global union network will be that much less prepared to confront the challenges that China and India offer to both global unionism and global labor policy.

Yet, talking to Southern unions is also not inclusive enough. Most of the unions in the South are in industry and services. Unionization among agricultural workers, including plantation workers, is less than 1 percent of the total number of agricultural workers. Most workers are unorganized and frequently considered unorganizable. Southern unions, in short, do not represent the range of workers of their countries. A fully egalitarian agenda linking the global economy and workers cannot be limited to organized workers—it must address all workers.[75]

While the above arguments suggest that the social-clause strategy does not go far enough, others believe that it goes too far.[76] Business, in both North and South, was quite united against the linkage (with a couple of exceptions).[77] Business leaders argue that better labor rights and standards are the long-term result of growth and that trade liberalization is the best path to it. Developmentalist elites from the South make the exact same argument but add a North-South dimension. Accordingly, Northern countries have historically used selective trade liberalization to better serve their interests. This pattern continues today as they refuse to liberalize agriculture at the same time that they seek the liberalization of services. This North-South debate has stalled negotiations both at the WTO and at the Free Trade Area of the Americas initiative. Yet, not all of these Southern countries share the same approach to labor rules. Brazil and South Africa, for instance, have supported the linkage, while India and China have rejected it. It also happens that the supporters are those countries with the strongest and most egalitarian union movements.

But what about the United States? It is truly strange to see the government of a country that has not ratified many of the core conventions insisting on a linkage.[78] What explains this counterintuitive stance? We can offer some plausible explanations without claiming to have the whole answer. When the AFL-CIO embarked on this strategy in the 1970s, it was much larger and more influential. Combined with its close collaboration in the anticommunist campaign, this had some purchase even during Republican administrations, leading to the adoption of trade-labor linkages during the Ford and Reagan administrations. As the neoliberal agenda picked up steam, the influence of the organization diminished, as evident by its defeat in the NAFTA debate. While the Clinton administration showed support, that support was not enough to place labor rights and standards at the same level as trade liberalization. The George W. Bush administration is generally hostile to labor rights and standards, but the 2002 Trade Act continues to call for the linkage—evidence that there remains a strong congressional alliance in support of the linkage.[79] Moreover, a number of analysts suggest that the new Democratic majority in the U.S. Congress is likely to adopt a more protectionist trade agenda, using the loss of "American jobs" as a justification. So long as there is a chance that unions, nationalists, industries, and other constituencies that are affected adversely can block the further liberalization of trade, U.S. administrations will keep the linkage on the agenda while also trying to weaken it—as was the case with the Clinton administration and NAFTA.[80] Thus, the trade-labor linkage strategy of the United States is the product of diverse forces. While the most multilateralist U.S. unions are sincere in their desire to create a global union agenda, this does not mean that they are the only force behind the linkage, nor that all U.S. unions are multilateralist.

Beyond Core Labor Rights

It would be unfair to leave the impression that there is nothing else to the global union agenda than the social-clause/core-labor-rights proposal. As we noted at the very beginning of this section, global unions have a much broader agenda. Here we want to highlight some aspects that, in our view, can very well amplify the "core labor rights" strategy. One agenda item, very much supported by global union federations such as the Public Services International and the Education International, is the resistance to the privatization that is being promoted by the financial organizations and the WTO.[81] Global union organizations have come up with a cohesive policy against privatization that goes beyond mere resistance. Large numbers of people in the world work in public services, there are public services in every country, and public services have become part of citizenship rights. Not only is this an issue that can help unions from both North and South work together, but it also can help build broader alliances. Moreover, this strategy can well serve as a compelling response to the liberalization/privatization discourse. We return to this in the conclusion to this volume.

The interactions of global union organizations with the global economic organizations have also allowed these organizations to address development, poverty, and democratic supervision. Unions, for instance, have adopted a more cohesive agenda on development in all relevant international forums and have sought to become more active participants in the formulation, implementation, and evaluation of poverty-reduction programs.[82] This, of course, is a double-edged sword. Legitimating liberal development and poverty-reduction programs can well aggravate concerns about the Northern bias of global union organizations. On the other hand, ensuring autonomous participation can well enhance democratic control of the economy as well as help build alliances between unions and other egalitarian forces.

The engagement of unions with fundamentally inegalitarian intergovernmental organizations raises important questions. How can they influence global governance—or any other kind of governance—without committing to the exclusively collaborative, insider strategy that these organizations prefer? How is it possible to pursue a global egalitarian strategy when the problem with these organizations is not simply that of misdirected policies but of an inegalitarian worldview? We address these questions in the conclusion to this chapter and, more broadly, in the conclusion to this volume.

Challenges to Global Multilateralism

The prominence of global economic organizations and the focus of global unions on them can easily obscure the continuing relevance of alternatives to global regulation as well as the deep crisis facing these organizations as powerful Southern countries challenge their authority. In line with the overall heuristic of this volume, these alternatives can be divided into national, international, and regional. As always, there are important variations within each one of these subcategories.

National policies continue to play an important role. Unilateral policies can be divided into two categories. The first category involves policies that aim at influencing the global political economy through laws whose goal is to attract or repel global trade or investment. A particular country, for instance, may prohibit imports produced using unacceptable child labor practices.[83] Countries and localities may change their labor laws or provide incentives to attract foreign investment or workers, or they may pass laws that make it difficult for capital or people to enter the country. Such provisions may well run afoul of the WTO, but that is not always the case. The second category involves unilateral policies with explicit extraterritorial reach. Various domestic laws promulgated by the United States and the European Union make the importation of commodities contingent on the labor practices in other countries. Primary examples of that are the Generalized Systems of Preferences.[84] In fact, U.S. or EU groups can make the case against an exporting country without any involvement by the latter.

Are all national or local strategies inimical to a multilateralist politics? We do not think so, and we believe that doctrinaire opposition to national initiatives can well deprive unions of an important strategic tool. When are national policies acceptable? In general, we think that national policies are acceptable and desirable when they are not particularistic and when they refuse to lower domestic standards. Multinational corporations and governments often request or demand exceptions in exchange for investment.[85] Another instance is when communities and workers demand that corporations pay for all the negative externalities that they leave behind—perhaps by setting up a fund at the time they start doing business. We find problematic those local or domestic strategies that lead to a regulatory competition between countries, localities, or unions. Here we must note that, in the absence of international collaboration, militant and just local struggles can well produce divisions and play into the hands of capitalist divide-and-conquer strategies. It is for this reason that we think that stronger global union networks and organizations, as well as global public rules, are necessary.

While unilateralism does remain a force, intergovernmental policies have become a more prominent alternative in recent years.[86] Over the past few years, in particular, the United States and other countries have signed many bilateral trade agreements, a few of which include labor and environmental standards. Many of these agreements include all core labor rights as well as some standards and have been hailed as important accomplishments by U.S. unions. Clearly, bilateral agreements that include labor rules can be considered a positive step. One can envision, however, a situation whereby national unions, frustrated by the resistance of global economic organizations and the strategies of other unions (see chapter 5), could well place their hopes on bilateralism rather than multilateralism. Bilateral and regional strategies, therefore, may become a stepping-stone toward global social regulation or may become an end in themselves. Such an outcome, in our view, is likely to divide more than unite the world's unions.

Bilateral strategies, therefore, require global union collaboration. A recent article, for instance, reported that there were gross violations of labor rights in Jordanian Export Processing Zones, despite the fact that the U.S.-Jordan bilateral agreement includes labor provisions that the Bush administration wanted to cancel. The problem here was made even more difficult because the workers affected were immigrants from Bangladesh working for Jordanian subcontractors to U.S. companies.[87] Without a network that is broader than U.S.-Jordanian unions and workers, an issue like this one cannot be addressed.

The third alternative is that of regionalism.[88] The important difference between bilateralism and regionalism is that the latter is more multilateral, requiring that major unions confront and negotiate each other. Yet, labor regionalism could well develop into larger-scale nationalism.[89] The reality is that the most advanced proposals for global labor regulation now appear at the regional level, particularly the European Union. Labor policies have also been adopted under NAFTA and Mercosur and are being hotly contested in the case of the Central American Free Trade Area and the Free Trade Area of the Americas.

Here we want to distinguish two models of regional labor policies—the European and the North American. In the European Union model, labor policies are freestanding and apply to the whole community—not only traded products or investments. The European Works Council Directive, for instance, applies to all companies, European or not, that satisfy certain employment conditions in Europe. On the other hand, the North American Agreement on Labor Cooperation is triggered only if trade is involved. In previous analyses, we have made the case that the North American agreement is an instance when a policy is more of a hindrance than a step toward something better, even though it has been used by some unions to build transnational ties.[90] One of the most serious issues, moreover, was the bitter disagreement between U.S. and official Mexican unions. Since then, there have been some important developments, the most significant being the negotiation of *Labor's Platform for the Americas*.[91] In addition to its broad coverage, what makes this document significant is the group of organizations that contributed to its drafting. These include national unions from throughout the continent, including some Mexican unions that had been resolutely opposed to NAFTA's labor provisions. In addition, the ICFTU's regional arm played a central role. The platform, submitted to the various heads of state that met in La Plata, Argentina, in December 2005, reflects a very high degree of convergence among the unions of the Americas.

During the NAFTA debates in the early 1990s, a number of U.S. union leaders spoke of the EU labor policies as the model that they envisioned for North America. Without a doubt, the labor laws and the structural programs of the EU would be an immense improvement over NAFTA's labor provisions. Yet, their strengths can also be exaggerated, so a few words are necessary here to put them in perspective.[92] Starting with the European Social Charter adopted in 1992, the EU has initiated a dual process toward pan-European labor legislation. One is the direct enactment of directives by the bodies of the EU. The other is the adoption by the EU of policies negotiated by what it considers as the social partners, that is, capital and labor. Even the choice of terms—"social partners" rather than "counterparts," which many unions would prefer—is indicative of the collaborative and largely compensatory labor policy of the European Union.

With respect to directives, the most important policy is that which created the European Works Councils (EWCs). Of great relevance, also, is the European Company Statute Directive that was passed in 2002, even though its labor implications are not the main reason why the directive was passed. The EWCs are organizations of workers employed in the same corporation and must be paid for by the company, thus solving the resource problem plaguing international labor organizations. Contrary to early hopes, they are not negotiating bodies and are entitled only to information and consultation, often perfunctory. Yet, some of them, prodded by national and regional union organizations, have signed "joint texts" with corporations that go beyond information and consultation and, in a few cases, are quite close to collective bargaining.[93] Here, therefore, is an instance of a regional policy with potentially significant implications for global union politics and policies, an issue we discuss in the next chapter. Until EU-level policies are strengthened significantly, however, they will be much inferior to national policies, and their adoption at the expense of national rules will weaken rather than strengthen unions.

Conclusion

The historical sketch that we have provided demonstrates that the adoption of international labor policies is a slow process, with periods of slow change interrupted by windows of opportunity. As we note in the previous chapter, a great deal of the inability of unions to exploit those windows has been due to their own lack of unity and coordination. In this sense, the ability of the ICFTU to bring unions from all parts of the world along around the social-clause strategy is an important development in global labor politics. The fact that this unity continues to our days is remarkable, as is the willingness of unions in both the North and the South to differ with their own governments. We find that the strategy can be criticized in a variety of ways. Some of these criticisms are valid, but others are disingenuous. The most disingenuous ones are those that equate global justice with developmentalism. It is not surprising that business, Southern governments, and neoliberals join in such an argument. In our view, development and equity can and should go hand in hand, and there is good evidence to support this approach.[94] However, most developmentalist elites, now and in the past, put their hopes in growth and the trickle-down effect to avoid redistribution and democracy. Moreover, those egalitarians that emphasize redistributive development are routinely the targets of external and internal hostility.

The leads us to the question of the effectiveness of global union organizations. Labor has formal representation in the ILO (and the OECD), a rare occasion of direct societal participation. While it has a voice, however, its voice is drowned out by that of the opposition. More importantly, the ILO does not have the power to balance the global economic organizations.

Global union organizations have managed to establish a formal consultation process with the IMF and the World Bank (but they are totally excluded from the WTO). Of the two, the World Bank is clearly more receptive, or it seems that way. Their influence does not go as far as shaping the programs of these organizations and, certainly, not their political priorities. Yet, they can point to the IFC's guidelines, discussed at the beginning of this chapter, as evidence of making some inroads. How far can this take them, however, short of a constitutional reorganization of these organizations? And how must they respond since such a constitutional change is not likely without major changes in domestic and global politics?

While global governance has become more prominent and is often used by national elites to justify their own unpopular decisions, it continues to depend on select states and their ruling alliances. Until global organizations are given significant policy autonomy and resources, the locus of power will be external to them. At this point they remain largely intergovernmental and subject to serious challenges from the industrializing world. Accordingly, change will have to come from concerted efforts by unions and like-minded societal and state entities at the national, regional, and global levels. An important role for global union organizations, then, would be to help integrate national and regional strategies into broader global strategies.

In this light, the ability of the global union organizations to forge a common agenda, centered around the social clause and core labor rights, is a noteworthy accomplishment. Not only does it bridge important historical differences, it also engenders an important role for global union organizations. To the degree that global union organizations are successful in inserting core labor rights into global governance, to that degree they are also enhancing their own role in the governance of global union politics.

A global union politics that limits itself to core labor rights and demands about intergovernmental organization behavior may at most be considered as countervailing regulation. There is evidence that the global union network has been engaged in a debate over a broader agenda and considers the core labor rights as one element within a broader strategy. Whether the overall politics will remain regulatory or will become more radical remains to be seen. We think that there are substantial forces within the global union network to at least force a profound debate about what kind of a world global union organizations will fight for.

REGULATING CAPITAL:
BEYOND CORPORATE
SOCIAL RESPONSIBILITY?

In 1966, at a meeting in Detroit, unions from various countries set up the first three of what came to be known as World Company Councils. These new organizations aimed at creating effective union power at the multinational corporation level to confront them across the chain of their activities. By 1974 a total of thirty-two had been set up. Corporations and business analysts took these union efforts seriously and were determined to avoid global industrial relations. Their opposition along with the limited resources of the global union organizations did not allow this far-reaching strategy to succeed. It did not wholly disappear, however. Fourteen years later, the International Union of Food, Agricultural, Hotel, Restaurant, Catering, Tobacco, and Allied Workers' Associations (IUF) and the French company Danone signed the first of a series of agreements committing Danone to certain labor rules. Seven years later, the IUF signed another such agreement with the French hotel company Accor. On January 22, 2007, Building and Wood Workers International (BWI) signed the fifty-fifth International Framework Agreement, that is, a negotiated agreement between a global corporation, on one side, and a global union federation and national unions or other workers' organizations, on the other (see table 5.1). In short, after more than thirty years of frustration, unions have finally managed to get some multinationals to the table at the same time that most of them are resisting unions and are treating workers and communities as mere factors of production. Many global union federations consider these agreements as one of their major accomplishments. Yet, they also think that future agreements ought to be stronger than the ones that they have signed so far. What is it that makes them both enthusiastic and cautious about this accomplishment? To fully answer this question, we must first place these agreements in the historical context. In line with our central questions, we ask whether global union organizations have managed to regulate the corporation but, also, whether in that process they have managed to carve for themselves a more important role in the self-governance of global union politics.

Table 5.1.   International Framework Agreements and Union Participation

Year	Company	Country	Union signatories
1988	Danone	France	IUF
1995	Accor	France	IUF
1998	IKEA	Sweden	BWI
1998	Statoil	Norway	ICEM, national union
1999	FaberCastell	Germany	BWI, national union
2000	Freudenberg	Germany	ICEM, national unions
2000	Hochtief	Germany	BWI, national union (general works council)
2001	Carrefour	France	UNI
2001	Chiquita	United States	IUF, COLSIBA (regional union)
2001	OTE Telecom	Greece	UNI, national union
2001	Skanska	Sweden	BWI
2001	Telefonica	Spain	UNI, national unions
2002	Merloni	Italy	IMF, national unions
2002	Endesa	Spain	ICEM, national unions
2002	Ballast Nedam	Netherlands	BWI, national union
2002	Fonterra	New Zealand	IUF, national union
2002	Volkswagen	Germany	IMF, Works Council
2002	Norske Skog	Norway	ICEM, national union
2002	AngloGold	South Africa	ICEM, national union
2002	DaimlerChrysler	Germany	IMF, Works Council
2002	Eni	Italy	ICEM, national unions

Table 5.1. *(Continued)*

Year	Company	Country	Union signatories
2003	Leoni	Germany	IMF, European Works Council
2003	ISS	Denmark	UNI
2003	GEA	Germany	IMF, European Works Council
2003	SKF	Sweden	IMF, EMF, European Works Council
2003	Rheinmetall	Germany	IMF, European Works Council
2003	RAG	Germany	ICEM, national union
2004	H&M	Sweden	UNI
2004	Bosch	Germany	IMF, European Works Council
2004	Prym	Germany	IMF, European Works Council
2004	SCA	Sweden	ICEM, national union, European Works Council
2004	Lukoil	Russia	ICEM, national union
2004	Renault	France	IMF, World Council
2004	Impregilo	Italy	BWI, national union
2005	Falck	Denmark	UNI, World Council
2005	Electricité de France	France	ICEM, PSI, other international unions, national unions, "Asia Pacific Concertation Committee"
2005	Rhodia	France	ICEM
2005	Veidekke	Norway	BWI, national unions
2005	BMW	Germany	IMF, European Works Council
2005	EADS	Netherlands	IMF, European Works Council
2005	Röchling	Germany	IMF, EMF, European Works Council
2005	Schwan-Stabilo	Germany	BWI, national union
2005	Lafarge	France	ICEM, BWI
2005	Arcelor	Luxembourg	IMF, EMF
2006	PSA Peugeot Citroen	France	IMF, EMF
2006	Portugal Telecom	Portugal	UNI, national unions
2006	Royal BAM Group	Netherlands	BWI
2006	Securitas	Sweden	UNI, national union
2006	Nampak	South Africa	UNI, national union
2006	Euradius	Netherlands	UNI, national union
2006	France Telecom	France	UNI, national unions
2006	Skanska, Hochtief/Turner	United States	BWI, national unions
2006	Staedtler	Germany	BWI, national union
2006	National Australia Group	Australia	UNI, national unions
2007	Volker Wessels	Netherlands	BWI, national unions

Sources: Based on *Hazards Magazine* table and our own research. See www.hazards.org/unioneffect/gufagreements.htm (accessed March 14, 2007).
Key to abbreviations:
BWI: Building and Wood Workers International (former International Federation of Building and Wood Workers)
EMF: European Metalworkers' Federation
ICEM: International Federation of Chemical, Energy, Mine, and General Workers' Unions
IUF: International Union of Food, Agricultural, Hotel, Restaurant, Catering, Tobacco, and Allied Workers' Associations
IMF: International Metalworkers' Federation
UNI: Union Network International

We start with a brief outline of the expansion of multinational corporations and their impacts on private and public governance followed by a discussion of the key factors that explain the emergence of global agreements. This account also allows us to provide an overview of important developments in global union politics vis-à-vis multinationals. We then examine global agreements from two angles. First, what makes them superior to corporate codes of conduct but much weaker than national industrial relations? Second, have they had any impacts that recommend them as a global union strategy? We close by discussing various alternatives and offering suggestions about how these agreements may become the foundations of global industrial relations.

Multinational Corporations and Global Governance

Multinationals have been in existence for centuries but have become a central element of global capitalism during the past fifty years.[1] Thus, while migration, trade, and finance remain three major economic processes that bring national unions into contact, foreign direct investment by multinational corporations is now a fourth entity. However, the multinational corporation is not simply an economic process. It is also an institution of private governance in dynamic interaction with public governance. In what follows we briefly outline the uneven growth of the multinational and its governance role.

Before WWI there was extensive global finance and some foreign direct investment in raw materials. After WWI an increasing number of U.S. companies from the automobile, chemical, and other manufacturing sectors established subsidiaries in Western Europe. The trend was interrupted by WWII and the reconstruction period that followed. In the 1950s, spurred by the formation of the European Economic Community (1957) and fears of regional protectionism, there was an explosion of U.S. investment in Europe, mostly in chemicals and automobiles. It is not surprising, then, that U.S. unions in the globalizing sectors were alarmed over corporate emigration while some European capitalists objected loudly to the "American challenge."

By the late 1960s, however, the Europeans, having exhausted the postwar reconstruction process, started reinvesting abroad, primarily in the United States and other parts of their erstwhile colonies and spheres of influence. The German "east policy" of the 1970s, for instance, had much to do with German desire to reenter central and Eastern Europe, which had been denied to them by the Soviet Union.[2] Up to the late 1970s, there were almost no Japanese multinationals. Thus, the explosion that followed allowed various pundits to argue that Japan was about to take over the world and, certainly, the United States and Europe. By the end of the 1980s, almost all foreign direct investment came from and went to the United States, Western Europe, and Japan. The South received a small portion of that investment but was very much dependent on it.[3]

Since the 1990s, there has been a growth of multinationals from the industrializing countries, such as China, Taiwan, India, Mexico, Brazil, South Africa, and a few others. Most of us own something made by South Korean or Taiwanese corporations or have flown in airplanes made in Brazil. The recent purchase of Arcelor by Mittal, an Indian-owned company, is also indicative of the changing patterns. Moreover, the significance of these countries in the global political economy is underscored by the fact that they account for the overwhelming majority of Northern investment into the South.[4]

This short outline was intended to show two things: first, that different countries, and thus unions, were affected at different times and in different ways by the flows of investment and the growth of multinationals; and, second, that a successful global labor politics must involve multinationals and unions from the United States, Western Europe, Japan, and the major industrializing countries, and unions must find ways to defuse the nationalist and regionalist dynamics involved.

How do multinationals exercise global governance, particularly since they are renowned for their opposition to strong business organizations?[5] First, we can think of a corporation as an agency of governance since its rights to manage its employees and place enforceable demands on its subcontractors are recognized by national laws. This direct form of governance over the lives of millions of people is largely the product of regulatory competition rather than global rules. Individual countries and localities pass laws enhancing the rights of corporations in order to attract them or keep them from leaving. Corporations, in fact, are vehemently opposed to a global legal definition of the multinational corporation because they are afraid that it will open the door to global social regulation.

In addition to national rules, global rules emanating from economic organizations, such as the IMF, the World Bank, and the WTO, buttress the structural power of multinationals. Rules that privilege private property and contractual rights, private dispute resolution, and commercial secrecy provide strong protection for corporations. Imagine, for instance, if there were global or national laws that required a corporation that is unionized in the country of origin to be unionized everywhere it operated. Imagine if global or national rules required that corporations treat the employees of their suppliers and subcontractors in the same ways that they treat their unionized employees.

Because corporations are so insulated, they are the only ones that have the information necessary for writing the rules of international trade and investment.[6] The veil of commercial secrecy that allows corporations to protect proprietary rights even from governments is exceptionally difficult to penetrate. Recently, for instance, the European Union sought to strengthen consumer and environmental protections by requiring that chemical corporations prove that a substance is safe before bringing it to the market. The response was that any process requiring the release of proprietary information was unacceptable and would lead to the movement of production outside the European Union.[7]

In summary, corporations exercise direct authority over millions of employees and indirect authority by influencing public governance and writing public rules. To the degree that they obscure themselves behind a self-serving private sphere, to that degree will they exercise more and more power without having to formally make the decisions. They can leave the dirty work to states and intergovernmental organizations. The reality of global corporations, however, presents unions with a major dilemma. Unions must deal with corporations. In fact, most unions would not exist if there were no need to regulate corporate capitalism. But how can unions both engage and regulate the corporation? On one hand, unions seek to get their "fair share" from the corporation while helping it do better, in the process strengthening the private sphere. On the other, unions aim to embed their interactions with corporations within broader public rules that limit the corporate private sphere. Reconciling the two can often be difficult in practice.

The Roads to International Framework Agreements

Analysts have offered various explanations for the emergence of global agreements. Of these we find that three are more persuasive, namely, the efforts of unions, the rise of corporate social responsibility, and developments in European Union industrial relations. Below we offer a historical narrative of each, starting with the earliest. (See table 5.2.) We close this part by offering our view of the relative influence of each one of these factors.

The Workers Themselves: From World Company Councils to International Framework Agreements

In light of the brief history of the multinationals sketched in the previous section, it is not surprising that it was not until the mid-1960s that U.S. unions sought to engage corporations at the global level, motivated by the internationalization of the lead sectors of the era, that is, automobiles and chemicals. The main response of unions was to call for national policies that would make it difficult for companies to

Table 5.2. Key Dates in Global Private Governance

Date	Event or organization
1966	First World Company Council meeting
1967	ILO International Institute for Labour Studies symposium on transnational industrial relations
1970s–	Corporate social responsibility
1972	ILO resolution on multinationals and social policy
1976	OECD Guidelines for Multinational Enterprises
1977	ILO Declaration on Multinational Enterprises
1988	First Danone agreement with IUF
1994	European Works Council Directive
1995	Accor agreement with IUF
1997	Global union basic code for multinational enterprises
1998	ILO Declaration on Fundamental Principles and Rights at Work
1998	Formation of Volkswagen World Works Council
1999	UN Global Compact
2000	Revised OECD Guidelines for Multinational Enterprises
2000	Revised ILO Declaration on Multinational Enterprises
2007 (Jan.)	Building and Wood Workers' International signs fifty-fifth International Framework Agreement

become multinational. As we note in the previous chapter, first the United States and then the European Union and others adopted unilateral laws connecting access to their markets to respect for certain labor rights. These policies have not stemmed the globalization of business and have often created bitter divisions among unions. They do remain, however, important tendencies within global labor politics.

In the 1960s, however, the United Automobile Workers decided to pursue an additional strategy. Not only was it a union that was losing control over its domain as the U.S. automotive companies resumed and increased their interwar direct investments in Europe, it was also a union with a history of international politics and closer connections with European counterparts, often in conflict with the AFL-CIO's foreign-policy approach to global union politics.

The UAW employed the International Metalworkers' Federation (IMF) to facilitate the creation of World Company Councils, networks that brought together workers of the same company.[8] The first World Company Council meeting took place in Detroit in 1966. Thereafter, the IMF created a number of them, to be followed shortly by the International Federation of Chemical, Energy, and General Workers' Unions (ICF), now part of the ICEM. The connection here was Charles Levinson, who had worked for the metalworkers' union and then became secretary general of the chemical workers' union.[9] The other organization prominently active in the World Company Councils strategy was the IUF.[10]

The views about and the expectations of unions from the World Company Councils varied a great deal.[11] Levinson envisioned international collective bargaining evolving out of the economic dynamics of corporate internationalization.[12] Others had more limited expectations, aiming at the sharing of information in order to avoid divide-and-conquer strategies by capital. Still others objected to the economistic rationale of the councils and argued that without some kind of political agenda it was not possible to build a long-term international union politics.[13] A related criticism of the councils was their formation in corporations and the potential that this would divide workers along corporate lines.

Despite these criticisms, the World Company Council strategy stands as one of the most innovative and proactive attempts by global union organizations to actually respond to globalizing capitalism. In the history of global labor politics, there have been very few instances of strategic and sustained efforts at cross-border collaboration.[14] That this was the case was amply recognized by capital; the Industrial Research Unit of the Wharton School of Business responded to it with a multivolume series on multinational industrial relations.[15]

Many things worked against the World Company Councils, the most important of which were corporate intransigence and limited resources.[16] The conflicting views of U.S. and European unions about industrial relations and ideology, combined with interunion competition, were also debilitating factors.[17] After the defeat of the strategy, the IMF simply preserved the "shells" of these councils while the ICF—now ICEM—allowed most of them to expire, later to revive some of them in the form of networks in the mid-1990s.

The IUF, however, continued to pursue this strategy in a variety of ways, and in 1988 its efforts produced results. Interestingly enough, it was neither Nestlé nor Coca-Cola, leading companies that the IUF had doggedly pursued for years, that signed the first agreement.[18] Rather, it was the French company Danone, where the IUF had set up a World Company Council in 1980.[19] Without a doubt, then, the IUF provides a bridge between the recent move to IFAs and the first generation of efforts at directly engaging multinationals. Its success provides strong evidence of the significance of perseverance and a focused strategy during a period of time that was characterized by the rise of hyperliberalism. Yet, it is also worth noting that it was not until the late 1990s that the dam broke and additional corporations decided to sign agreements. This brings us to the second road to global agreements.

The Good Company

Throughout modern times, there have been corporations that have adopted strong social commitments.[20] In some cases this was due to the paternalistic views of the owner. The owner and founder of the Pullman car company, for instance, provided a great deal for his workers but also expected them to follow certain moral rules and stay away from unions. The Pullman strike, one of the most bitter in U.S. labor history, shows how paternalists react toward errant children. *Good Housekeeping* magazine has long committed itself to improving the lot of housewives by giving its seal of approval to products that were more user friendly and safer. The point, then, is that corporate social responsibility is not a new phenomenon. What is new is that it has become a global phenomenon with significant implications for the governance of the global political economy.[21]

As a starting point in this move toward global corporate social responsibility, we consider a set of activities by the ILO and related entities that took place during the late 1960s. Influenced by unions, the ILO was responding to the rise of multinational enterprises (to include public and private companies) and concerns about their lack of commitment to social policy.[22] This was followed by a 1972 ILO resolution "concerning the social problems raised by the activities of multinational enterprises." The process thus set in motion resulted in the 1977 Tripartite Declaration of Principles concerning Multinational Enterprises and Social Policy. Like all of the ILO's policies, resistance by business and its allies resulted in the declaration establishing a voluntary commitment to respecting fundamental principles and rights at work. The declaration has served to provide unions with a generally accepted statement that corporations do have social obligations. This was strengthened in 2000 when it was revised to include the language of the 1998 Declaration on Fundamental Principles and Rights at Work, the ILO's statement of what unions consider to be the core labor rights.[23]

While the ILO was moving toward its own declaration, the OECD was also working on rules aiming at regulating the behavior of corporations in a variety of areas.[24] The end result was the adoption of the Guidelines on Multinational Enterprises (1976). The guidelines were revised in 2000 and provide a mechanism for their implementation. On one hand, corporations cannot pick and choose which of the rights mentioned in the guidelines they will adhere to. In that sense, it reinforces the unity of core labor rights. On the other hand, the implementation mechanism is very weak and its best end result is that of shaming rather than enforcement.[25]

As Jenkins points out, there had been a 1970s wave of corporate codes of conduct "predominantly concerned with issues of questionable payments."[26] The new wave was significantly different from the codes of the 1970s in its emphases on social issues such as labor, the environment, and consumer protection. The motivation behind this shift was a widespread if not always connected activism focusing on the behavior of particular multinationals.[27]

120

Early on, much of that activism focused on particular companies, mainly from the United States or operating in the United States, with unions playing a leading role.[28] During the 1980s and in conjunction with the antiapartheid movement, a broader variety of societal actors, particularly faith-based and human-rights organizations, got involved in such campaigns. More recently global union organizations have become more involved, often taking a leading role.[29] Increasingly, moreover, non-U.S. companies, such as Nestlé, Shell, and Rio Tinto, have also been targeted.

It is fair to say that corporate social responsibility has become the dominant discourse in our days, receiving additional legitimacy by the United Nations' Global Compact.[30] The Global Compact was the product of a confluence between the United Nations' search for a more active role in global social policies and the reaction of the most enlightened business leaders to the social unrest generated by hyperliberalism.

As far back as the early 1990s, the organizers of the World Economic Forum, which has been bringing state and business leaders to Davos since the early 1970s, pointed to the need for a social component to global integration and a rejection of hyperliberalism.[31] This call became even more pronounced with the financial crises of the mid-1990s and the activism around business practices. As a result, some union leaders were again invited to attend Davos after twenty years of being excluded. It is worth noting that the World Economic Forum invitations to unions coincide with periods of heightened activism, that is, the 1970s and late 1990s.[32]

Building on this ground, the secretary general of the United Nations first proposed the Global Compact at the World Economic Forum in Davos in January 1999.[33] A year later, he held discussions with a global union delegation. There they agreed "that while governments continued to have prime responsibility for implementing internationally agreed standards, the novel feature of the Global Compact—asking corporations directly to demonstrate good corporate citizenship by translating the nine principles into practice—offered new opportunities to reconcile economic imperatives with social priorities."[34] The Global Compact was then formally launched in July 2000. It was based on nine key principles involving human rights, labor rights, and the environment. A tenth principle, against corrupting activities, was added in 2004. The early involvement of global unions is evident by the fact that the labor principles enumerated are precisely the core labor rules found elsewhere.

Most unionists think that the direct value of the Global Compact is limited, both because it is not binding and because it does not give the ILO a central role. Others, however, recognize these limitations but see the Global Compact as another arena in which to engage employers and promote additional IFAs. In short, they find some tactical value to the initiative. The global union organizations most involved are the ICFTU, the ICEM, and to a lesser degree the Union Network International (UNI).

Judging from the over 2,000 companies that have signed the Global Compact, many see some value in corporate social responsibility.[35] At one extreme are those who see simply public relations. At the other are those that consider socially responsible behavior and good relations with labor to be the right thing, as well as a smart strategy. None see corporate social responsibility as a prelude to binding regulation; in fact, it is exactly the opposite. Nor do they think that there is an automatic connection between corporate social responsibility and dialogue with unions.

Justifiably, unions have been very cautious in entering corporate social responsibility arrangements with corporations. They have uniformly criticized unilateral and voluntary codes of conduct, which constitute the overwhelming majority of these instruments. They have also been opposed to or have kept at a long arm's distance from any multistakeholder codes or arrangements that are not binding and do not involve unions—with the exception of the textiles and leather sectors.[36] They have been involved, however, in a few that are binding and that do not depend on the discretion of the corporation. In the late 1990s, the ICFTU and the ITSs formulated a strategy whose aim was to take advantage of the rise of corporate social responsibility and the first global agreements.[37] It is subsequent to that strategy that all but two global agreements have been negotiated.

The Europeans

Our exploration of the emergence of global agreements has looked, so far, at the efforts of unions to regulate the corporation and those of corporations to legitimate corporate social responsibility rather than more profound forms of regulation. Yet, we do not think that these two explanations fully account for the emergence of global agreements. As one looks at the political geography of global agreements, they are overwhelmingly European, even though most earlier corporate campaigns and corporate social responsibility schemes came from the United States and the United Kingdom.[38] Of the fifty-five agreements negotiated as of March 1, 2007, forty-eight involve European multinationals. Outside of Europe, there are two from the United States and South Africa and one each from Australia, New Zealand, and Russia.[39] Moreover, European union and worker organizations have also negotiated agreements with extra-European reach with corporations or subsidiaries incorporated in Europe.[40] What factors account for the central role of Europe?

We have noted earlier that the first wave of foreign investment came from the United States and that the Europeans followed in the 1970s. Even so, for much of the 1970s and 1980s the social welfare state held its own, with the exception of the United Kingdom. Multinationals from continental Europe could not easily fire workers and break the postwar understandings between government, unions, and business that had contributed so much to European reconstruction. Increasingly, however, European companies are becoming more like U.S. and British companies, shedding excess workers as they move more operations abroad or are reorganizing in order to become more competitive within the EU itself. As a result, European unions have increasingly decided to do what the UAW tried to do in the 1960s, that is, shadow their corporations as these become more global.

They have been aided in this effort by developments in European-level industrial relations, starting with the adoption of the European Social Charter in 1992. A major outcome of this general policy change was the negotiation of the European Works Councils (EWC) Directive. European Works Councils came into existence in 1994 but were the product of long negotiations at the EU level whose origins go back into the 1970s. Early proposals envisioned them as collective bargaining instruments. Partly as a result of disagreements among unions—the council system is common in a number of but not all European countries—but mostly as a result of corporate resistance, the end result has been much more modest. Presently, EWCs are forums in which corporations must provide information about plans and activities and where consultation can take place. They cannot formally negotiate with corporations. Moreover, EWCs are not union organizations but, rather, workers' organizations. While unions tend to control them, there are instances of their manipulation by corporate human resources managers.

Even so, the EWCs have had two important side effects. First, they have offered unions forums where they can actually talk to each other and, in some cases, develop common strategies. Some EWCs have become more active and have forced companies to discuss restructuring issues, while a few have also signed global agreements as well as their own agreements that have extra-European reach. This is the result of the influence and initiative of some national and EU-level unions that, for the most part, hold the majority in existing EWCs.[41]

Second, the European Works Councils have provided an impetus for the creation of World Works Councils. Works councils of various types are common in continental Europe. The European Works Councils legitimated them at the European Union level. Union initiatives are now introducing them to the global level.

We think that all three explanations have something to contribute to our understanding of the rise of global agreements. Without the activation of global union organizations, there would have been no agreements, and without corporate social responsibility, there would have been no window of opportunity for unions. In light of the distribution of these agreements, however, it is evident that these two factors would not have worked without developments at the European level.

In light of the European bias of the IFAs, the important question is whether they can become truly global or whether Europe will remain an "island" in an otherwise unregulated globe. This is an important question that informs much of the analysis that follows.

The Content and Impacts of Global Agreements

Are global agreements moving us beyond corporate social responsibility and social dialogue? This is a particularly important question because the 2003 report of the International Organisation of Employers notes that at a high-level meeting of executives of companies that have signed agreements "perhaps the key observation was that companies that have signed IFAs principally see them as a vehicle for deepening dialogue, first and foremost, and *not* as an industrial relations exercise. The difficulty however is that International Trade Unions see them very much so as the latter."[42] This is a particularly important issue because, according to some global unionists directly familiar with the history of the phenomenon, there has been a shift over time. While some of the earlier agreements asserted the demands of unions, most of the more recent ones seem to value social dialogue rather than creating "countervailing power" against global capital.

We approach these questions from two angles. First, we look at the formal content of the agreements. Then we examine their impacts to see whether they have served their goals and whether they have helped establish relations with unions beyond those envisioned in the agreements themselves.

The Content of the International Framework Agreements

Without a doubt, the most important element of the agreements is that they are negotiated between unions and corporations. This, in itself, distinguishes them from all codes of conduct. Since global union federations have signed all of them, the agreements also establish an important role for the global union network, another factor that makes them different from codes of conduct, which are unilateral. Here we want to identify two important issues. We analyze these agreements to discern their differences with respect to the relative role of European and non-European unions and the relative role of unions and workers' organizations.[43]

Reflecting the European bias of the global agreements, national and regional European unions exert a preponderant influence. Of the forty-eight agreements that cover European companies, only a few involve non-European unions formally. This, of course, can be a problem in the long term if unions from other countries see the agreements as a self-serving European strategy or even as a good strategy implemented in a Eurocentric way.[44] There are some reasons to be hopeful, however, because global union federations are involved in all agreements, providing some voice for non-European unions. Also, a number of agreements provide for involvement by non-European unions through corporation-based organizations of workers, known as World Works Councils, of which, however, there are currently very few.[45] Finally, a fall 2006 development gives us hope that non-European unions, including unions that have been skeptical, may be willing to try the strategy. This involves the formation by a number of South and North American unions of a Global Workers Council in the Brazilian-owned steelmaker Gerdau, a major aim of which is to persuade the company to sign a framework agreement.

In terms of regulatory provisions, the global unions have three goals. First, the agreement must cover all core labor rights, thus further legitimating them. Second, it must not be limited to the official workers of the company but must also cover subcontractors and suppliers. If limited to local workers then only a small portion of Coca-Cola or IBM workers would be covered. Third, it must institutionalize the relationship in the sense that there are permanent arrangements for interactions between the company and the unions for monitoring and implementation.

Unions have been quite successful in including core labor rights in IFAs. According to an ILO study, and supported by our own analysis, freedom of association and collective bargaining are covered in more than 95 percent of IFAs, forced labor is covered in more than 90 percent, employment discrimination in about 85 percent, and child labor in more than 75 percent. While some IFAs do not include some core standards, many include additional provisions such as safety and health or minimum wages.[46] Global agreements signed by European organizations show similar patterns.

By contrast, many of the voluntary labor codes of conduct cover a wide variety of labor rules, some of them beyond the core labor rights. Most of them, however, do not include freedom of association.[47] Moreover, the majority do not include one or more of the core labor rights. In that sense, the IFAs are much more consistent and do reinforce a common minimum set of rules.

A related major goal of global unions has been for the codes to have the broadest coverage possible. This includes the coverage of all employees, regardless of where they are located. The fact that a country has not ratified a particular convention or conventions does not release the company from the relevant prescriptions of the global agreement. Most agreements do cover all corporate employees and allow no derogations, at least explicitly. This provision is particularly significant because it prevents companies from segmenting their own labor force and using national rules to justify adopting lower standards. It clearly has important implications for countries with weak labor rules, such as China, India, and the United States, which also attract a great deal of foreign investment. Until these provisions are applied across the whole labor force, global agreements will be but a promise.

Global union federations have been less successful in including suppliers and subcontractors in IFAs. This is particularly important in labor-intensive and primary-product industries where the majority of the people actually employed by a corporation work for the suppliers. Nike, for instance, owns no plants. Furniture companies like IKEA depend very much on subcontractors and suppliers outside of their core markets. The pattern, however, is not limited to these sectors but is increasingly evident in services, telecommunications, high technology, manufacturing, and so on. The rise of hiring agencies and of sophisticated assembly-line companies is bound to accelerate this trend.

A third goal for global union federations has been to institutionalize the global agreements by setting up permanent organizational arrangements and procedures for discussions, monitoring, and implementation. While the structures and procedures that have been set up do vary, we can identify two patterns of institutionalization: new organizations and extensions of existing ones. In most cases, the agreements create new organizational arrangements. In fewer but an increasing number of cases, the global agreement is added to the responsibilities of a European Works Council or a World Works Council. The advantages of the first, less formal end of the spectrum, are that the union side is purely union and that it is flexible. On the negative side, it is costly for unions and it is less permanent. The advantages of the second, more formal end of the spectrum (Councils) are that the costs are absorbed by the company and that these institutions are more permanent. The disadvantages are that they are not union organizations and that they may be more collaborative than some unions may desire.[48] On balance, then, global agreements do provide for some institutionalization while in a few cases multinationals have committed to providing material support, an important demand of unions.

The proliferation of organizations involved in global agreements creates important problems for global unionism. While unions have been successful in controlling most EWCs and the few existing World Works Councils, there is no guarantee that this will always be the case because corporations often seek to manipulate or co-opt these organizations. Moreover, even if unions were to be in control of them, there is a strong possibility of fragmentation along corporate or national lines.[49] For these reasons, we think that the involvement of global union federations is desirable in order to avoid fragmentation along corporate lines as well as the manipulation of workers' organizations by corporations. If affiliates do not transfer more resources and authority to global union federations, however, they will not be able to respond to these important challenges.

The Impacts of Global Agreements

There is general agreement that global agreements must be evaluated in terms of whether they help organize the unorganized and empower the organized.[50] Most of the agreements have been in existence for too short a time to pass comprehensive judgment on the strategy. Their dismissal at this point in time would be premature. Some of the earlier ones, however, have been the subject of in-depth studies, and it is possible to start drawing some preliminary lessons.[51]

There is a second dimension that we also need to take into account, however. As we have noted, most of the companies that have signed agreements are European companies. It follows that the unions most directly involved are also European. If global agreements are to become a means toward global unionism, rather than a European strategy, there must be participation from unions throughout the world, and that participation has to start at the planning stage. This is important for two reasons. First, the global agreement strategy will not be adequately tested unless all important unions in a corporation's production and supply chains are involved. Imagine, for instance, if Brazilian unions refused to collaborate with German unions on a common strategy vis-à-vis DaimlerChrysler or Volkswagen, or if Japanese unions refused to collaborate with French unions with respect to Renault/Nissan. This brings us to the second reason why more inclusive union participation is important. In some cases, unions outside of Europe have taken an indifferent or even a hostile approach to global agreement strategy. If those unions that are interested in and affected by the strategy are not included as full partners, then they can be alienated and side with the opponents.

In what follows we provide some evidence that global agreements have produced positive results, albeit not enough to let unions rest on their laurels. We also pay particular attention to whether the strategy, in the course of implementation or in the course of campaigns to get multinationals to the table, has broadened the universe of unions involved beyond Europe. We start by looking at instances where agreements helped empower and protect unionized workers. We then do the same with examples when agreements helped workers unionize.

The developments surrounding Danone's plans to reorganize its biscuit sector during 2001 are indicative of the potential of global agreements for protecting unionized workers, even though Danone is a special case with a profound commitment to social responsibility. In response to an article in the January 10, 2001, issue of *Le Monde* regarding company plans to close ten factories resulting in loss of 3,000 jobs, the IUF demanded an emergency meeting of the Danone Information and Consultation Committee, as the company's EWC is called. The company agreed to it, and the meeting took place on January 17. The company admitted that there were such plans under consideration but also stated that there were no final plans, that it remained committed to its dialogue with workers' organizations, and that it would communicate "any plans to reduce the Group's over-capacity in the biscuit sector" to the committee and the national consultation bodies in two to three months. The company did announce such plans to its EWC on March 29, 2001. National unions, particularly in France, responded vocally, albeit in a variety of ways. The IUF and the EWC contributed to a network of solidarity demanding that the company devise a more socially responsible transition period in which plants would be closed. As it turned out, the only plant that would be closed was in Hungary. The IUF pressed the company to extend the period for consultations "and the development of trade union counter-proposals" beyond the three months as envisioned in the 1997 Joint Understanding in the Event of Changes in Business Activities Affecting Employment or Working Conditions. They were successful in extending the period to the end of October 2001. During that time, they managed to negotiate a detailed agreement regarding restructuring. The October agreement dealing with the biscuit sector both affirms and expands the 1997 understanding. In short, the Danone case exhibits a longevity and an application that bring us as close to collective bargaining as one can get among IFAs. Yet, it is important to note that actual collective bargaining is still in the hands of national unions and that international agreements cannot negate national ones.[52]

Jane Wills has examined the contribution of the Accor-IUF agreement and has argued that it has generated a space within which unions have been able to contest certain activities by the company in various parts of the world, including the United States and Australia.[53] While Accor is generally underunionized, it has been consistent in its application of the agreement. One possible explanation for that, of course, is its unwillingness to expose itself to protracted labor disputes. A review of the Chiquita agreement has found mixed results but has also shown how unions can collaborate with other societal actors on a worldwide basis in order to accomplish common goals.[54]

Another positive experience comes from the collaboration between the Norwegian Statoil and the ICEM. Statoil is one of the first multinationals to sign and renew an IFA. More importantly, Statoil has collaborated with the ICEM in training national unions on how to implement the agreement and has incorporated its experience in its annual report to the Global Compact. Finally, Statoil played an important role in helping the ICEM and its affiliates successfully solve a bitter dispute between a U.S. union and Crown Central Petroleum in Texas. Specifically, the ICEM and the Norwegian union that had negotiated the agreement persuaded Statoil that it should sever its ties with Crown Central Petroleum, which depended a great deal on Statoil. Statoil's decision to abide by the global agreements played a key role in getting Crown to abandon its antiunion practices and come back to the negotiating table.[55]

There is also some evidence of IFAs helping workers unionize or choose a union of their own. One example is the case of the Turkish company Ditas. Once it became apparent that the company was a DaimlerChrysler supplier, the IMF adopted a strategy articulated around the relevant global agreement. The end result was that DaimlerChrysler did exercise pressure on Ditas, leading to successful unionization.[56]

A more recent example involves the use of UNI's agreement with the French retailer Carrefour to facilitate the conclusion of a collective agreement between its subsidiary and the Korean commerce trade union. According to UNI, Carrefour sped up negotiations after discussions took place between UNI and the company's headquarters to ensure that the agreement was concluded before the company sold its subsidiary to a Korean investor.[57]

One should not exaggerate these results. In fact, the IUF, the global union federation with the oldest and most evaluated agreements, has been critical of most existing agreements. Rather than abandoning the strategy, however, it wants to move it toward Global Union Recognition Agreements, committing companies to actively and positively encourage unionization. Such a shift may make it more difficult to negotiate global agreements, but corporations that do negotiate them will know that the end goal is not social dialogue but some form of global industrial relations.

These examples also show that non-European unions are involved in the process of the implementation of the agreements.[58] So far, however, direct involvement by U.S. and UK unions is very limited, and that of Asian unions is nonexistent. An important U.S. development is the October 2006 announcement that the construction company Turner has negotiated the first agreement that applies to activities in the United States. This, we think, is a very important development for various reasons. First, it shows that agreements can "travel" because Turner is a subsidiary of Hochtief, with which Skanska has a joint venture, and both of these companies have signed global agreements. Second, it involves a number of U.S. unions, which may exercise a positive impact throughout the U.S. labor movement. Finally, it involves unions from both the AFL-CIO and its competitor Change to Win. The participation of the United Steel Workers and the Canadian Auto Workers in the Gerdau Global Workers Council, mentioned earlier, is also encouraging because of the centrality of these unions in U.S. and Canadian labor politics.

Additional U.S. unions are also becoming more open to the IFA strategy. The Service Employees International Union, for instance, has been collaborating with UNI in the security sector. This involves an ongoing campaign as well as one that has produced one of the most recent IFAs, with Securitas. The Teamsters have collaborated with the same global union federation in a successful campaign against Quebecor. The company, however, has not signed an agreement yet. The United Food and Commercial Workers union has also expressed its support for IFAs.

There is some evidence that the scene may be changing in the United Kingdom, as well. For example, a UK union directly participated in the recent agreements with Electricité de France and the National Australia Group, while a number of UK unions are involved in campaigns with global union federations whose aim is to sign agreements.

So far there have been no signs of involvement by Japanese unions. This is particularly important since Japanese industrial relations differ from those found in the United States and Europe. Like European industrial relations, they are much more collaborative. Unlike them, however, they are based on corporation-based paternalism rather than the broader laws of the social welfare state. A recent statement by Japan's largest union confederation indicates that Japanese unions are now considering the IFA strategy. Analysts have also suggested that the strategy is quite suitable to Japan's industrial relations tradition.[59] Yet, while Japanese companies are open to negotiating agreements with their unions, they are strongly opposed to global union federations cosigning these agreements. In short, they are opposed to global industrial relations, preferring instead the corporation-based pattern of industrial relations prevalent in Japan.

On balance, then, there is some evidence that unions beyond Europe are becoming more engaged in the global agreement strategy. As things stand, however, union participation remains largely European and/or colored by the European tradition. How can the strategy move beyond Europe? This is a question we take on below.

Beyond Global Agreements

Global agreements may prove to be a passing phenomenon. It is also possible, however, that they are here to stay. This will not necessarily be a positive development for global union collaboration unless they are the right kinds of agreements, that is, agreements that do not segment workers along corporate lines and that strengthen rather than weaken global union organizations. After outlining the most negative scenarios, we move on to some positive ones and close by suggesting ways in which the strategy can become truly global.

Negative Scenarios

The most negative scenario is that global agreements will prove to be nothing but a public-relations triumph for multinationals. While that may be possible for some of the agreements, we do not think that this scenario is likely for all of them. Not only are some of these agreements grounded in regional or national laws and industrial traditions, but, also, there is a push among corporate human resources managers to harmonize the behavior of corporations across subsidiaries. What is possible, however, is that future agreements will not be more profound and may become the rationale that corporations will use to avoid more consequential arrangements in the same way that General Motors uses the Sullivan Principles to avoid signing a global agreement.[60] As things stand, a review of sustainability reports to the Global Reporting Initiative by corporations that have signed such agreements indicates that they see them as instances of corporate responsibility.

A directly related negative scenario is the proliferation of agreements that do not raise additional demands but, by their numbers, stretch the resources of national and global unions. This is a problem that all global union federations recognize. Both the IUF and the IMF have gone through reviews of the strategy with an eye to raising the bar. Other federations are seeking the same ends by improving the content of every new agreement.

A third negative scenario has to do with the very practice of organizing on the basis of corporations. Nobody disagrees that corporations ought to be the target of unionization. If not placed within broader public rules and strong union organizations, however, corporation-based unionization can fragment unions and help corporations divide and conquer. The worst part of such an outcome is that it may look like a success, that is, a corporation agreeing to a strong agreement or even collective bargaining in exchange for a loyal workforce that sides with the company and against other workers. None of the agreements is explicitly predatory, but some of them do contain language that places a high premium on corporate competitiveness and survival. The possibility of such a development further recommends the involvement of global union federations and highlights the need for broader arrangements.

Positive Scenarios

What are the positive scenarios? Starting small, agreements could be revised to accent some things already there. Rather than asking corporations to abstractly recognize the right to organize, they can ask corporations to accept it and facilitate it. Rather than leaving implementation up to future arrangements, they can ask corporations to absorb the costs of institutional arrangements without calling the shots. IFAs could move from negative commitments to positive regulations, redrawing the boundaries of the public and the private to the advantage of workers. Currently, for instance, unionization drives in the United States have to go through two stages. First, organizers must get workers to sign cards indicating that they want to have a union certification vote. Then, they must vote. The first step often serves as a warning to the company to take countermeasures. Doing away with this two-step process would greatly facilitate unionization.

Moving from enterprise to sectoral agreements is a major goal for global unions and would be a second positive scenario.[61] Capital is generally unwilling to commit to binding agreements of any kind. Equally significant is the systematic weakness of industry associations at the global level. The International Organisation of Employers at the ILO, for instance, is renowned for its lack of authority. Moreover, almost no global sectoral organizations have been given suprasocietal authority by their members. This is partly because there are serious disagreements among corporations, partly because of different traditions of industrial relations, and partly a result of strategic calculations.[62] Stronger business organizations can well strike agreements with their union counterparts and thus open the door to global social regulation. While various advocacy organizations, such as the International Chamber of Commerce, provide some discursive guidance, capital is not rationalized at the global level.

As we have noted, there are similar dynamics among unions. Global union organizations are still confederal, with key national unions objecting to stronger global union organizations. Whether with respect to bipartite or sectoral arrangements, global union organizations must always navigate a difficult road between suprasocietal arrangements and national industrial relations. On balance, however, global union organizations have been more willing to explore bipartite and sectoral agreements than are corporations.

The most promising scenario, but also the one that carries the highest risks, is the use of European industrial relations as the springboard to global industrial relations.[63] We have already noted the problems with this approach. Until non-European companies and unions join, it could be very divisive. It is for this reason that the Turner agreement is so encouraging. Marginalizing global union organizations would certainly make it difficult for unions from other continents to join. Yet, there are three advantages to Europe. First, unions remain strong and the social welfare state resists being dismantled, despite the prominence of Tony Blair's "third way." This is the case even in countries with low union membership, such as France. Second, there is some institutionalization in the form of EWCs. Finally, European industrial relations cover foreign companies operating in Europe. In light of the above, we see two possible routes to the globalization of European industrial relations.

First, it is possible that non-European multinationals that have agreed to EWCs and other arrangements in Europe, such as General Motors, Ford, and General Electric, will eventually decide to adopt them globally rather than deal with multiple systems of industrial relations. Since multinationals have a lot of experience in dealing with diverse systems of industrial relations, this is not foreordained. But coordinated pressure by unions, where unions exist, may actually encourage corporations to do so.

Alternatively, we can envision a scenario of European companies operating abroad unionizing in countries where unionization is difficult. Accordingly, if a European company's workers were unionized throughout the corporation, including, for example, in China and the United States, the implications would be momentous. If subcontractors and suppliers were forced by companies who have signed agreements to respect their provisions as a condition of continuing to do work with them, the impact would be multiplied. As it stands, DaimlerChrysler has intervened in at least eleven cases to get its suppliers throughout the world to respect the labor rules outlined in its global agreement. For such a strategy to work, it will be necessary for European unions to ally with unions throughout the world. Moreover, they must be willing to recognize the existence of different labor traditions rather than speak the language of superiority or foreign policy.

CHAPTER FIVE

But how can this European phenomenon be propelled to the global level? Is collaboration enough? When must European unions, accustomed to collaborative industrial relations, adopt other strategies? When must non-European unions accustomed to more confrontational relations adopt collaboration?

We have used the term *campaign* without any discussion. Here we want to clarify what the term means and how campaigns and agreements can be articulated with each other in a manner that also bridges diverse industrial traditions. Campaigns against corporations have become the dominant U.S. union strategy over the past twenty years[64] and have been necessitated by the recalcitrance of U.S. companies, aided as they were by the hyperliberal turn since the early 1980s. The common characteristic of these campaigns is that they focus on corporations rather than governments or broader practices, such as child labor. Beyond that, there are many variations. Accordingly, a corporate campaign tries to influence the top managers, a comprehensive campaign attacks everything that the corporation does, an organizing campaign aims at unionization, and so on.

Campaigns are generally militant and confrontational precisely because corporations are being recalcitrant. They are not necessarily radical in their demands, however. Most campaigns by U.S. unions are quite limited in their demands, focusing mostly on economic and union issues rather than the nature of the corporation or the overall rules of the economy. Moreover, U.S. campaigns have been criticized for their lack of long-term commitments. Once the goal has been achieved, the networks and the alliances created are allowed to fade away. In recent years there is some evidence of longer-term commitments, but even then it is not clear what the goal is: permanent union networks? global bargaining with a corporation? solving a labor dispute in the United States?

We agree with various analysts and unionists that the more sophisticated and comprehensive campaigns have a great deal to offer to the global union movement, and it is encouraging that global union federations have become more active participants over time.[65] We also think, however, that in order for campaigns to become a permanent and positive aspect of global unionism, they must create permanent networks and stronger global union federations and must aim at some global goals. In line with the discussion in this chapter, stronger framework agreements are one such goal.

While campaigns have been criticized for their ad hoc nature and their narrow horizons, the collaborative nature of the framework agreements is also problematic. Most continental European unions, certainly German and Scandinavian, are accustomed to formal industrial relations arrangements that go beyond economic issues and underpin the welfare state. Yet, the industrial relations common in many European countries, certainly in Germany, are well below what even interwar social democrats had in mind. In fact, the collaborative industrial relations system used in Germany owes a great deal to a Christian Democratic effort to engage the largely devastated German unions after WWII. In short, European unions are important but not the central elements of the post-WWII industrial relations system.[66] As governments are becoming more liberal and corporations more transnational, the limitations of the collaborative model are becoming more apparent. For German or Japanese or any other unions to reject out of hand the need for more militant tactics is to narrow their options and leave their fate to the discretion of multinationals.

Articulating campaigns with framework agreements at this point in time is a promising strategy for a variety of reasons. First, it takes advantage of those corporations that are willing to transfer the European system to the global level but warns them that other tactics may be employed if they are not willing to deepen their commitment. Thus, Volkswagen has been a leader and set up a World Works Council earlier than any other company. It would be a mistake, however, to exempt it from demands for a stronger agreement. Second, it warns companies that they cannot change their tune when operating in other countries, less they be subject to more militant strategies. This applies to both U.S. companies, which have entered some serious agreements with European regional unions but refuse to sign global agreements, and European companies that refuse to cover their workforce outside of Europe. Finally, it warns generally antiunion companies that they are going to confront the collective power of all unions wherever they are, especially in union-friendly countries. Attacking Wal-Mart with an eye toward unionization only in the United States is a valiant but difficult task. Making the strategy global, as is the direction, by not allowing the company to open nonunion stores, or any stores, in Europe or elsewhere in the world will both limit its choices and will bring workers from other countries on board.

It is our view that unions have to go beyond corporations and take on the public rules about the corporation. We briefly suggest two routes here. The first is through the reform of corporate governance. The second is through reforming global economic rules and organizations. As we note earlier in the chapter, corporate social responsibility is not the same as corporate governance. Social issues are but one aspect. Shareholders, for instance, may be more interested in transparency and returns than in social impacts. In recent years, however, national and global unions have sought to influence global debates on corporate governance, particularly the guidelines offered by the OECD. To that end, they have also created the Committee on Workers' Capital, whose aim is to marshal the momentous amounts of union pensions invested throughout the global economy, particularly the U.S. economy.[67] Labor intervention is already broadening the debate. Yet, unions may choose to offer a more or less profound critique of the corporations. The less profound will focus on including labor rights and ensuring that unions get a seat at the table next to private capital. The more profound could lead to a rethinking of the options available in our world today by attacking the idea that private bureaucracies are inevitable or preferable. It seems to us that trying to regulate individual corporations without regulating or reforming the institution of the corporation may be successful for particular unions and groups of workers but not necessarily internationalist and egalitarian.

Ultimately, we think there must be global public rules for corporations and states. The most plausible scenario would be the promulgation of global-union-enabling policies. While the current global situation is not encouraging, giving up the fight for public rules is, in our view, a bad strategy. The enhanced relations between global union federations and the ITUC, reflected in the Council of Global Unions, will hopefully lead to a better articulation of private and public strategies. In any case, the pursuit of advantageous public policies is not solely a global union matter. States continue to matter, contrary to what liberal internationalists tell us. For that reason, the continued coordination of national, regional, and global strategies remains central in order to take advantage of another opening like the one that occurred in the late

1990s. The ICFTU did a good job making the social clause a common demand in the 1990s. A number of criticisms can be raised with respect to the social clause and core labor rights, as well as the tactics of the ICFTU. Yet, the fact that the ICFTU got most unions in the world to agree on a common agenda compares well to any other examples of global union collaboration.

Conclusion

Have global unions formulated a global agenda vis-à-vis corporations, and have they been able to engage and regulate the corporation? What are the implications for global unionism? We think that they have accomplished both goals but certainly not to the degree they have done domestically or to the degree that is needed globally.

Over the past ten years or so, many global union federations have been admirably focused on the IFA strategy. While there are variations in their interpretations of the strategy, this is another example of long-term commitment to an agenda. The agenda can be criticized on many grounds, including its collaborative nature and its geographic bias. Yet, it is clearly a strategic agenda.

The political vision of global union federations, as it emerges from the global agreement strategy, is one of countervailing regulation. The global agreements do not seek to change the rules of capitalism, nor do they touch upon the managerial prerogatives of multinational corporations, for example, where to invest, what to invest, and so on. Rather, the goal is to create a space within which workers can organize to advance their rights as workers. One can argue, with some validity, that this is a necessary tactical move by global union organizations, some of which may hold reformist rather than regulatory views. Accordingly, the approach taken by unions in the public service sectors, represented globally by the Public Services International and Education International, offers an alternative. The approach here is not simply one of regulating the activities or even governance of the corporation but actually advocating an alternative to private authority. On that view, certain goods must be taken out of the market and must be provided in an increasingly more efficient and more equitable fashion. The implication here is that private corporate authority cannot be democratized while remaining private. By its nature, it assumes that owners and managers have discretionary powers that are not subject to democratic scrutiny. It is for this reason that we think that to the degree that unions do not question the legitimacy of private authority, they can at most regulate corporations.

Have global unions managed to engage the multinational corporation? It is important to underscore the fact that while modest in their regulatory provisions, global agreements are the first instance of agreements negotiated between corporations and unions at the global level. Before dismissing them, one must offer alternatives or must show that their existence is foreclosing other and better alternatives.

Global agreements are not unilateral codes of conduct, but they are also not binding industrial relations instruments. Unless they mutate into something binding, they will become an interesting and painful footnote in global union politics the way that World Company Councils of the 1960s have done. Or, they may serve to foreclose other options. In short, they raise the same dilemma as the ILO. When should unions engage policies and organizations that are less than what they would like? When do such arrangements become a stepping-stone to something more profound, and when do they become an end in themselves? In our view, global union federations and national unions are at a moment when some strategic thinking is necessary, even if this means fewer global agreements. Getting many more agreements will be just that. Getting a few stronger agreements and perhaps some collective bargaining agreements, by any name, will finally realize the hopes of the 1970s and will lead to global industrial relations.

Finally, we think that the direct involvement of the global union federations in all global agreements is a qualitative improvement over their pre-1990s history. Like global public governance, global private governance has exerted a very powerful pull that national unions cannot address through ad hoc alliances and foreign policies. Stronger global union organizations are necessary before unions can pursue more ambitious global initiatives. There is likely to be a time, in the very near future, when corporations will prefer to talk to global union federations, albeit for many different reasons. In some cases, they may find them spread thin and easy to manipulate; in other cases, they may find that acting like a national rather than a transnational corporation may limit its appeal; in still other cases, they may find it easier to work with one body rather than many national unions. Finally, future success of the global agreement strategy is probably the best reason why global unions must be strengthened. As we noted earlier, the proliferation of corporate-level workers' organizations makes the specter of divisions all the more plausible as workers align with their companies in the spirit of competitiveness. Successful framework agreements that are not part of a larger whole, in fact, may be the worst outcome. For all of these reasons, we think that stronger global union networks and organizations are as much of a necessary response to the uneven growth of global private governance as they are to the uneven growth of public governance.

CONCLUSION: THE
CHALLENGES OF THE PRESENT

Globalization and global governance have exerted a noticeable influence on global union politics. There is, in fact, a trend toward healing the wounds of the past, there are global agendas, and there are efforts at accomplishing them. Yet, global integration is both an opportunity and a challenge. Unions may well continue to move toward more collaboration or may fragment along interstate, regional, or national lines. The future depends very much on both the legacies of the past and the strategies that unions adopt. In what follows we return to the major themes of the volume and close with a few comments on the implications of the lessons from global union politics for global justice politics.

Engaging Each Other

The unification of the global union movement is an encouraging development even though it is only partial. Some unions will not join, as is the case with the official Chinese unions. Others are guaranteed regional autonomy, as is the case with the Europeans. Equally importantly, the global union network may gain in terms of coordination as a result of the unification and the formation of the Council of Global Unions, but there has been no dramatic change in terms of the organizational and political powers of global union organizations. Yet, better and sustained coordination could help make labor a more formidable force.

Throughout the volume, we argue that a vibrant global union movement requires stronger global union organizations and networks. Why are they necessary? What will they be like? Is there any evidence of them emerging? We think that the uneven nature of global integration mandates stronger organizations for two reasons. First, stronger organizations are needed in order to respond more effectively to the global state and to global capital. If national unions are alarmed over the increasing influence of global public and private governance, then it makes sense to have strong global union organizations (in the same sense that nationalization of the political economy resulted in national unions). Second, global integration is uneven. If unions are to avoid the divisive influences of nationalism, regionalism, and intergovernmentalism, they need stronger organizations to bring them together to at least negotiate their differences.

We do not have in mind centralized organizations like the Catholic Church or the Third International. Regional, national, and local unions are desirable and are not likely to go away. Rather, national and global organizations must work out a division of labor, much as has happened in national union movements and federal political systems, with global union organizations and networks gaining some authority with respect to institutions of global governance and with respect to the internal governance of the global union movement.

The creation of stronger global organizations does not require the massive transfer of resources. A great deal can be accomplished, and probably more effectively, through the integration of global politics into the activities of national unions and the pooling of the resources of national and global unions. Such integration can build on existing patterns but should be consequential enough to prevent foreign policy from overcoming global policy.

As we suggest throughout, the first steps have been taken. Not only have there been some modest organizational developments over the past fifteen years, but, equally importantly, global union organizations have "used" global governance to start carving a niche for themselves. In this sense, global governance is exerting the same kind of influence that national governance has exerted in the past. But opposition to strong global unions remains formidable, and success is not foreordained. One important question, therefore, is where the push toward stronger global unions is likely to come from.

According to many analysts and activists, it is likely to come "from below."[1] We agree with them if this means that for workers or any other people to be empowered, they must be active participants and take authorship of their destiny. We do not think, however, that commitment to such an approach ought to preclude the possibility of finding allies at various levels and for various reasons.

Historically, profound change has often been catalyzed "from above." John Lewis, the leader of the United Mine Workers during the interwar period, was not the most democratic or likable of union leaders. Yet, he was instrumental in helping launch the Congress of Industrial Organizations (CIO) and change the landscape of U.S. labor politics. The CIO, however, was not his complete creation. Communists and other radicals, who had long been working for a more inclusive union movement, grabbed the opportunity to create industrywide unions with a broader political agenda.

Change can also come from the middle, whether that is a large local union, a national union, or some other kind of network. We think that paying closer attention to the potential of second-tier organizations is worthwhile. Not only do they possess important material and human resources, but they are also more closely connected to workers than national federations or global organizations.

Finally, impetus will also come from the formation of "super unions" through the merger of national unions, as envisioned by the recent discussions between IG-Metall, Amicus, and the United Steel Workers, or the formation of global unions centered around strategic nodes, such as global cities, as proposed by the Service Employees

International Union (SEIU).[2] It is worth noting that such unions bring us full circle back to transnational unions created by the Knights of Labor in the second part of the nineteenth century and the Industrial Workers of the World during the first part of the twentieth century. It is also worth noting that transnational unions in the past created serious problems, even among friends, such as the AFL and the British unions.

We are personally supportive of actual global unions, provided that they are not particularistic and do not create jurisdictional problems. The proposed "super union," for instance, is silent about unions from Asia or the industrializing world. The SEIU's proposal could well create conflicts with national unions by creating a two-tiered workforce, that is, with one tier more integrated into the global economy and another tier less so. For these reasons, we believe that the relevance of stronger global union organizations and the need for effective self-governance will increase even more as the traditional national boundaries of unions are challenged by unions themselves.

Yet, even if the global union organizations were to become stronger, they would still be representing a small minority of the world's workers, even in industry and services. That would be less of a problem if the largest reservoirs of labor were not in countries with weak union systems, such as India or Indonesia, or compromised union systems, such as China or Vietnam.

But where should unions look for additional members? We think that they should look both up and down the socioeconomic ladder. Paying attention to those categories of professionals who are finally recognizing that they are workers, such as physicians, engineers, college professors, and others, should be an important priority for unions. It took unionism a long time to realize that white-collar workers were workers. Missing another opportunity by accepting the argument, often coming from professional workers themselves, that they are not workers would be a strategic blunder.

Unions have also paid more attention to gender, but a great deal more needs to be done. Not only must they integrate women, but they must also address gender and the question of work more broadly. A number of unions have made the argument that bringing up children and keeping a household should be recognized as work. As more men are also engaged in child care and housework, this is an opportunity for unions to address gender roles more broadly.

We also think that appealing to less-skilled or precarious workers, such as migrants, is very important, and there is encouraging evidence in that direction. We do not think so just because that is a way to increase the ranks of the unionized. If unions do not represent and advocate for the unprotected labor force, then others, with often very hostile attitudes toward unions, will do so. That certainly was the case with Hitler and could well be the case with the likes of Patrick Buchanan. Finally, we think that advocating for the large numbers of workers who make up the vast hinterland of the working class can establish long-term legitimacy that passes from generation to generation.

Historically, global union organizations have been organizations of the industrial and service workers in the industrial North and, more recently, the South. Many national union movements realize that one or another aspect of doing business as usual and appealing only to these same categories of workers is shortsighted. Global union organizations can play a very important role as promoters of best practices among the world's unions, thus broadening the horizons of their affiliates.

In general, we think that unions must increasingly offer themselves as organizations that represent the full spectrum of working people and their needs rather than narrow economistic organizations. Here we can learn a great deal from a comparison of the U.S. and French union movements. Both of them represent a low percentage of the labor force—about 14 percent for the United States and even less for the French. Moreover, the French are divided into many confederations. When U.S. workers take to the streets, it is to protest a narrow economic issue. When French workers take to the streets, they do so to protest the organization of the political economy, whether against contingent employment by the young or in favor of the thirty-five-hour work week. These are rules that apply to everyone—not only unions. This is one of the major reasons why French unions enjoy a great deal of legitimacy, even though they are divided and declining in numbers.

Regulating the State

A number of liberal advocates have posed societal politics as the antithesis of the state. Where the state is oppressive and unrepresentative, societal forces are more tolerant and inclusive. Where the state divides the world into separate territorial units, societal forces help people break away from the parochialism of the nation. As we anticipate in chapter 2, we have serious problems with such an approach. States, that is, the rules and organizations that organize political authority and rights, vary both across time and in time. The present U.S. state, for instance, is not the same one that it was a hundred and fifty years ago, when slavery was still allowed in much of the country and African Americans, women, and many poor people could not vote or be elected to office. It is not the same as it was a hundred years ago, when senators were elected by state legislatures and there was no social security. In 2007, the U.S. state is not the same as the Swedish state with its emphasis on rights rather than philanthropy or the Chinese state with its combination of liberalization and authoritarianism.

Nor are states the guarantors of territoriality. More often than not, they are its major enemies. How else could we make sense of various governments rejecting labor policies in the name of sovereignty at the same time that they submit to the discipline of the global economic organizations? Similarly, societal forces are often the most trenchant supporters of territoriality. Many environmentalists, often the most cosmopolitan among societal entities, justify national energy policies in the name of national security and oppose migration in the name of sustainability.

It is not our argument that there are no similarities and common patterns. We are saying, however, that it is important to not reify the state in the same sense that we should not reify the corporation or the individual. Sometimes patterns of similarity are more pronounced and sometimes not. Sometimes states are the product of egalitarian alliances, other times of inegalitarian alliances, and more often of some mixture of social forces.

Labor unions have generally not shared this disdain for the state, even though they have sought to avoid political issues (or what they claim are political issues). Sooner or later they all realize that without public rules, it is more difficult to unionize and empower workers. Most unions, however, are not simply interested in influencing the state and its rules. They actually want to shape the state. In many cases, this involves organic relations with political parties that circulate in power. Whether directly or indirectly, their goal is to put in place rules that organize political authority and make it difficult for opponents to dismiss unions without undoing the state. One of the major reasons why Mexican unions have not passed into oblivion, given their own internal problems and the country's move to the right, is the fact that about ninety years ago they managed to include labor rights into the constitution. One of the sources of power of the French unions is their role in managing pensions through state organizations.

In chapter 4, we review the efforts of global unions to engage and regulate the global state, such as it is. The results are very modest but noticeable. In the late 1990s, the global union movement almost succeeded in inserting social regulation into the WTO. As has been the case throughout history, the global union movement has to prepare for the next round, whether that is another attempt at the public regulation of trade, investment, or corporate governance. Then, as in the past, global unions will be confronted with a major dilemma. At what point should unions reject legitimating a state entity because it offers them participation but at the cost of power? How should they approach any opportunities that such organizations offer?

It seems to us that there are instances when unions ought to walk away or resist international arrangements, even if they offer them some representation, as they have done at the domestic level. We do not think that the argument "anything is better than nothing" is always valid. Quite often, "anything" may very well close the road to something more consequential or lead to the waste of resources, as has largely been the case with the North American Agreement on Labor Cooperation.

Yet, we also think that there are situations where global union organizations cannot walk away from weak organizations, such as the ILO and the OECD, both of which offer unions a formal status. In such instances, unions are better served when they approach such organizations as part of their broader tactics and strategy—not as the fulfillment of their political goals. Thus, they ought to keep the reform of these organizations on their agenda, even if that means breaking with their collaborative tradition. For unions to foreclose the possibility of outsider strategies vis-à-vis friendly organizations is to legitimate their own subordinate role.

On the other hand, how should they deal with stronger organizations that keep them at arm's length and whose priorities are vastly inimical to social regulation and reform? Here, the articulation of both

149

insider and outsider strategies, with the latter playing a more important role, is necessary. It is not surprising that the modest global social regulatory provisions that we have were enacted in the late 1910s, the 1970s, and the late 1990s, all periods of systematic mobilization.

Global and national unions have participated in various demonstrations against organizations of global governance during various global meetings. Such militant tactics are both useful and necessary. They are not sufficient, however. In order to be fully effective, they must be part of a multilevel union strategy that integrates the national and the regional. Global campaigns to change global organizations must target power, which also means those states that control global organizations. Had the Europeans decided to side with the United States, for instance, it is likely that there would have been a social clause in the WTO by now. It is important to realize that even the most powerful intergovernmental organizations are controlled by particular states. Until the time when they gain authority above and beyond that of the leading states, attention to intergovernmental organizations should not detract attention from the real sources of power.

The successful pursuit of such a multilevel strategy vis-à-vis the state further underscores the need for stronger global unions and networks. How can unions be effective if they are scrambling to rebuild their relations after the opportunities have become apparent? How can they develop a long-term strategy unless global union organizations are authorized to play a more consequential role in developing such a strategy?

Regulating Capital

International Framework Agreements are an accomplishment for global unions. As we note in chapter 5, the negotiation of stronger agreements is a necessary development, provided that these agreements are not at odds with each other and do not promote competition rather than collaboration among unions. The prospects of sectoral agreements are quite limited at this time, but more agreements with leading companies in particular sectors could well create a pattern and may lead to sectoral negotiations. That certainly is possible in the automobile sector. For that to happen, global union federations must have more authority, and global business organizations even more, compared to the present.

Yet, global unions must confront questions similar to those they must confront with respect to the global state. How should they respond to private governance when it offers them incentives? How should they respond to private governance when it excludes them? It is worth noting that unions did reject unilateral codes of conduct. It is also worth noting that the sector where unions did get involved in some codes of conduct—textiles—is the sector with no global agreements. Perhaps this is a case where "anything" got in the way of "something."

But engaging corporations, even recalcitrant ones, is a necessity for unions. This raises a broader issue. While there are states where unions have strong legal rights, there are no global corporations where that is the case. Moreover, most unions do not question the right of private corporations to exist—they only question aspects of their behavior. It is not necessary to reject capitalism in order to reject the liberal claim that most economic activity should be in private hands with the state doing only what capitalists cannot do or are unwilling to do. We do think, however, that unions should not simply respond to liberals. They should actually offer an alternative program that asserts the social priorities that have helped empower people over the past two centuries. In fact, we think that global and national union politics offer proposals that keep this vision alive. A prominent example is resistance to privatization while calling for the reform of the public sector. This argument can be taken further. Some arguments against privatization take a very narrow approach and contest the privatization of what is currently public. Why not broaden the public sphere? Analysts and activists have done so in a variety of ways. The existence of the public sector offers unions a concrete place from which to "reclaim the commons."[3] In some parts of the world, making such arguments is easier than in others. It is certainly very difficult to make those arguments in the United States. Yet, even in the United States there are vast sectors of the economy that are directly socialized, including water, education, and libraries. Others, such as social security and health care, are indirectly socialized. Finally, some activities that seem liberalized, such as research and transportation, would not function if the costs were not undertaken by the state. No airline has built a major airport, and no car company has built a highway.

The long-standing debates over corporate governance offer another opportunity. Here, as well, unions and their allies can move beyond regulating the company and ensuring that it behaves in an ethical fashion; they can address the nature and role of large private bureaucracies. The move from shareholder to stakeholder democracy should go beyond demanding voice and must address the rules of the whole economy since it is these rules that empower private authority.

We want to highlight the significance of public rules that regulate capital and empower workers. We think that the greatest success of capital has been its ability to create a private space within which it can operate without democratic supervision. Anyone who chooses to contest capital by conceding the autonomy of that space has already conceded the war and may die in battle. Some unions have done very well within these parameters. A global unionism that wants to globalize justice and solidarity cannot.

Beyond Labor

Are these lessons relevant for other societal forces? How can labor and other societal forces committed to social justice find common ground? We close by briefly addressing these two questions.

Environmentalists promoting energy policy on national security grounds rather than ecological grounds? Human-rights advocates opposing universal human rights? Feminists who want to join the militaries of their countries? All societal politics has and is confronting the questions of internationalism and egalitarianism. In some cases, it is possible to bypass the issue through mechanistic claims, for example, that since environmental problems are global, anyone who offers a solution must be a cosmopolitan.

Those unions that are committed to global egalitarianism can learn a great deal from other social movements, keeping in mind that global egalitarians are a particular thread or tendency in all societal politics, sometimes hegemonic and sometimes marginalized. Other social movements can learn even more from labor, particularly as they confront the reality of their differences and the cynicism of the powers that be.

One of the most important issues that global egalitarians must confront is that of scale, for lack of a better word. This volume is about global union organizations as indicators of the willingness and ability of national unions to bridge their differences and redirect some of their energies. The history of labor, and other social movements, is populated with local or particular struggles. The people participating in these struggles are regularly up against the wall. But as the world is becoming more global if not globalized, local struggles have implications well beyond their geography. How can local struggles against environmental harm be integrated into a broader strategy? The point we want to make is that all societal movements, particularly those that aspire to global justice, must guard against "militant particularism" or the glorification of particularistic struggles, whether local or global.[4]

This brings us to the last issue. A number of analysts have argued that global union politics has not fully engaged the global justice movement, primarily manifested in societal politics. In light of our approach, the delineation of the global justice movement out of the many societal networks and movements is not a simple task.[5] Certainly, the global justice movement could not include all those who protest against global economic organizations nor even those who attend the World Social Forum. Some of the people protesting global organizations are nationalists, while others are opposed to specific measures that may seem just within certain parameters but rather unjust within other parameters. Demanding protections for farmers in France or South Korea, for instance, does raise questions about the impacts on farmers in West Africa. In general, we think that a global justice movement must be characterized by both strong internationalism and strong egalitarianism, neither of which is a homogeneous category. Now, as throughout the history of international egalitarianism, it will be necessary to be inclusive of various interpretations of equality and internationalism without becoming an aimless gathering of fundamentally conflicting views. This combination has proven difficult to accomplish but is certainly worth aiming at.

We argue that global union politics is moving between nationalism and multilateralism with internationalism being less prominent and cosmopolitanism even less so. Yet, we think that as global governance becomes more profound, there will be strong incentives for more global union action. Whether this will move global union politics

153

beyond what Richard Hyman has called "imagined solidarities," which are heavy on symbolism and light on practice, remains to be seen.[6] We think that the potential is there and that a central element must be the further strengthening of the existing global union network.

What about egalitarianism? It is our view and we think that there is strong evidence that unions have been one of the principal architects of the democratic state. Yet, unions have often been blind to or have discriminated against particular constituencies, and some continue to do so to our days. For a long time many unions excluded women and migrants and were racist. Many unions have aspired to particularistic gains at the expense of others. Unions have been strong supporters of imperialist wars and practices.

These dynamics, unfortunately, are present in our days as well. However, the rise of other social movements has made it difficult for unions to act as if they do not matter. What should be done, then? There are two routes, we believe. One is the route of alliances; the other is the route of internalization. The route of alliances assumes that environmentalists deal with the environment, women with gender, and workers with work. Accordingly, the various societal forces should collaborate with each other to accomplish common ends, in the process gaining a better understanding and more respect for each other.

Alliances are often the best means for collaboration, and they are certainly a necessary beginning of a relationship. A global justice movement, however, cannot simply be one of alliances. Unions must internalize gender, the environment, or human rights in a programmatic rather than instrumental fashion and must accept the fact that narrow priorities are a choice and not a destiny. It is through the internalization of all of those values that unions and other egalitarian forces will themselves become more democratic and will be able to forge the comprehensive programmatic and organizational arrangements that are necessary for another, more democratic world.

Unions can bring a great deal to the global justice movement, provided that they keep broadening and deepening their horizons. Their most important contribution, in our view, will be their serious if contested engagement with the state, at all levels. While capital has been successful in creating its own private sphere, it is not possible to think of capitalism without the modern capitalist state. Nor, in our view, is it possible to regulate, reform, or transform capitalism without changing the capitalist state. Global societal politics that avoid the question of the state, and the social power that it embodies, are destined to become global interest group politics without a broader vision of democracy and justice.[7]

NOTES

Introduction

1. The World Social Forum brings together a wide array of social forces from all over the world and has been taking place in late January since 2001. The first three forums, as well as the fifth forum, took place in Porto Alegre. The fourth forum (2004) took place in New Delhi, India, and the sixth (2006), in Caracas, Venezuela. The seventh took place in Nairobi, Kenya. Its motto is "another world is possible." For more information, see www.forumsocialmundial.org.br (accessed June 6, 2006). Also see Boaventura de Sousa Santos, *The Rise of the Global Left: The World Social Forum and Beyond* (London: Zed Books, 2006).

2. Global union organizations represent national unions at the global level. Their history and politics will be discussed in chapter 3.

3. Ronaldo Munck, *Globalisation and Labour: The New 'Great Transformation'* (London: Zed Books, 2002); Jeffrey Harrod and Robert O'Brien, eds., *Global Unions? Theory and Strategies of Organized Labour in the Global Political Economy* (London: Routledge, 2002); George Myconos, *The Globalizations of Organized Labour, 1945–2005*

(New York: Palgrave, 2005); Ronaldo Munck, ed., *Labour and Globalisation: Results and Prospects* (Liverpool: Liverpool University Press, 2004).

4. Kim Moody, *Workers in a Lean World: Unions in the International Economy* (London: Verso, 1997); Peter Waterman, *Globalization, Social Movements and the New Internationalisms*, rev. ed. (London: Continuum, 2001); Stuart Hodkinson, "Is There a New Trade Union Internationalism? The International Confederation of Free Trade Unions' Response to Globalization, 1996–2002," *LABOUR, Capital and Society* 38, nos. 1 & 2 (2005): 37–65.

5. There is a host of additional works that have addressed global union politics in recent years and that we have found useful. The following are just some of them. These include Jeremy Waddington, ed., *Globalization and Patterns of Labor Resistance* (London: Munsell, 1999); Annie Fouquet, Udo Rehfeldt, and Serge Le Rouf, eds., *Le syndicalisme dans la mondialisation* (Paris: Editions l'Atelier / Editions Ouvrières, 2000); Mark Bray and Gregory Murray, eds., "Globalisation and Labour Regulation," thematic issue, *Journal of Industrial Relations* 42, no. 2 (June 2000); Michael Gordon and Lowell Turner, eds., *Transnational Cooperation among Unions* (Ithaca, NY: Cornell University Press, 2000); Frank Emspak and María-Luz D. Samper, eds., "Unions in the Global Economy," thematic issue, *Labor Studies Journal* 26, no. 1 (Spring 2001); Peter Waterman and Jane Wills, eds., "Space, Place and the New Labour Internationalisms," thematic issue, *Antipode* 33, no. 3 (2001); Beverly Silver, *Forces of Labor: Workers' Movements and Globalization since 1870* (New York: Cambridge University Press, 2003); Nathan Lillie, *A Global Union for Global Workers: Collective Bargaining and Regulatory Politics in Maritime Shipping* (New York: Routledge, 2006); Kate Bronfenbrenner, ed., *Global Unionism: Challenging Capital through Cross-Border Campaigns* (working title) (Ithaca, N.Y.: Cornell University Press, forthcoming).

Chapter One   Globalization and Global Governance

1. The foreign companies finally signed contracts with Bolivia on October 29, which significantly shifted the balance in favor of the country. See Reuters, "Energy Firms Bow to Demands Set by Bolivia," *New York Times*, October 30, 2006, at www.nytimes.com/2006/10/30/world/americas/30bolivia.html (accessed December 6, 2006).

2. Mercosur stands for Mercado Común del Sur or Market of the South. It now includes Argentina, Uruguay, Paraguay, Brazil, and Venezuela. Chile and Bolivia have associate status, while additional countries, including Mexico, want to join.

3. It is informative to contrast the 2002 National Security Strategy of the United States to that of 2006. While the earlier one was largely unilateralist and did not use the term *globalization* one single time, the more recent strategy exhibits a very profound tension between unilateralism in military affairs and multilateralism in economic affairs. Even here, however, the United States seems conflicted as it advances bilateral trade and investment agreements that can very well gut the WTO's multilateralism. Compare The White House (2006), *The National Security Strategy of the United States of America*, March 16, 2006, at www.whitehouse.gov/nsc/nss/2006/ (accessed

December 6, 2006), and The White House (2002), *The National Security Strategy of the United States of America*, September 17, 2002, at www.whitehouse.gov/nsc/nss.html (accessed December 6, 2006).

4. On globalization, see Manfred Steger, *Globalism: Market Ideology Meets Terrorism*, 2nd ed. (Lanham, Md.: Rowman & Littlefield, 2005); David Held, Anthony McGrew, David Goldblatt, and Jonathan Perraton, *Global Transformations* (Stanford, Calif.: Stanford University Press, 1999); David Held and Anthony McGrew, eds., *The Global Transformations Reader: An Introduction to the Globalization Debate*, 2nd ed. (Cambridge: Polity Press, 2003); John Baylis and Steve Smith, eds., *The Globalization of World Politics: An Introduction to International Relations*, 3rd ed. (Oxford: Oxford University Press, 2005).

5. Kenichi Ohmae, *The Borderless World: Power and Strategy in the Interlinked Economy* (New York: HarperBusiness, 1990); Susan Strange, *The Retreat of the State: The Diffusion of Power in the World Economy* (New York: Cambridge University Press, 1996).

6. Paul Hirst and Grahame Thompson, *Globalization in Question*, 2nd ed. (Cambridge: Polity Press, 1999); Linda Weiss, *The Myth of the Powerless State* (Ithaca, N.Y.: Cornell University Press, 1997).

7. Nikolai Bukharin, *Imperialism and World Economy* (1917; New York: Monthly Review Press, 1973); Elmar Rieger and Stephan Leibfried, *Limits to Globalization* (Cambridge: Polity Press, 2003).

8. Ohmae, *Borderless World*; Kenichi Ohmae, *The End of the Nation State: The Rise of Regional Economies* (New York: Free Press, 1995).

9. Weiss, *Myth*; Hirst and Thompson, *Globalization in Question*; Robert Gilpin, "The Retreat of the State?" in *Strange Power: Shaping the Parameters of International Relations and International Political Economy*, ed. Thomas Lawton, James Rosenau, and Amy Verdun (Aldershot, UK: Ashgate, 2000), 197–213.

10. To highlight the problems with globalization as both a concept and a reality, it should suffice to state that most liberal analysts and practitioners are actually using the term *globalization* to mean global capitalism. This includes critics of hyperliberalism such as Joseph Stiglitz. In our discussion below, we assume that *globalization* may denote a much broader set of developments and that global egalitarians have long offered alternative visions of global integration.

11. David Held and Anthony McGrew, "The Great Globalization Debate: An Introduction," in Held and McGrew, *Global Transformations Reader*, 1–50; Aseem Prakash and Jeffrey Hart, eds., *Globalization and Governance* (London: Routledge, 1999).

12. See Jan Aart Scholte, *Globalization: A Critical Introduction*, 2nd ed. (New York: Palgrave Macmillan, 2005), for a similar approach but, also, divergence on what is globalized.

13. Held et al., *Global Transformations*.

14. Karl Polanyi, *The Great Transformation: The Political and Economic Origins of Our Time* (1944; Boston: Beacon, 1957).

15. Charles Kindleberger, *A Financial History of Western Europe*, 2nd ed. (New York: Oxford University Press, 1993).

16. John Braithwaite and Peter Drahos, *Global Business Regulation* (Cambridge: Cambridge University Press, 2000), chapter 8.

17. Daniel Yergin and Joseph Stanislaw, *The Commanding Heights* (New York: Simon and Schuster, 2002), chapter 9.

18. The financial crisis of 1997–1998 affected the East Asian industrializing countries, such as South Korea and Thailand. Given the increasingly central role that this region plays in the global political economy, the crisis had broad repercussions and highlighted both the limitations of the International Monetary Fund, the major global financial organization, and the social costs of its policies. See Paul Blustein, *The Chastening: Inside the Crisis That Rocked the Global Financial System and Humbled the IMF* (New York: Public Affairs, 2003).

19. Manuel Castells, *The Rise of the Network Society*, 2nd ed. (Oxford: Blackwell, 2000); Eric Hobsbawm, *The Age of Capital, 1848–1875* (1975; New York: New American Library, 1979), chapter 3.

20. Ronnie Phillips, "Digital Technology and Institutional Change from the Gilded Age to Modern Times: The Impacts of the Telegraph and the Internet," *Journal of Economic Issues* 34, no. 2 (June 2000): 267–289.

21. Quite possibly two or more countries may decide to break down the boundaries among them, often called transnationalization. Yet, so long as there are firmly drawn boundaries between insiders and outsiders, the world will remain partially internationalized. For instance, the United States is currently negotiating or has negotiated many bilateral trade agreements that transnationalize interactions and connections between the United States and its counterparts. On a world scale, this leads to further internationalization since outsiders do not enjoy the same benefits.

22. B. Hans-Henrik Holm and Georg Sorensen, eds., *Whose World Order? Uneven Globalization and the End of the Cold War* (Boulder, Colo.: Westview, 1995).

23. See International Labor Rights Fund, "Fairness in Flowers Campaign," at www.laborrights.org (accessed May 15, 2006).

24. The amounts and impacts of nationalized sectors are and will remain significant, even though their most profitable components will be globalized. During 2003, for instance, the U.S. government employed, directly and indirectly, about 18 million people, more than at any time in its history, reversing a decline that had been taking place in the early 1990s. In fact, careful research has shown that the most globalized countries also have the largest states, in terms of personnel and expenditures. See Dani Rodrik, "Why Do More Open Economies Have Bigger Governments?" *Journal of Political Economy* 106, no. 5 (1998): 997–1032; also Vincent Navarro, "The Worldwide Class Struggle," *Monthly Review*, September 2006, 18–33.

25. Scholte, *Globalization*; Robert Keohane, "Global Governance and Democratic Accountability," in *Taming Globalization: Frontiers of Governance*, ed. David Held and M. Koenig-Archibugi (Cambridge: Polity Press, 2003), 130–159.

26. James Mittelman, ed., *Globalization: Critical Reflections* (Boulder, Colo.: Lynne Rienner, 1996), 3. Also Wolfgang Reinicke, *Global Public Policy: Governing Without Government?* (Washington, D.C.: Brookings Institution Press, 1998).

27. For two views, see Yakub Halabi, "The Expansion of Global Governance into the Third World: Altruism, Realism or Constructivism?" *International Studies Review* 6

(2004): 21–48; M. Shamsul Haque, "Globalization, New Political Economy, and Governance: A Third World Viewpoint," *Administrative Theory and Praxis* 24, no. 1 (2002): 103–124.

28. This same process accounts for country and empire building. Very few people had ventured to the American West before it was annexed and integrated into the United States. Subsequent to annexation, the U.S. government played the leading role in nationalizing the U.S. political economy by building railways, agricultural universities, and irrigation systems. See William Goetzmann, *Exploration and Empire: The Explorer and the Scientist in the Winning of the American West* (New York: Knopf, 1966).

29. Ever since the events in Seattle, there have been demonstrations at various meetings of the WTO, the World Bank, and the IMF as well as other institutions of global governance.

30. Rorden Wilkinson, *Multilateralism and the World Trade Organization: The Architecture and Extension of International Trade Regulation* (London: Routledge, 2000), chapter 1.

31. Joan Spero and Jeffrey Hart, *The Politics of International Economic Relations*, 6th ed. (Belmont, Calif.: Wadsworth / Thomson Learning, 2003), 72–86.

32. Spero and Hart, *International Economic Relations*, 87–90.

33. Spero and Hart, *International Economic Relations*, 97–105.

34. Spero and Hart, *International Economic Relations*, 202–214.

35. Blustein, *Chastening*.

36. Yergin and Stanislaw, *Commanding Heights*, 231–234.

37. See Bello's argument regarding the declining legitimacy of the IMF and the World Bank in the South as important Southern countries are less willing to compromise domestic goals in the altar of repayments. Walden Bello, "The Crisis of Multilateralism," International Relations Center, Foreign Policy in Focus, September 13, 2006, at www.fpif.org/pdf/gac/0609CrisisMultilateralism.pdf (accessed December 8, 2006).

38. For overviews, see Martin Hewson and Timothy Sinclair, "The Emergence of Global Governance Theory," in *Approaches to Global Governance Theory*, ed. Martin Hewson and Timothy Sinclair (Albany: State University of New York Press, 1999), 3–22; Aseem Prakash and Jeffrey Hart, "Globalization and Governance: An Introduction," in Prakash and Hart, *Globalization and Governance*, 1–24.

39. For origins of the ILO, see James Shotwell, *The Origins of the International Labor Organization*, 2 vols. (New York: Columbia University Press, 1934).

40. Wilkinson, *Multilateralism*, chapter 6.

41. Thus, while the ILO's Declaration on Fundamental Principles and Rights at Work is binding on all member countries, its implementation depends on suasion rather than enforcement.

42. Loukas Tsoukalis, *The New European Economy Revisited*, 3rd ed. (Oxford: Oxford University Press, 1997).

43. International Confederation of Free Trade Unions, *Behind the Wire: Anti-Union Repression in the Export Processing Zones* (Brussels: ICFTU, 1996). For information from the promoters, visit the World Economic Processing Zones Association at www.wepza.org (accessed March 15, 2006). For more comprehensive information,

visit the ILO at www.ilo.org/public/english/dialogue/sector/themes/epz.htm (accessed March 15, 2006).

44. The White House, *The National Security Strategy of the United States of America* (September 2002). Compare this with *The National Security Strategy of the United States of America* (March 2006). While the basic thrusts remain the same, the latter seeks to accent the global linkages and employs the term *globalization* throughout, while the former does not use it one single time.

45. See also James Petras and Henry Veltmeyer, *Globalization Unmasked: Imperialism in the 21st Century* (London: Zed Press, 2001).

46. Kim Moody and Mary McGinn, *Unions and Free Trade: Solidarity vs. Competition* (Detroit: Labor Notes, 1992).

47. International Confederation of Free Trade Unions, *No Time to Play: Child Workers in the Global Economy* (Brussels: ICFTU, 1996). For more comprehensive and up-to-date information, visit the ILO at www.ilo.org/public/english/standards/ipec/ (accessed March 15, 2006).

48. "Official" Mexican unions refers to all those unions that were supportive of the policies of the Revolutionary Institutional Party (PRI) ever since the 1940s. The dominant one for many decades was the Confederación de los Trabajadores Mexicanos (CTM). Since the defeat of the PRI in 2000, these unions have declined a great deal. Other unions, however, were opposed to NAFTA and/or willing to collaborate with their U.S. counterparts. These included a new federation that brought together disaffected leaders of the official unions. Two of the most sustained and principled collaborations, however, involve the Frente Autentico del Trabajo (FAT) and the United Electrical, Radio, and Machine Workers of America (UE) and the various members of Coalition for Justice in the Maquiladoras (CJM). As we note in the introduction, this book is motivated by those acts of cross-border solidarity that have kept internationalism and egalitarianism alive in the midst of predatory capitalism. For more information on the UE-FAT strategic alliance, visit www.ueinternational.org/Solidarity Work/fat.html#vision (accessed December 8, 2006); for more information on the CJM, visit www.coalitionforjustice.info/CJM_Website/New_Sites/CJM_WebPage/Home_ Page.html (accessed December 8, 2006).

49. Rachael Kamel and Anya Hoffman, eds., *The Maquiladora Reader: Cross-Border Organizing since NAFTA* (Philadelphia: American Friends Service Committee, 1999).

50. Terry Boswell and Christopher Chase-Dunn, *The Spiral of Capitalism and Socialism: Toward Global Democracy* (Boulder, Colo.: Lynne Rienner, 2000); Ronaldo Munck and Barry Gills, eds., "Globalization and Democracy," *Annals of the American Academy of Political and Social Science* 581 (May 2002).

51. Stephan Leibfried and Paul Pierson, eds., *European Social Policy: Between Fragmentation and Integration* (Washington, D.C.: Brookings Institution, 1995); Dimitris Stevis and Terry Boswell, "Labor Politics and Policy in International Integration: Comparing NAFTA and the European Union," in *The Politics of Social Inequality: Research in Political Sociology*, vol. 9, ed. Betty Dobratz, Lisa Waldner, and Timothy Buzzell (Amsterdam: Elsevier, 2001), 335–364.

52. Dimitris Stevis, "Unions, Capitals and States: Competing (Inter)nationalisms in North American and European Integration," in *Global Unions? Theory and Strategies of*

Organized Labour in the Global Political Economy, ed. Jeffrey Harrod and Robert O'Brien (London: Routledge, 2002), 130–150.

53. A social clause is a clause inserted into trade agreements specifying that certain labor rules must be respected in producing for the international market and that measures can be taken if they are not. Please see chapter 4. For a thorough account, see Gerda van Roozendaal, *Trade Unions and Global Governance: The Debate on a Social Clause* (London: Continuum, 2002).

54. International Confederation of Free Trade Unions, *Building Workers' Human Rights into the Global Trading System* (Brussels: ICFTU, 1999).

55. George Kell and John Ruggie, "Global Markets and Social Legitimacy: The Case for the 'Global Compact,'" *Transnational Corporations* 8, no. 3 (2001): 101–120.

56. Ingeborg Wick, *Workers' Tool or PR Ploy? A Guide to Codes of International Labour Practice*, 4th ed. (Bonn: Friedrich-Ebert-Stiftung, 2005).

57. International Confederation of Free Trade Unions, *Trade Union Guide to Globalization*, 2nd ed. (Brussels: ICFTU, 2004), chapter 6.

58. Samir Amin, *Re-reading the Postwar Period: An Intellectual Itinerary* (New York: Monthly Review Press, 1994).

59. The strategy of the social clause has a long history that we discuss in chapter 4. Its resurgence in the 1970s, however, owes much to the move of the AFL-CIO from "free trade" to "fair trade." Without a doubt, the U.S. unions were trying to protect benefits that they had long fought for. There is a great deal of merit, however, to the argument that this was a unilateral strategy that came to the fore only after U.S. capital started breaking its pact with U.S. unions.

60. van Roozendaal, *Trade Unions and Global Governance*, chapter 5; Gerard Griffin, Chris Nyland, and Anne O'Rourke, "Trade Unions and the Trade–Labour Rights Link: A North-South Union Divide?" *International Journal of Comparative Labour Law and Industrial Relations* 19, no. 4 (Winter 2003): 469–494.

61. Ronnie Lipschutz, "Reconstructing World Politics: The Emergence of Global Civil Society," *Millennium: Journal of International Studies* 21, no. 3 (1992): 389–420; Paul Wapner, "The Normative Promise of Nonstate Actors: A Theoretical Account of Global Civil Society," in *Principled World Politics: The Challenge of Normative International Relations*, ed. Paul Wapner and Lester Edwin J. Ruiz (Lanham, Md.: Rowman & Littlefield, 2000), 261–274.

62. Mustapha Kamal Pasha and David L. Blaney, "Elusive Paradise: The Promise and Peril of Global Civil Society," *Alternatives* 23, no. 4 (1998): 417–450; Elisabeth Jay Friedman, Kathryn Hochstetler, and Ann Marie Clark, *Sovereignty, Democracy, and Global Civil Society: State-Society Relations at UN World Conferences* (Albany: State University of New York Press, 2005).

Chapter Two   Societal Politics and Global Governance

1. See, for example, Eddie Yuen, George Katsiaficas, and Daniel Burton Rose, eds., *The Battle of Seattle: The New Challenge to Capitalist Globalization* (New York: Soft Skull Press, 2001). For an important debate over the meaning of Seattle, see the

exchange entitled "Seattle: December '99?" between Mary Kaldor, Jan Aart Scholte, Fred Halliday, and Stephen Gill in *Millennium: Journal of International Studies* 29, no. 1 (2000): 103–140. More on the significance of Seattle can be found in chapter 4.

2. See Rupert Taylor, ed., *Creating a Better World: Interpreting Global Civil Society* (Bloomfield, Conn.: Kumarian Press, 2004). For two incisive studies that place global union politics within broader contexts, see Jeffrey Harrod, *Trade Union Foreign Policy: A Study of British and American Trade Union Activities in Jamaica* (Garden City, N.Y.: Doubleday, 1972); and Peter Waterman, *Globalization, Social Movements and the New Internationalisms*, rev. ed. (London: Continuum, 2001).

3. We use the term *societal politics* to denote the politics of organizations, movements, and networks that are formally distinct from states and corporations. As will become apparent, we do not consider societal politics to be immanently separate from state or corporate politics. Rather, we think that there are frequently more organic relations between state, societal, and corporate entities than there are between societal entities.

4. For example, see Ronnie Lipschutz, "Reconstructing World Politics: The Emergence of Global Civil Society," *Millennium: Journal of International Studies* 21, no. 3 (Winter 1992): 389–420; Paul Wapner, "The Normative Promise of Nonstate Actors: A Theoretical Account of Global Civil Society," in *Principled World Politics: The Challenge of Normative International Relations*, ed. Paul Wapner and Lester Edwin J. Ruiz (Lanham, Md.: Rowman & Littlefield, 2000), 261–274; Jan Aart Scholte, "Civil Society and Democracy in Global Governance," *Global Governance* 8 (2002): 281–304.

5. For the political economy perspective, see Mustapha Kamal Pasha and David L. Blaney, "Elusive Paradise: The Promise and Peril of Global Civil Society," *Alternatives* 23 (1998): 417–450. Also see Alejandro Colás, *International Civil Society* (Cambridge: Polity Press / Blackwell Publishers, 2002); and Elisabeth Jay Friedman, Kathryn Hochstetler, and Ann Marie Clark, *Sovereignty, Democracy, and Civil Society: State-Society Relations at UN World Conferences* (Albany: State University of New York Press, 2005). See also the *Global Civil Society Yearbook* published by Oxford University Press since 2001.

6. Nativists are virulent nationalists. Here and elsewhere we use the term *nationalist* to include people who espouse national solutions for a wide variety of reasons, including the protection of egalitarian policies.

7. See Jackie Smith, Ron Pagnucco, and Charles Chatfield, "Social Movements and World Politics: A Theoretical Framework," in *Transnational Social Movements and Global Politics: Solidarity Beyond the State*, ed. Jackie Smith, C. Chatfield, and Ron Pagnucco (Syracuse, N.Y.: Syracuse University Press, 1997), 59–77.

8. We want to be very clear here. We are not arguing that societal politics must be reduced to organizational politics nor that organizations are inherently good. We are arguing that strong and long-term transnational ties that will allow societal politics to move from particularistic politics to global politics will require permanent and strong global organizations.

9. "Weak" organizations may be called intersocietal while "strong" ones may be called suprasocietal to mirror the intergovernmental and supragovernmental terminology used in international politics.

10. It is worth noting here that "strong" organizations may be organized in a variety of ways, and their power may be the result of various arrangements. Multinational corporations, for instance, are centralized organizations in the sense that they own their subsidiaries. A subsidiary cannot simply walk away. On the other hand, affiliates of sports federations do have the right to withdraw, but the costs are very high, for example, exclusion from world cups or the Olympics.

11. We discuss this issue with respect to labor politics in Dimitris Stevis and Terry Boswell, "Globalizing Justice All the Way Down? Agents, Subjects, Objects, and Phantoms in International Labor Politics," in *Poverty and the Production of World Politics: Unprotected Workers in the World Political Economy*, ed. Matt Davies and Magnus Ryner (New York: Palgrave Macmillan, 2006).

12. This, we think, is important for a variety of reasons. At one level, it is a measure of an organization's sensitivity to the broader political economy. At another level, organizations often advocate for others in ways that are paternalistic, thus obscuring the real preferences of those they advocate for.

13. See Manfred Steger, *Globalism: Market Ideology Meets Terrorism*, 2nd ed. (Lanham, Md.: Rowman & Littlefield, 2005), especially chapter 4. Also Mary Kaldor, "'Civilising' Globalisation? The Implications of the 'Battle in Seattle,'" *Millennium: Journal of International Studies* 29, no. 1 (2000): 105–114, especially table on page 109.

14. For much of their early history, unions excluded women, foreign-born people, or people of color. There were also important exceptions, such as the Knights of Labor in the United States. Even today there are unions that are based on particular religious or ethnic identities. In some instances these give voice to the weak, while in others they serve to discriminate.

15. *Multilateralism* is a term historically used to refer to negotiations and organizations involving many states, and thus it is differentiated from unilateralism, bilateralism, and even regionalism. *Multistakeholder* broadens multilateralism to include not only states but also other social entities affected by a particular activity. Accordingly, unions see themselves as legitimate stakeholders in deliberations over corporate governance. For different views on multilateralism, see Robert Cox, "Multilateralism and World Order," *Review of International Studies* 18, no. 2 (1992): 161–180; on unions and corporate governance, see Trade Union Advisory Committee and Committee on Workers' Capital, *Workers' Voice in Corporate Governance—A Trade Union Perspective*, 2005, at www.tuac.org/statemen/communiq/0512cgpaper.pdf (accessed November 7, 2006).

16. Accordingly, many unionists and other egalitarians are not willing to abandon domestic labor or environmental rules in favor of weaker or nonexistent rules at the global or regional level. Others argue that in light of the totalitarian tendency of neoliberal capitalism to commodify everything, states are the most promising bastion of democracy. See Marti Koskenniemi, "The Future of Statehood," *Harvard International Law Journal* 32, no. 2 (Spring 1991): 397–410.

17. As we noted earlier, we are using these concepts in a heuristic manner. For views and debates over cosmopolitanism, see Daniele Archibugi, "Cosmopolitan Democracy and Its Critics: A Review," *European Journal of International Relations* 10, no. 3 (2004): 437–473; Molly Cochran, "A Democratic Critique of Cosmopolitan

Democracy: Pragmatism from the Bottom-up," *European Journal of International Relations* 8, no. 4 (2002): 517–548.

18. On hyperliberalism, see Robert Cox, "The Global Political Economy and Social Choice," in *Approaches to World Order*, ed. Robert Cox with Timothy Sinclair (Cambridge: Cambridge University Press, 1996), 191–208. Hyperliberalism should not be equated with international trade or investment but, rather, socially unregulated trade and investment. One of the great successes of hyperliberals is to equate open trade and investment with unregulated trade and investment.

19. OECD, *Societal Cohesion and the Globalising Economy: What Does the Future Hold?* (Paris: OECD, 1997); OECD, *Governance in the 21st Century* (Paris: OECD, 2001).

20. Vito Tanzi, Ke-young Chu, and Sanjeev Gupta, eds., *Economic Policy and Equity* (Washington, D.C.: IMF, 1999).

21. We want to distinguish here between generalized laws that provide rights for categories of people, such as workers, women, or immigrants, from rules that apply to particular subgroups within them. For instance, it is possible that particular workers may strike collective agreements with employers whose benefits apply only to them. Sometimes unions do not have a choice but to accept such rules. In some instances, however, unions and other societal entities prefer to strike bilateral agreements with employers while keeping general public rules at an arm's length. Such arrangements are more managerial rather than social regulatory policies.

22. Some definitions are appropriate at this point. *Social democracy* originally referred to radical parties, largely Marxist, whose aim was the abolition of capitalism. As the major social democratic parties, such as those of Germany, became more reformist, the term *social democrat* came to refer to conservative socialists to distinguish them from those socialists who continued to advance the drastic overhaul of the capitalist system. Communists are one of the more radical versions of socialism. Syndicalists were also inspired by socialist ideals but differed from socialists of all hues with respect to strategic and tactical issues. More detail can be found in chapter 3.

23. These are two examples of a communist and a socialist party, respectively, seeking to fuse political democracy and egalitarian economic policies. In the case of Czechoslovakia, the experiment ended with the invasion of the Soviet army. In the case of Chile, it ended with a military coup instigated and supported by the United States. A third such effort involved the Italian Communist Party, which adopted the road of political democracy but continued to advance more radical reforms during the 1970s. When it seemed as if it could win the 1976 elections, the United States came out resolutely against them and used various means to defeat them. The Soviet Union was also opposed to the Italian brand of Eurocommunism.

24. See Dimitris Stevis, "Agents, Subjects, Objects or Phantoms? Labor, the Environment and Liberal Institutionalization," *Annals of the American Academy of Political and Social Science* 582 (May 2002): 90–105. Also see Terry Boswell and Christopher Chase-Dunn, *The Spiral of Capitalism and Socialism: Toward Global Democracy* (Boulder, Colo.: Lynne Rienner, 2000).

25. The mechanisms of global democracy can and have been the subject of vigorous debate. We do not have a specific proposal here, but we are skeptical of views that reject the potential of global democracy by contrasting it to reified notions of domestic or local democracy. After all, we would not consider the Athenian system a democratic one since women, slaves, the poor, and recent immigrants had no rights.

26. On the history of the concept of governance, see Martin Hewson and Timothy Sinclair, "The Emergence of Global Governance Theory," in *Approaches to Global Governance Theory*, ed. Martin Hewson and Timothy Sinclair (Albany: State University of New York Press, 1999), 3–22. For a collection of key statements on global governance, see Rorden Wilkinson, ed., *The Global Governance Reader* (London: Routledge, 2005).

27. For the long-term perspective, see L. S. Stavrianos, *Global Rift: The Third World Comes of Age* (New York: William Morrow, 1981); for a case study involving Versailles, see Margaret Macmillan, *Paris, 1919: Six Months That Changed the World* (New York: Random House, 2001).

28. John G. Ruggie, "Reconstituting the Global Public Domain—Issues, Actors and Practices," *European Journal of International Relations* 10, no. 4 (2004): 499–531; A. Claire Cutler, "Critical Reflections on the Westphalian Assumptions of International Law and Organization: A Crisis of Legitimacy," *Review of International Studies* 27, no. 2 (2001): 133–150.

29. See A. Claire Cutler, Virginia Haufler, and Tony Porter, eds., *Private Authority and International Affairs* (Albany: State University of New York Press, 1999); John Braithwaite and Peter Drahos, *Global Business Regulation* (Cambridge: Cambridge University Press, 2000).

30. For a history of societal involvement with global governance, see Steve Charnovitz, "Two Centuries of Participation: NGOs and International Governance," *Michigan Journal of International Law* 18 (Winter 1997): 183–286.

31. See Darel Paul, "Re-scaling IPE: Subnational States and the Regulation of the Global Political Economy," *Review of International Political Economy* 9, no. 3 (2002): 465–489.

32. For an illustration of related difficulties in global societal politics, see Deborah Avant, "Conserving Nature in the State of Nature: The Politics of INGO Policy Implementation," *Review of International Studies* 30 (2004): 361–382.

33. For example, see Elisabeth Corell and Michele Betsill, "A Comparative Look at NGO Influence in International Environmental Negotiations: Desertification and Climate Change," *Global Environmental Politics* 1, no. 4 (2001): 86–107; Friedman, Hochstetler, and Clark, *Sovereignty, Democracy, and Civil Society.*

Chapter Three   Engaging Each Other, 1864–2006

1. The process and the details of the unification had been negotiated well in advance (background interviews). For more information on the ITUC, see its website at

www.ituc-csi.org/spip.php?rubrique1&lang=en (accessed November 7, 2006). Also see the website of the World Confederation of Labor at www.cmtwcl.org/cmt/ewcm.nsf/_/ 31A6B28E68DD82FFC12571F6006E4CDF?opendocument (accessed November 7, 2006).

2. One such example is the collaboration between Mexico's Frente Autentico del Trabajo and the United States' UE that we mention in chapter 1. There are also many examples of global campaigns that involve unions from various countries but do not involve global union organizations. See Kate Bronfenbrenner, ed., *Global Unionism: Challenging Capital through Cross-Border Campaigns* (working title) (Ithaca, N.Y.: Cornell University Press, forthcoming).

3. A relatively recent case that engendered a serious debate on the role of GUFs involved the Liverpool dockworkers during the 1990s. The differences, in fact, gave rise to an alternative international network of dockworkers.

4. This chapter revises and amplifies Dimitris Stevis, "International Labor Organizations 1864–1997: The Weight of History and the Challenges of the Present," *Journal of World-Systems Research* 4 (1998): 52–75.

5. See Lewis L. Lorwin, *Labor and Internationalism* (New York: Macmillan, 1929), 33. This volume offers the most detailed and authoritative history of early labor internationalism in the English language. For diverse discussions of the First International, see G. M. Stekloff, *History of the First International* (New York: International Publishers, 1928); R. W. Postgate, *The Workers' International* (London: Swarthmore Press / Labour Publishing Company, 1921); Julius Braunthal, *History of the International, Volume 1: 1864–1914* (1961; New York: Frederick A. Praeger, 1967), parts 1 and 2. For documents, see Jacques Freymond, ed., *La Première Internationale*, 2 volumes (Geneva: Librairie Droz, 1962). Stekloff's work, mentioned above, as well as extensive documentary and witness material about the First International and its precursors, can also be found at www.marxists.org/history/international/index.htm (accessed March 17, 2006).

6. The First International followed a number of previous attempts and brought together organizations with different political and organizational preferences. See Lorwin, *Labor and Internationalism*, chapter 1; Braunthal, *History, Volume 1*, part 1; Stekloff, *History*, chapters 1–3; and D. E. Devreese, "An Inquiry into the Causes and Nature of Organization: Some Observations on the International Working Men's Association, 1864–1872/1876," in *Internationalism in the Labour Movement, 1830–1940*, ed. Frits van Holthoon and Marcel van der Linden (Leiden: E.J. Brill, 1988), 283–303.

7. See Freymond, *La Première Internationale*, xiii–xv; Braunthal, *History, Volume 1*, 113–116; Wilhelm Eichhoff, *The International Workingmen's Association: Its Establishment, Organisation, Political and Social Activity* (from *Marx-Engels Collected Works*, volume 21, pp. 322–380), chapter 8, at www.marxists.org/history/international/ iwma/archive/eichhoff/iwma-history/ch08.htm (accessed March 17, 2006); Knud Knudsen, "The Strike History of the First International," in *Internationalism in the Labour Movement, 1830–1940*, ed. Frits van Holthoon and Marcel van der Linden (Leiden: E.J. Brill, 1988), 304–335.

8. Countries where First International sections existed at any one time were Austria-Hungary, Belgium, France, Germany, Holland, Italy, Poland, Spain,

Switzerland, the United Kingdom, and the United States. An Australian section was also represented in the 1872 Congress, while an Argentinian section made of European immigrants may have also joined. See Ricardo Melgar Bao, *El Movimiento Obrero Latino-Americano* (Madrid: Allianza America, 1988), 425.

9. See Lorwin, *Labor and Internationalism*, 47–48; Braunthal, *History, Volume 1*, 116–119.

10. See Freymond, *La Première Internationale*, vol. 1, 21.

11. See Braunthal, *History, Volume 1*, chapter 15.

12. Th. van Tijn, "Closing Address: Nationalism and the Socialist Workers' Movement," in *Internationalism in the Labour Movement, 1830–1940*, ed. Frits van Holthoon and Marcel van der Linden (Leiden: E.J. Brill, 1988), 611–623.

13. See Nikolai Bukharin, *Imperialism and World Economy* (1917; New York: Monthly Review Press, 1973); Paul Bairoch, *Economics and World History: Myths and Paradoxes* (Chicago: University of Chicago Press, 1993), chapters 2–4. Even today, economists of the right and the left argue that financial globalization was more profound before WWI than it is today. In any event, it seems to us that it is important to distinguish between the globalization of the pre-WWI decades and the globalization that has emerged since the 1970s. In the first case, this was a globalization that emerged as a result of protectionist countries competing for world markets while there was no hegemon to prevent a war. During the latter, there are global efforts to lower protection and a hegemon that can prevent global war. It is possible that this second wave will end up like the first. Their differences, however, are profound, one of them being the growth of institutions of global governance. For a useful study whose comparisons and conclusions, however, are affected by not paying attention to these differences, see Robert Flanagan, *Globalization and Labor Conditions: Working Conditions and Worker Rights in a Global Economy* (New York: Oxford University Press, 2006). For a major study on globalization and labor since the nineteenth century, see Beverly Silver, *Forces of Labor: Workers' Movements and Globalization since 1870* (New York: Cambridge University Press, 2003).

14. See Michael Mann, *The Sources of Social Power, Volume 2: The Rise of Classes and Nation-States, 1760–1914* (New York: Cambridge University Press, 1993), chapters 17–19.

15. See Charles Tilly, "Globalization Threatens Labor's Rights," *International Labor and Working-Class History* 47 (Spring 1995): 1–23.

16. The Second International was formed in Paris in 1889. The disagreements about whether this was an appropriate time for another international and about the political priorities of the organization became evident in the fact that there were two simultaneous meetings of socialist, syndicalist, and labor organizations, each with its own priorities.

17. The most important development of this period, from the point of view of labor politics, is the emergence to hegemony within continental radicalism of social democracy, led by the German Social Democratic Party and, increasingly, the Austrian socialists. *Social democracy* was a term covering all parties that adhered to Marxism and espoused the socialist reorganization of society. After WWI, the term applied to the more reformist or least radical socialists, while the term *socialist* applied to those that

advocated deeper changes, sometimes revolutionary. *Communism* applied to those that advocated revolutionary changes. This differentiation has continued, with some modifications, to our days. See Braunthal, *History, Volume 1*, part 3; G. D. H. Cole, *The Second International, 1889–1914*, volume 3, part 1, of his *A History of Social Thought* (London: Macmillan, 1960); Lorwin, *Labor and Internationalism*, chapter 3.

18. See Harry J. Marks, "The Sources of Reformism in the Social Democratic Party of Germany, 1890–1914," *Journal of Modern History* 11, no. 3 (September 1939): 334–356; Sinclair Armstrong, "The Internationalism of the Early Social Democrats in Germany," *American Historical Review* 47, no. 2 (January 1942): 245–258; Susan Milner, *The Dilemmas of Internationalism: French Syndicalism and the International Labour Movement, 1900–1914* (New York: Berg, 1990).

19. See Robert F. Wheeler, "Revolutionary Socialist Internationalism: Rank-and-File Reaction in the USPD," *International Review of Social History* 22, no. 3 (1977): 329–349; Milner, *Dilemmas of Internationalism*.

20. On syndicalism, see Milner, *Dilemmas of Internationalism*; Wayne Thorpe, *'The Workers Themselves': Revolutionary Syndicalism and International Labour, 1913–1923* (Dordrecht: Kluwer Academic Publishers / International Institute of Social History, 1989). The earliest syndicalists were anarchists in inspiration. Increasingly, however, syndicalism came to refer to unions that sought to combine political and economic action rather than depend on political parties for political initiatives. The major difference between syndicalists and trade unionists, such as the AFL, who also sought to avoid politics, is that the latter did so because they fundamentally accepted the primacy of capitalism. In reality, of course, trade unionists did not avoid politics—they just picked and chose.

21. See Lorwin, *Labor and Internationalism*, chapter 4; Peter Rütters, "Histoire et developpement des Secretariats Professionels Internationaux (SPI)," in *Syndicalisme: Dimensions Internationales*, ed. Guillaume Devin (La Garenne-Colombes, France: Editions Européennes ERASME, 1990), 251–266; Denis Macshane, "Reflexions sur l'historire de la Federation Internationale des Ouvriers de la Metallurgie (FIOM)," in *Syndicalisme*, Devin, 267–296; for a chronological tracing of the subsequent evolution and unifications of ITSs, see Rainer Gries, "Overview of the Development of International Trade Union Organizations," in *International Trade Union Organizations: Inventory of the Archive of Social Democracy and the Library of the Friedrich-Ebert-Stiftung*, ed. Peter Rütters, Michael Schneider, Erwin Schweißhelm, and Rüdiger Zimmerman (Bonn: Friedrich-Ebert-Stiftung, 2002), 85–94.

22. Madeleine Reberioux, "Naissance du Secretariat Typographique International," in *Syndicalisme: Dimensions Internationales*, ed. Guillaume Devin (La Garenne-Colombes, France: Editions Européennes ERASME, 1990), 37–52.

23. Michel Dreyfus, "The Emergence of an International Trade Union Organization," in *The International Confederation of Free Trade Unions*, ed. Marcel van der Linden (Bern: Peter Lang, 2000), 27–28. It is worth noting here that some British unions as well as the U.S. Knights of Labor (1870s and 1880s), the Industrial Workers of the World (early twentieth century), and the American Federation of Labor did have

affiliates in other countries. This is not to say that the territorial organization of unions is never necessary but, rather, that the territorialization that took place was part of a nationalist political agenda and not simply demanded by the practical exigencies of union work.

24. It seems to us that the strict division of labor between parties and unions is problematic. On the other hand, there is a great deal of merit in distinguishing between parties and unions if one wants parties that retain some ideological cohesion and unions that unite rather than divide the working class.

25. Milner, *Dilemmas of Internationalism*, 100.

26. Johann Sassenbach, *Twenty-five Years of International Unionism* (Amsterdam: International Federation of Trade Unions, 1926); Walther Schevenels, *Forty-five Years: International Federation of Trade Unions* (Brussels: Board of Trustees of the IFTU, 1956); Milner, *Dilemmas of Internationalism*, chapter 4.

27. Milner, *Dilemmas of Internationalism*, 101–103.

28. In 1911, for instance, the AFL asked and was invited to join the Secretariat largely in order to prevent the Industrial Workers of the World from joining.

29. This was an issue that attracted a lot of discussion within the Second International. For discussions, see Braunthal, *History, Volume 1*, chapter 20; Preben Kaarsholm, "The South African War and the Response of the International Socialist Community to Imperialism Between 1896 and 1908," in *Internationalism in the Labour Movement, 1830–1940*, ed. Frits van Holthoon and Marcel van der Linden (Leiden: E.J. Brill, 1988), 42–67; Fritjof Tichelman, "Socialist Internationalism and the Colonial World," in *Internationalism in the Labour Movement*, van Holthoon and van der Linden, 87–108.

30. See Gries, "Development of International Trade Union Organizations." The relevant table does not have numbers of the textile workers where women were the overwhelming majority. It is possible that in this case women were the majority although we do not have any evidence one way or another.

31. Unions in both the United States and Europe had already sought to include unskilled workers of all nations as well as to organize across whole industries rather than crafts. The more craft-based unions of the United States and the United Kingdom, however, insisted on organizing along craft lines and were often racist and xenophobic.

32. Patrick Pasture, *Histoire du syndicalisme chrétien international: la difficile recherche d'une troisième voie* (Paris: Éditions L'Harmattan, 1999).

33. A number of unions and groups influenced by syndicalism became increasingly disenchanted or marginalized, and just before WWI they formed the International Working Men's Association. See Thorpe, *'The Workers Themselves.'*

34. Bairoch, *Economics and World History*, chapter 1.

35. Karl Polanyi, *The Great Transformation: The Political and Economic Origins of Our Time* (1944; Boston: Beacon, 1957), 249.

36. In our view, the organismic ontology of Karl Polanyi, consistent with his Christian Socialism, tends to produce structural-functional interpretations and predictions, rather than historically based analyses. For a critique of Karl Polanyi's impact on

Marxist archaeology, see Mary Van Buren, "Rethinking the Vertical Archipelago: Ethnicity, Exchange, and History in the South Central Andes," *American Anthropologist* 98, no. 2 (1996): 338–351.

37. Eric Hobsbawm, *The Age of Extremes: A History of the World, 1914–1991* (New York: Vintage Books, 1996), 142–147.

38. Julius Braunthal, *History of the International, Volume 3: 1943–1968* (1971; Boulder, Colo.: Westview, 1980); background interviews by authors.

39. Lorwin, *Labor and Internationalism*, 191. The international trade secretariats were reconstituted immediately after WWI. Most of them were then located outside of Germany and were under the hegemony of the IFTU, but some did preserve a significant degree of independence. Due to the activism of the IFTU and the intensity of the subsequent conflicts, however, most of the ITSs remained even more inactive than they had been before WWI. One important exception was the International Transport Workers' Federation. By WWII there were twenty-seven ITSs, five fewer than the thirty-two before WWI.

40. Geert Van Goethem, "Conflicting Interests: The International Federation of Trade Unions (1919–1945)," in *The International Confederation of Free Trade Unions*, ed. Marcel van der Linden (Bern: Peter Lang, 2000), 73–163, at 84. Also Geert Van Goethem, *The Amsterdam International: The World of the International Federation of Trade Unions (IFTU), 1913–1945* (Aldershot, UK: Ashgate, 2006). For an account by a participant, see Samuel Gompers, *Seventy Years of Life and Labor: An Autobiography* (1925; New York: E.P. Dutton, 1943), 2:501–512. Also see Edo Fimmen, *The International Federation of Trade Unions: Development and Aims* (Amsterdam: International Federation of Trade Unions, 1922). Its activities were to take place through regular congresses with the number of delegates reflecting the size of national unions—but not proportionally as the AFL and its British allies demanded. In addition, the IFTU was equipped with standing organizational forms whose role was to improve communications among the members but, also, initiate a labor agenda as well as coordinate collective action. Decision making was to be by majority rather than unanimity, as the AFL preferred. Dues were kept lower than continental unions demanded because of the opposition of the AFL and the Trade Union Congress. In short, the IFTU was envisioned as a more federal organization than its predecessor; due to internal opposition, however, it did not become as strong as the socialists would have liked it to be.

41. The Congress of Industrial Organizations aimed at industrywide unionization, rather than the craft-based system preferred by the AFL. Under the leadership of John Lewis, head of the United Mine Workers and a Republican, the organization pursued a very aggressive international policy, joining in the formation of a pan-American organization and seeking to affiliate with the IFTU. See Melvyn Dubofsky and Warren Van Tine, *John L. Lewis: A Biography*, abridged ed. (Urbana, Ill.: University of Illinois Press, 1986); Art Preis, *Labor's Giant Step: Twenty Years of the CIO* (New York: Pioneer, 1964). The AFL's decision to join in order to block the CIO was the same strategy that the organization had used in 1911 against the Industrial Workers of the World.

42. Fimmen was the secretary of the International Transport Workers' Federation and had also served as one of the secretaries of the IFTU in the early post-WWI period. His proposal came after he had been forced to resign his second position.

43. Here we should pay tribute to those socialist internationalists who formed the short-lived Vienna or "two and half" International. What distinguished them from the Third International was a commitment to socialist democracy, and from the Second International, a commitment to socialist internationalism.

44. For background and overviews, see R. Palme Dutt, *The Two Internationals* (London: George Allen and Unwin, 1920); Lorwin, *Labor and Internationalism*, chapters 10, 14, 20, and 21; E. H. Carr, *A History of Soviet Russia: The Bolshevik Revolution, 1917–1923*, volume 3 (New York: Macmillan, 1953), 116–147 and 567–570; G. D. H. Cole, *Communism and Social Democracy, 1914–1931*, volume 4, parts 1 and 2, of his *A History of Socialist Thought* (London: Macmillan, 1958); Julius Braunthal, *History of the International, Volume 2: 1914–1943* (1963; New York: Frederick A. Praeger, 1967), chapters 7, 10, and 13; James W. Hulse, *The Forming of the Communist International* (Stanford, Calif.: Stanford University Press, 1964); E. H. Carr, *The Twilight of the Comintern, 1930–1935* (New York: Pantheon Books, 1982).

45. Syndicalist tendencies continued to play an important, if diminishing, role during the interwar period. Syndicalist unionists, for instance, remained important in countries such as France, Spain, Sweden, and the Netherlands and, increasingly, in Latin America. Syndicalism as an important autonomous force came to an end with the destruction of the Spanish National Confederation of Labor (CNT) during the Spanish civil war.

46. A. Losovsky, *The International Council of Trade and Industrial Unions* (New York: Union Publishing Company, 1920); Arthur Rosenberg, "Communism and the Communist Trade Unions," originally published in German in the *Internationales Handwortebuch des Gewerkschaftswesen* (Berlin, 1932), translation at whatnextjournal .co.uk/Pages/History/Rosenberg.html (accessed March 18, 2006); Geoffrey Swain, "Was the Profintern Really Necessary?" *European History Quarterly* 17 (1987): 57–77; Reiner Tosstorff, "'Moscow' or 'Amsterdam'? The Red International of Labour Unions, 1920/21–1937," *Communist History Network Newsletter* 8 (July 2000), accessible online at les.man.ac.uk/chnn/CHNN08AOM.html (accessed March 18, 2006).

47. The "social-fascism" strategy lumped together socialists and fascists. The "popular front" strategy reversed this destructive policy and advocated collaboration of a broad spectrum of democratic forces.

48. Carr, *History of Soviet Russia*, 607–610 and passim.

49. The RILU was disbanded in 1936, so it was not directly involved in the formation of the Confederación de Trabajadores de América Latina (CTAL). Previously, however, it had set up a Latin American section whose unions participated in this process. On CTAL, see Julio Godio, *Historia del Movimiento Obrero Latinoamericano/3: Socialdemocracia, Socialcristianismo y Marxismo, 1930–1980* (Caracas: Editorial Nueva Sociedad, 1985), 27–30.

50. Schevenels, *Forty-five Years*, 191–194 and 425 for member unions from Latin America, Africa, and Asia; Van Goethem, "Conflicting Interests," 115–116.

51. H. J. Simmons and R. E. Simmons, *Class and Colour in South Africa, 1850–1950* (London: Penguin Books, 1969), chapter 16; Carr, *History of Soviet Russia*, 605–638.

52. Simmons and Simmons, *Class and Colour*, 362.

53. Lorwin, *Labor and Internationalism*, 389–395.

54. While most workers were forced to join fascist and national socialist fronts, some workers did form fascist and national socialist organizations. In general, however, working-class organizations were in the forefront of resistance to fascism and national socialism.

55. For a comprehensive and systematic overview of Latin American labor, see Ruth Berins Collier and David Collier, *Shaping the Political Arena: Critical Junctures, the Labor Movement, and Regime Dynamics in Latin America* (Princeton, N.J.: Princeton University Press, 1991).

56. See Lutz Niethammer, "Structural Reform and a Compact for Growth: Conditions for a United Labor Union Movement in Western Europe after the Collapse of Fascism," in *The Origins of the Cold War and Contemporary Europe*, ed. Charles Maier (New York: New Viewpoints, 1978).

57. Gøsta Esping-Andersen, *The Three Worlds of Welfare Capitalism* (Princeton, N.J.: Princeton University Press, 1990); Alexander Hicks, *Social Democracy and Welfare Capitalism: A Century of Income Security Politics* (Ithaca, N.Y.: Cornell University Press, 1999).

58. Lewis L. Lorwin, *The International Labor Movement: History, Policies, Outlook* (New York: Harper and Brother Publishers, 1953), chapters 19–22; John Windmuller, *American Labor and the International Labor Movement 1940 to 1953* (Ithaca, N.Y.: Cornell University Press, 1954); Schevenels, *Forty-five Years*, 329–361; Anthony Carew, "A False Dawn: The World Federation of Trade Unions (1945–1949)," in *The International Confederation of Free Trade Unions*, ed. Marcel van der Linden (Bern: Peter Lang, 2000), 165–184.

59. See Denis Macshane, *International Labour and the Origins of the Cold War* (Oxford: Clarendon Press, 1992). The ITF's resistance was probably as consequential, however (background interview by authors).

60. Carew, "A False Dawn." Some communist unions in the West, including two major ones, the French Confédération Générale du Travail (CGT) and the Italian Confederazione Generale Italiana del Lavoro (CGIL), stayed within the WFTU. The CGT was one of the unaffiliated unions that joined the ITUC in November 2006 (the CGIL was already a member of the ICFTU).

61. Everett Kassalow, *National Labor Movements in the Postwar World* (Evanston, Ill.: Northwestern University Press, 1963); Robert Cox, "Labor and Transnational Relations," in *Transnational Relations and World Politics*, ed. Robert Keohane and Joseph Nye Jr. (Cambridge, Mass.: Harvard University Press, 1971), 204–234; Gary K. Busch, *The Political Role of International Trades Unions* (New York: St. Martin's Press, 1983).

62. There are good reasons to suggest that WFTU unions were less likely to resist Soviet policies because most of them had lost their autonomy vis-à-vis state and party.

63. Labor imperialism refers both to the role of some unions in supporting their ruling classes in their imperial endeavors and to the particularistic attitude of unions from

Northern countries toward their counterparts in the South. Robert Cox, "Labor and Hegemony," *International Organization* 31 (Summer 1977): 385–424; Dave Spooner, *Partners or Predators? International Trade Unionism and Asia* (Hong Kong: Asia Monitor Resource Center, 1989).

64. John Windmuller, "ICFTU after Ten Years: Problems and Prospects," *Industrial and Labor Relations Review* 14, no. 2 (January 1961): 257–272; and "Internationalism in Eclipse: The ICFTU after Two Decades," *Industrial and Labor Relations Review* 23, no. 4 (July 1970): 510–527; Anthony Carew, "Conflict Within the ICFTU: Anti-Communism and Anti-Colonialism in the 1950s," *International Review of Social History* 41 (1996): 147–181. Interestingly enough, the ICFTU employed more people then than it does now.

65. In many cases the reason why the members could contribute very limited amounts was due to their own limited resources. Both the British and German confederations, for instance, are very weak and poor when compared with their member unions. Others, such as the AFL-CIO (which is not that powerful but is certainly more so than the ones just mentioned), were not interested in a strong international organization.

66. Robert Alexander, "Labor and Inter-American Relations," *Annals of the American Academy of Political and Social Science* 334 (March 1961): 41–53.

67. Here, of course, we must also lay the major blame on various local dictators who destroyed, co-opted, or divided the labor movement in a number of South American countries.

68. Recognizing that it could not compete with the WFTU and the ICFTU in Europe, it placed its energies in Africa, Latin America, and Asia. During the 1950s it formed a regional organization in Latin America and brought non-European unionists into its leadership. By 1961, African delegates accounted for 37 percent and Latin American delegates for 29 percent of those participating at its congress. In 1968 the International Federation of Christian Trade Unions reduced its denominational character and adopted a more class-struggle approach. At that point it changed its name to World Confederation of Labour (WCL) (Pasture, *Histoire du syndicalisme chrétien*, chapter 5). Christian-based unions, particularly the Belgian one, continued to play a central role (background interviews).

69. Carew, "Towards a Free Trade Union Centre," in *The International Confederation of Free Trade Unions*, ed. Marcel van der Linden (Bern: Peter Lang, 2000), 286–291; Busch, *Political Role*, chapter 6.

70. Barbara Barnouin, *The European Labour Movement and European Integration* (London: Frances Pinter, 1986); Corinne Gobin, *L'Europe Syndicale* (Bruxelles: Éditions Labor, 1997); Rebecca Gumbrell-McCormick, "Facing New Challenges: The International Confederation of Free Trade Unions (1972–1990s)," in *The International Confederation of Free Trade Unions*, ed. Marcel van der Linden (Bern: Peter Lang, 2000): 341–517, at 347–359.

71. At least one important unionist with direct experience of the era believes that ideological differences were less important than lack of resources.

72. Gumbrell-McCormick, "Facing New Challenges," 367–376.

73. For a critical view of the AFL-CIO's policy, see Beth Sims, *Workers of the World Undermined: American Labor's Role in U.S. Foreign Policy* (Boston: South End Press, 1992).

74. Gumbrell-McCormick, "Facing New Challenges," 460–463.

75. Sadahiko Inoue, *Japanese Trade Unions and Their Future: Opportunities and Challenges in an Era of Globalization* (Geneva: International Institute for Labour Studies, Labour and Society Programme, DP/106/1999, 1999).

76. Rosalind E. Boyd, Robin Cohen, and Peter C. W. Gutkind, eds., *International Labour and the Third World: The Making of a New Working Class* (Aldershot, UK: Avebury, 1987); Roger Southall, ed., *Trade Unions and the New Industrialization of the Third World* (London: Zed Books, 1988). Many Northern unions extended support to Southern unions during the 1980s although their motivations were often questioned. See Roger Southall, *Imperialism or Solidarity? International Labour and South African Trade Unions* (Cape Town, South Africa: University of Cape Town, 1995).

77. The UAW's motivations also had to do with its disagreement with the AFL-CIO's obsession with anticommunism. In fact, the immediate reason why the AFL-CIO withdrew from the ICFTU in 1969 was the evidence that some ICFTU leaders were looking positively toward a UAW application for membership.

78. On balance, unions have managed to avoid divisions among themselves along the line of the "war on terrorism."

79. The movement toward unification started with the Millennium Review that was initiated at the 2000 congress of the ICFTU and whose aims may have been more profound than the ones currently adopted. See "Launching the Millennium Review—The Future of the International Trade Union Movement," at www.icftu.org/www/english/congress2000/econres2000_XII.pdf (accessed March 16, 2006). At the 2004 congress it became the centerpiece. See ICFTU, *Globalizing Solidarity* (Brussels: ICFTU, 2004); and ICFTU, *Decisions of the Eighteenth World Congress* (Brussels: ICFTU, 2004), 1–7. Also background interviews with ICFTU, ETUC, and GUF officials.

80. The formal employees and the financial resources of the global union organizations do not reflect their potential. Under circumstances of close collaboration with national unions, these human and material resources get multiplied. As we have noted, the major issue is that most major unions choose to pursue their own foreign policies.

81. The end of the Cold War has left the WFTU but a shell of its previous self. Notably, it includes a preponderant number of unions from West Asia, mostly state controlled, highlighting the fact that the region is one of the last frontiers for the ITUC and its line of politics. Moreover, efforts at its reorganization and revitalization continue. Its fifteenth congress took place in Havana, Cuba, in late November 2005, while a week earlier the Communist Party of Greece hosted a global conference of communist and related radical parties. The communist left is fighting both against some of the legacies of the Soviet Union and the formation of socialist parties, such as the European Party of the Left, which offer a radical but also more democratic option. Even so, we must note that WFTU-affiliated unions play an important and even dominant role in a

number of countries, such as Cyprus, Peru, Colombia, and India. Additionally, communist tendencies and unions not affiliated with the WFTU play an important role in a number of countries, such as Greece, Italy, France, Spain, South Africa, Brazil, South Korea, the Philippines, and elsewhere.

82. The emergence of regional unions is more likely in the Mercosur area. One can also envision a similar process emerging in North America now that the traditional Mexican unions have declined and have been replaced by unions more open to collaboration with U.S. unions. The ETUC's special status, however, can very well stoke the unilateralist attitudes of the AFL-CIO, the Japanese RENGO, and other national unions.

83. Additionally, the new confederation preserves the existing regional organizational subdivisions, which are associated with geographic regions rather than common political targets. The regional organizations in Africa and Asia, for instance, do not have any continental counterparts in the sense that the ETUC has the European Union and ORIT may have the Free Trade Area of the Americas.

84. See ICFTU, *Whose Miracle? How China's Workers Are Paying the Price for Its Economic Boom* (Brussels: ICFTU, 2006). Accessible at www.workersvoiceatwto.org/www/pdf/WhoseMiracleChinaReport.pdf (accessed March 17, 2006).

85. See ICFTU, *Decisions of the Eighteenth World Congress*.

86. See the Teamster website at www.teamster.org/divisions/Port/secureamericanports.htm (accessed March 17, 2006).

87. The Teamsters have reason to be concerned about the lack of unions in Dubai and the pressures upon Mexican drivers to work dangerously long hours. Yet, the framing of the discourse on the Mexican drivers was contentious even within the union.

88. On SIGTUR, see Robert Lambert and Edward Webster, "Social Emancipation and the New Labour Internationalism: A Southern Perspective," at www.ces.uc.pt/emancipa/research/en/internacionalismo.html (accessed March 17, 2006). Also see Robert Lambert and Edward Webster, "Global Civil Society and the New Labor Internationalism: A View from the South," in *Creating a Better World: Interpreting Global Civil Society*, ed. Rupert Taylor (Bloomfield, Conn.: Kumarian Press, 2004), 82–115.

89. Even though a number of Russian unions are struggling for a more democratic union movement and a more democratic Russia, there are also those who seem more intent upon preserving good relations with the state in order to keep substantial resources from the Soviet era.

90. For a debate on the significance of the unification, see Peter Waterman, "The International Union Merger of November 2006: Top-Down, Eurocentric and . . . Invisible?" at info.interactivist.net/article.pl?sid=06/10/28/1410212&mode=nested&tid=4 (accessed February 1, 2007); and Rebecca Gumbrell-McCormick, "From the Old Trade Union Internationals to the New," at www.labourstart.org/docs/en/000382.html (accessed February 1, 2007).

Chapter Four   Regulating the Global State

1. "Action by World Bank's IFC on Workers' Rights a Major Step Forward," *ICFTU Online*, February 22, 2006, at www.icftu.org/displaydocument.asp?Index=991223448 &Language=EN (accessed March 26, 2006). For more information on the case, see ICFTU, "Haiti–Dominican Republic Export Processing Zones: Taking on Grupo M," *Trade Union World Briefing*, no. 15, November 2005, at www.icftu.org/www/PDF/ LMSDossier15-05HaitiDomre.pdf (accessed March 26, 2006).

2. International Finance Corporation, *International Finance Corporation's Policy and Performance Standards on Social & Environmental Sustainability*, 2006, at www.ifc.org/ifcext/policyreview.nsf/AttachmentsByTitle/Policy+and +Performance+Standards+FINAL+03-06-06/$FILE/Policy+&+Performance+ Standards+PUBLIC+FINAL-03-06-06.pdf (accessed April 19, 2006).

3. A social clause is a clause included in trade agreements that specifies the implications of violating certain core labor standards and rights in the production of export products. Quite easily a social clause could be included in investment or financial agreements. In all of these cases, it would be limited to violations that are related to the areas covered by these agreements. Core labor standards and rights, however, may also be employed independent of economic agreements. That is the approach of the ILO as well as the European Union, and that is also the broader strategy of the global union organizations. *Labor rights* refers to labor policies that empower workers, such as the right to form unions. *Labor standards* refers to policies that protect workers, such as improved working conditions. As we will see, global union organizations use the term *core labor standards* when they are actually referring to core labor rights. We distinguish between the two and use *rules* when referring to both rights and standards. For a distinction between labor conditions and labor rights, see Robert Flanagan, *Globalization and Labor Conditions: Working Conditions and Worker Rights in a Global Economy* (New York: Oxford University Press, 2006).

4. The labor regulation proposals of the First International included proposals on an eight-hour workday and work by women and children. See G. M. Steckloff, *The History of the First International* (London: Martin Lawrence Limited, 1928), chapter 8, also at marx.org/archive/steklov/history-first-international/ch06.htm (accessed May 30, 2006).

5. U.S. Department of Labor, Bureau of Labor Statistics, Bulletin 268, *Historical Survey of International Action Affecting Labor* (Washington, D.C.: Government Printing Office, 1920), 64.

6. The German initiative owes more to Bismarck than the kaiser. Bismarck, however, was soon to be fired as chancellor for a variety of reasons. This strategy was consistent with Bismarck's earlier adoption of labor policies (1870s) intended to stem the growth of socialism and unionism. This kind of preemptive strategy, based on compensatory reforms involving better standards and conditions of work, has been frequently used in order to prevent countervailing and egalitarian reforms involving labor and political rights. The Greek social security system, for instance, was put in place by a right-wing dictator in the late 1930s in order to weaken the appeal of the left. The same process

took place in much of South America with Juan Perón importing the Italian fascist system, where he had served in a diplomatic capacity, to Argentina.

7. For the development of global labor regulation during the prewar period, see L. Chatelain, *La protection internationale ouvrière* (Paris: Librairie Nouvelle de Droit et de Jurisprudence, 1908); Ernest Mahaim, *Le droit international ouvrier* (Paris: Librairie de la Société Recueil Sirey, 1913); Ignace Sinzot, *Les traités internationaux pour la protection des travailleurs: Leur sanction* (Louvain: Imprimerie Ch. Peeters, 1911); Stephan Bauer, *International Labor Legislation and the Society of Nations* (U.S. Department of Labor, Bureau of Labor Statistics, Bulletin 254, 1919); U.S. Department of Labor, *Historical Survey*.

8. See U.S. Department of Labor, *Historical Survey*, chapter 7.

9. See Virginia Leary, "Workers' Rights and International Trade: The Social Clause," in *Fair Trade and Harmonization: Prerequisites for Free Trade?* vol. 2, *Legal Analysis*, ed. Jagdish Bhagwati and Robert E. Hudec (Cambridge, Mass.: MIT Press, 1996), 185.

10. Bauer, *International Labor Legislation*, 11.

11. See Dimitris Stevis and Terry Boswell, "Labor Politics and Policy in International Integration: Comparing NAFTA and the European Union," in *The Politics of Social Inequality: Research in Political Sociology*, vol. 9, ed. Betty Dobratz, Lisa Waldner, and Timothy Buzzell (Amsterdam: Elsevier, 2001), 335–364, for discussion of the labor provisions of the European Union and the North American Agreement on Labor Cooperation along those lines. Also Flanagan, *Globalization and Labor Conditions*.

12. See Margaret Macmillan, *Paris 1919: Six Months That Changed the World* (New York: Random House, 2001); James T. Shotwell, *At the Paris Peace Conference* (New York: Macmillan, 1937).

13. Edo Fimmen, *The International Federation of Trade Unions: Development and Aims* (Amsterdam: IFTU, 1922), 11–12.

14. Samuel Gompers, *Seventy Years of Life and Labor: An Autobiography*, vol. 2 (1925; New York: E.P. Dutton, 1943), chapters 45 and 46; Stephen Charnovitz, "Two Centuries of Participation: NGOs and International Governance," *Michigan Journal of International Law* 18 (Winter 1997): 183–286, at 212–216.

15. The literature on the ILO is vast. For an accessible overview, see U.S. Department of Labor, Bureau of Labor Statistics, *Monthly Labor Review: Special Issue Commemorating the 75th Anniversary of the International Labor Organization* (Washington, D.C.: U.S. Department of Labor, September 1994).

16. For easily accessible information on the history, structure, and goals of the ILO, visit www.ilo.org/public/english/about/index.htm (accessed May 30, 2006).

17. Except for article 3 in Convention 135 (the Workers' Representatives Convention).

18. Conventions are regular international treaties. Recommendations are specific guidelines and suggestions to accomplish a specific goal, for example, improve health and safety. For a concise account, see George Tsogas, *Labor Regulation in a Global Economy* (Armonk, N.Y.: M.E. Sharpe, 2001), chapter 2. This is a superb overview of global labor regulation.

19. The same situation applies to the OECD's Guidelines for Multinational Enterprises.

20. See Rorden Wilkinson, "Peripheralizing Labour: The ILO, WTO and the Completion of the Bretton Woods Project," in *Global Unions? Theory and Strategies of Organized Labour in the Global Political Economy*, ed. Jeffrey Harrod and Robert O'Brien (London: Routledge, 2002), 204–220.

21. Leary, "Workers' Rights and International Trade," 198.

22. The term *social welfare state* refers to states with extensive social programs, ranging from the protection of vulnerable categories to the expansion of economic and social rights for all citizens. The term *developmental state* refers to the strategies of Southern states, common from the 1930s to the 1970s, whose aim was to industrialize by producing domestically manufactured items that they had historically imported (import substitution). Since the rise of globalism, it has been forgotten that this strategy produced spectacular results in a number of countries over a number of decades from the interwar period to the 1960s. The same strategy, incidentally, was used by the North during the nineteenth and much of the twentieth century. See Paul Bairoch, *Economics and World History: Myths and Paradoxes* (Chicago: University of Chicago Press, 1993). For Southern perspectives, see Sarah Anderson, ed., *Views from the South: The Effects of Globalization and the WTO on Third World Development* (n.p.: Food First Books / International Forum on Globalization, 2000).

23. For a thorough account, see Gerda van Roozendaal, *Trade Unions and Global Governance: The Debate on a Social Clause* (London: Continuum, 2002), chapter 7. Also see Leary, "Workers' Rights and International Trade," 190–197.

24. For more information, visit www.ilo.org/public/english/standards/norm/index.htm (accessed June 5, 2006).

25. For more information on the Bureau for Workers' Activities, visit www.ilo.org/public/english/dialogue/actrav/ (accessed June 5, 2006).

26. For more information on GURN, visit www.gurn.info (accessed June 5, 2006). For more information on the Global Labor University, visit www.global-labour-university.org (accessed June 5, 2006).

27. For more information on the ILO's work on the "informal economy," visit www.ilo.org/public/english/employment/infeco/index.htm (accessed June 5, 2006). For global union views, see International Labor Office, Bureau for Workers' Activities, Labor Bulletin 2002/2, no. 127, *Unprotected Labor: What Role for Unions in the Informal Economy?* (Geneva: International Labor Office, 2002).

28. This debate has also allowed many in the global union network to recognize the potential of the organizations in the informal economy as allies and, even more, as members. One major example of that is the admission of the Indian Self-Employed Women's Association into a number of global union federations as well as the ICFTU.

29. On decent work, visit www.ilo.org/public/english/bureau/integration/decent/index.htm (accessed June 5, 2006).

30. The text can be accessed at www.ilo.org/public/english/fairglobalization/report/index.htm (accessed May 30, 2006).

31. We would like to point out that we are not talking about the South and the North as homogeneous entities. Class divisions are as important if not more important since the impacts of liberalization policies are at the expense of the poor and the working class and to the benefit of capitalist and ruling elites in both North and South.

32. On the WTO, see Rorden Wilkinson, *Multilateralism and the World Trade Organization: The Architecture and Extension of International Trade Regulation* (London: Routledge, 2000); also Jagdish Bhagwati and Robert E. Hudec, eds., *Fair Trade and Harmonization: Prerequisites for Free Trade?* 2 vols. (Cambridge, Mass.: MIT Press, 1997).

33. On the status of negotiations as of early March 2007, see www.wto.org/ english/news_e/sppl_e/sppl56_e.htm (accessed March 14, 2007).

34. See Carew, "A False Dawn: The World Federation of Trade Unions (1945–1949)," in *The International Confederation of Free Trade Unions*, ed. Marcel van der Linden (Bern: Peter Lang, 2000), 165–185.

35. For a detailed historical overview, see van der Linden, ed., *International Confederation of Free Trade Unions*. For a summary of global union views on global economic governance, see ICFTU, *Trade Union Guide to Globalization*, 2nd ed. (Brussels: ICFTU, 2004).

36. See Robert O'Brien, "The Varied Paths to Minimum Global Labor Standards," in *Global Unions? Theory and Strategies of Organized Labour in the Global Political Economy*, ed. Jeffrey Harrod and Robert O'Brien (London: Routledge, 2002), 221–234.

37. See van Roozendaal, *Trade Unions and Global Governance*; Tsogas, *Labor Regulation*, chapter 1; Pharis Harvey, Terry Collingsworth, and Bama Athreya, *Developing Effective Mechanisms for Implementing Labor Rights in the Global Economy* (Washington, D.C.: International Labor Rights Fund, 1998).

38. Peter Donohue, "'Free Trade', Unions and the State: Trade Liberalization's Endorsement by the AFL-CIO, 1943–1962," *Research in Political Economy* 13 (Greenwich, Conn.: JAI Press, 1992), 1–73. The same discursive move from "free" to "fair" trade was adopted by British unions in the late nineteenth century as competition from abroad became more pronounced.

39. van Roozendaal, *Trade Unions and Global Governance*, chapter 4.

40. See Tsogas, *Labor Regulation*, chapter 5; American Center for International Labor Solidarity/AFL-CIO, *Justice for All: A Guide to Worker Rights in the Global Economy* (Washington, D.C.: American Center for International Labor Solidarity, 2003), chapter 3. As we discuss in the last part of this chapter, these are unilateral measures to be distinguished from negotiated bilateral agreements. Tsogas, in his otherwise strong analysis, labels them "bilateral."

41. ILO, *Final Report of the Working Party on International Labour Standards*, Official Bulletin, Series A, special issue (Geneva: ILO, 1979).

42. On the positions of the various participants, see van Roozendaal, *Trade Unions and Global Governance*, chapter 3 and throughout; also Robert O'Brien, Anne Marie Goetz, Jan Aart Scholte, and Marc Williams, *Contesting Global Governance: Multilateral Economic Institutions and Global Social Movements* (Cambridge: Cambridge University Press, 2000), chapter 3.

43. ICFTU, *International Workers' Rights and Trade: The Need for Dialogue* (Brussels: ICFTU, 1994).

44. ICFTU, *Building Workers' Human Rights into the Global Trading System* (Brussels: ICFTU, 1999), 42–45.

45. "EU Trade Ministers Agree to Exclude Labor Standards from WTO Guidelines," *Daily Labor Report*, no. 212 (November 1, 1996): A-1.

46. Robert O'Brien, "Globalization, Imperialism and the Labor Standards Debate," in *Labor and Globalization: Results and Prospects*, ed. Ronaldo Munck (Liverpool: Liverpool University Press, 2004), 52–70.

47. van Roozendaal, *Trade Unions and Global Governance*, chapter 5. See also Jagdish Bhagwati's *In Defense of Globalization* (New York: Oxford University Press for Council on Foreign Relations, 2004), chapter 10. Bhagwati has consistently argued against the inclusion of labor and environmental standards in trade agreements.

48. ICFTU, *Building Workers' Human Rights*; Mark Anner, "The International Trade Union Campaign for Core Labor Standards in the WTO," *Working USA* 5, no. 1 (Summer 2001): 43–63.

49. A great deal of useful information and interviews with participants has been collected by the WTO History Project of the University of Washington. It can be accessed at depts.washington.edu/wtohist/ (accessed May 30, 2006).

50. ICFTU, *The Doha Declaration: A Trade Union Analysis*, at www.icftu .org/displaydocument.asp?Index=991214586&Language=EN (accessed May 30, 2006).

51. Daniel Pruzin, "U.S. Silent on Labor, Trade Issues as WTO Prepares for Ministerial Meeting," *Daily Labor Report*, no. 197 (October 15, 2001), A-5.

52. Pascal Lamy, "The WTO in the Archipelago of Global Governance," Speech to the Institute of International Studies, Geneva, May 14, 2006, at www.wto.org/English/ news_e/sppl_e/sppl20_e.htm (accessed May 30, 2006).

53. Transcript of Internet Chat with WTO Director-General Pascal Lamy, February 21, 2006, at www.wto.org/english/forums_e/chat_e/chat_transcript_e.doc (accessed May 30, 2006).

54. It is worth underscoring that the ITUC continues to believe in the necessity of including labor rights in the WTO and/or strengthening the ILO's role in order to ensure the respect of these rights by the WTO. For example, Pascal Lamy was invited to participate in one of the roundtables during the ITUC's inaugural meeting. See www.ituc-si.org/spip.php?article281 (accessed March 14, 2007). Moreover, the organization welcomed the first ever report jointly authored by the ILO and the WTO as "an unprecedented step forward towards achieving genuine coherence in the way the world's major institutions work together" (see www.ituc-csi.org/spip.php?article749 [accessed March 14, 2007]).

55. See van Roozendaal, *Trade Unions and Global Governance*, chapter 7.

56. For the text and follow-up work, visit www.ilo.org/dyn/declaris/ DECLARATIONWEB.INDEXPAGE (accessed May 30, 2006).

57. For an earlier overview, see Göte Hansson, *Social Clauses and International Trade* (London: Croom Helm, 1983). For a recent overview, see Werner Sengenberger,

Globalization and Social Progress: The Role and Impact of International Labor Standards, 2nd ed. (Bonn: Friedrich-Ebert-Stiftung, 2005).

58. Gilbert Van Liemt, "Minimum Labor Standards and International Trade: Would a Social Clause Work?" *International Labour Review* 128, no. 4 (1989): 433–448.

59. Harvey, Collingsworth, and Athreya, *Developing Effective Mechanisms*, D:2.

60. ICFTU, *Building Workers' Human Rights*, 45.

61. See National Research Council of the National Academies, *Monitoring International Labor Standards: Techniques and Sources of Information* (Washington, D.C.: National Academies Press, 2004), chapter 8.

62. See Robert Kyloh, Faith O'Neill, and Carmel Whelton, *Trade Unions and the Global Economy: An Unfinished Story*, Labour Education 124–125 (Geneva: ILO, 2001); ICFTU, *IMF & World Bank–Sponsored Privatization and Its Impact on Labor* (Brussels: ICFTU, 2002); ICFTU, *Fighting for Alternatives: Cases of Successful Trade Union Resistance to the Policies of the IMF and the World Bank* (Brussels: ICFTU, 2006).

63. Gerard Greenfield, "Democratic Trade Union Responses to Globalisation: A Critique of the ICFTU-APRO's 'Asian Monetary Fund' Proposal," September 6, 1999, at www.labournet.de/diskussion/gewerkschaft/greenf.html (accessed June 5, 2006).

64. World Bank, *World Development Report 1995: Workers in an Integrating World* (New York: Oxford University Press for the World Bank, 1995); World Bank, *World Development Report 2006: Equity and Development* (New York: Oxford University Press for the World Bank, 2006).

65. This is particularly evident whenever there are studies that purport to show how labor rights are not inimical to economic growth. Such an argument is tantamount to saying that slaves or women should not have rights unless these rights contributed to economic growth. For such examples, see Organization for Economic Cooperation and Development, *International Trade and Core Labor Standards* (Paris: OECD, 2000); Toke Aidt and Zafiris Tzannatos, *Unions and Collective Bargaining: Economic Effects in a Global Environment* (Washington, D.C.: World Bank, 2003). For the World Bank's current policies on labor rights, visit web.worldbank.org/WBSITE/EXTERNAL/TOPICS/EXTSOCIALPROTECTION/EXTLM/0,,contentMDK:20224298~menuPK:584854~pagePK:148956~piPK:216618~theSitePK:390615,00.html (accessed June 5, 2006).

66. See ICFTU, "World Bank Publication Promotes Elimination of Worker Protection," September 6, 2006, at www.icftu.org/displaydocument.asp?Index=991224962&Language=EN (accessed November 9, 2006).

67. See International Trade Union Confederation, "World Bank Takes Major Step on Labour Standards," December 13, 2006, at www.ituc-csi.org/spip.php?article491 (accessed December 15, 2006).

68. International Finance Corporation, *Policy and Performance Standards*, 7.

69. International Financial Corporation, *Policy and Performance Standards*, 7.

70. ICFTU, *Fighting for Alternatives*.

71. For historical accounts, see Hansson, *Social Clauses and International Trade*; Steven Charnovitz, "The Influence of International Labor Standards on the World Trade Regime: A Historical Overview," *International Labour Review* 126, no. 5 (1987): 565–584. For an overview of different ways of thinking about labor rights, see Brian

Langille, "Eight Ways to Think About Labour Standards," *Journal of World Trade* 31, no. 4 (August 1987): 27–53. See also Virginia Leary and Daniel Warner, eds., *Social Issues, Globalisation and International Institutions: Labour Rights and the EU, ILO, OECD and WTO* (Leiden: Martinus Nijhoff, 2006), particularly chapters by Philip Alston and Brian Langille.

72. Peter Waterman, "Capitalist Trade Privileges and Social Labor Rights," *Working USA* 5, no. 1 (Summer 2001): 70–86.

73. See Robert O'Brien et al., *Contesting Global Governance*, chapter 4; Marc Williams, "In Search of Global Standards: The Political Economy of Trade and the Environment," in *The International Political Economy of the Environment: Critical Perspectives*, ed. Dimitris Stevis and Valerie Assetto (Boulder, Colo.: Lynne Rienner, 2001), 39–61.

74. See Anner, "International Trade Union Campaign"; Gerard Griffin, Chris Nyland, and Anne O'Rourke, "Trade Unions and the Social Clause: A North-South Union Divide?" *International Journal of Comparative Labour Law & Industrial Relations* 19, no. 4 (December 2003): 469–494.

75. See Jeffrey Harrod, *Power, Production, and the Unprotected Worker* (New York: Columbia University Press, 1987); and Matt Davies and Magnus Ryner, eds., *Poverty and the Production of World Politics: Unprotected Workers in the Global Political Economy* (Houndmills, UK: Palgrave Macmillan, 2006).

76. See Ajit Singh and Ann Zammit, *The Global Labour Standards Controversy: Critical Issues for Developing Countries* (Geneva: South Centre, 2000), at www.southcentre .org/publications/labour/labour.pdf (accessed June 6, 2006).

77. See International Organization of Employers (IOE), *Policy Statement on the Social Clause* (Geneva: IOE, 1996), at www.ioe-emp.org/fileadmin/user_upload/ documents_pdf/papers/statements_resolutions/english/state_1996june_socialclause.pdf (accessed June 6, 2006); also International Organization of Employers, *The ILO and the Social Dimensions of Globalization: Position Paper* (Geneva: IOE, 2001).

78. van Roozendaal, *Trade Unions and Global Governance*, chapter 4.

79. National Research Council, *Monitoring International Labor Standards*, chapter 8.

80. See Steve Weisman, "G.O.P. Shift Seen on Trade," *New York Times*, March 6, 2007, C1.

81. ICFTU, *IMF and World Bank–Sponsored Privatisation*; ICFTU, *Fighting for Alternatives*. For information on PSI's views, visit www.world-psi.org (accessed June 6, 2006), as well as the associated Public Services International Research Unit at www.psiru.org (accessed June 6, 2006), which has produced a number of outstanding analyses. This is an example of productive collaboration between academia and unions.

82. Global Unions, "Equitable Development and Poverty Reduction Require Improved Protection of Workers' Rights," statement by Global Unions to the 2006 spring meeting of the IMF and the World Bank, Washington, D.C., April 22–23, 2006, at www.icftu.org/displaydocument.asp?Index=991223584&Language=EN (accessed June 6, 2006).

83. See Tsogas, *Labor Regulation*, chapter 4.

84. American Center for International Labor Solidarity/AFL-CIO, *Justice for All*, chapter 3.

85. We are not saying here that domestic firms are better. In fact, they often ask for lower labor practices in order to compete with foreign corporations.

86. See Thomas Greven, *Social Standards in Bilateral and Regional Trade and Investment Agreements: Instruments, Enforcement, and Policy Options for Trade Unions*, Friedrich-Ebert-Stiftung Dialogue on Globalization Occasional Papers 16 (Geneva: Friedrich-Ebert-Stiftung, 2005). For up-to-date information, go to www.bilaterals.org (accessed May 31, 2006).

87. Steven Greenhouse and Michael Barbaro, "An Ugly Side of Free Trade: Sweatshops in Jordan," *New York Times*, May 3, 2006.

88. American Center for International Labor Solidarity/AFL-CIO, *Justice for All*, chapter 4; Tsogas, *Labor Regulation*, chapters 8 and 9; Dimitris Stevis, "Unions, Capitals and States: Competing (Inter)nationalisms in North American and European Integration," in *Global Unions? Theory and Strategies of Organized Labour in the Global Political Economy*, ed. Jeffrey Harrod and Robert O'Brien (London: Routledge, 2002), 130–150.

89. Please see chapter 3.

90. Stevis and Boswell, "Labor Politics and Policy in International Integration."

91. *Labor's Platform for the Americas* at www.gpn.org/research/orit2005/labour_platform_eng_web.pdf (accessed June 6, 2006).

92. For a comparison of NAFTA and EU labor policies, see Stevis and Boswell, "Labor Politics and Policy in International Integration."

93. European Works Councils Bulletin, "GM, Ford and GE Highlight EWC's Bargaining Role," *European Works Councils Bulletin* 56(2005): 7–13.

94. See Amartya Sen, *Development as Freedom* (New York: Knopf, 1999); Samir Amin, *Re-reading the Postwar Period: An Intellectual Itinerary* (New York: Monthly Review Press, 1994).

Chapter Five Regulating Capital

1. For the expansion of U.S. corporations abroad, see Mira Wilkins, *The Emergence of Multinational Enterprise: American Business Abroad from the Colonial Era to 1914* (Cambridge, Mass.: Harvard University Press, 1970); and *The Emergence of Multinational Enterprise: American Business Abroad from 1914 to 1970* (Cambridge, Mass.: Harvard University Press, 1974). See also B. C. Roberts, "Multinational Enterprise and Labour," in *Industrial Relations in International Perspective: Essays on Research and Policy*, ed. Peter B. Doeringer with Peter Gourevitch, Peter Lange, and Andrew Martin (New York: Holmes and Meier, 1981), 365–400.

2. The German "east policy" was promulgated by the Social Democratic Party and broke with the punitive strategy of the German Christian Democrats and the United States. The goal was to engage the communist countries through the strategic use of rewards and punishments.

3. As we note in chapter 1, the decline of governmental development aid in the 1970s and the focus of foreign direct investment on the North led to excessive Southern borrowing and the debt crisis. The liberalization of the South during the 1980s and the 1990s, along with the increasing economic weight of what are often called the newly industrialized or industrializing Southern countries, has increasingly attracted more investment. We must note, however, that about ten Southern countries, such as China, Brazil, India, and Mexico, account for the overwhelming majority of Northern investment into the South.

4. See Pam Woodall, "The New Titans," *The Economist*, September 16, 2006.

5. See A. Claire Cutler, "Critical Reflections on the Westphalian Assumptions of International Law and Organization: A Crisis of Legitimacy," *Review of International Studies* 27 (2001): 133–150. More directly on corporations and governance, see Dan Danielson, "How Corporations Govern: Taking Corporate Power Seriously in Transnational Regulation and Governance," *Harvard International Law Journal* 46, no. 2 (Summer 2005): 411–425; and Trade Union Advisory Committee and Committee on Workers' Capital, *Workers' Voice in Corporate Governance—A Trade Union Perspective. Global Unions Discussion Paper* (September 2005), at www.tuac.org/statemen/communiq/0512cgpaper.pdf (accessed April 6, 2006).

6. Jeff Gerth, "Where Business Rules: Forging Global Regulations That Put Industry First," *New York Times*, national edition, January 9, 1998, C1, C17. For a more comprehensive view, see John Braithwaite and Peter Drahos, *Global Business Regulation* (Cambridge: Cambridge University Press, 2000).

7. *Irish Times*, "Watering Down of EU Regulations on Chemicals Proves Power of Lobbyists," January 16, 2006, at www.alter-eu.org/IrishTimes20060116 (accessed June 7, 2006).

8. It is very important here to distinguish World Company Councils from what are often called World Works Councils—which we discuss later in this chapter. World Company Councils were and are union networks not recognized by the corporation; World Works Councils may vary in their composition, but the critical difference is that they are recognized by the corporation.

9. See Charles Levinson, *A Concrete Trade Union Response to the Multinational Company: ICF's Emerging Countervailing Power* (Geneva: ICF, 1974) and *International Trade Unionism* (London: Allen and Unwin, 1972). According to Dan Gallin's "Funeral Speech for Charles Levinson, January 26, 1997," at www.globallabour.org/levinson.htm (accessed March 21, 2006), Levinson (1920–1977) "served as Assistant Director at the European Office in Paris of the Congress of Industrial Organizations. . . . Between 1956 and 1964 he was Deputy General Secretary of the International Metalworkers' Federation. From 1964 to 1983 he was General Secretary of the International Chemical, Energy and General Workers' Federation, which now has become the ICEM."

10. The best explanation is that of the socialist internationalist commitments of Levinson and Dan Gallin, the IUF secretary general. As Gallin's funeral speech indicates (see note 9), he thought very highly of Levinson.

11. For discussions and comparisons, see Harvie Ramsay, "Solidarity at Last? International Trade Unionism Approaching the Millennium," *Economic and Industrial*

Democracy 18, no. 4 (1997): 503–537; Harvie Ramsay, "In Search of International Trade Union Theory," in *Globalization and Patterns of Labor Resistance*, ed. Jeremy Waddington (Los Altos, Calif.: Mansell, 1999), 192–239.

12. Levinson, *A Concrete Trade Union Response* and *International Trade Unionism*.

13. Werner Olle and Wolfgang Schoeller, "World Market Competition and Restrictions Upon International Trade Union Policy," *Capital and Class*, no. 2 (1977): 56–75.

14. While global unions politics can show many instances of heroic and imaginative acts of cross-border collaboration, they are mostly around specific corporations and unions.

15. See Herbert R. Northrup and Richard Rowan, *Multinational Collective Bargaining Attempts: The Record, the Cases and the Prospects*, Multinational Relations Series 6 (Philadelphia: Industrial Research Unit, The Wharton School, University of Pennsylvania, 1979). Then and now the interests of the Industrial Research Unit are more than academic as people working with it advise corporations on how to avoid or manage unions. Also see David Hershfield, *The Multinational Union Challenges the Multinational Company* (New York: Conference Board, 1975).

16. Northrup and Rowan, *Multinational Collective Bargaining Attempts*.

17. See Olle and Schoeller, "World Market Competition"; Nigel Haworth and Harvie Ramsay, "Workers of the World Untied: A Critical Analysis of the Labour Response to the Internationalization of Capital," *International Law of Sociology and Social Policy* 6, no. 2 (1986): 55–82; background interview.

18. The IUF and the member unions, however, were able to defeat the antilabor practices of Nestlé in 1979 and Coca-Cola in 1980 and 1984 through international campaigns.

19. This breakthrough owed much to the continuous efforts of the IUF but, also, to the specific characteristics of Danone. Antoine Riboud, the company's CEO, was actually pro-union and "sincerely and profoundly democratic." On Danone-IUF relations and the origins of early IUF agreements, see part 7 of Dan Gallin's interview with Peter Rütters, August 24–26, 2001, at www.globallabour.org/dan_interview.htm (accessed February 16, 2006). We follow standard practices and count the IUF-Danone agreements as one IFA.

20. Clive Crook, "The Good Company: A Survey of Corporate Social Responsibility," *The Economist*, January 22, 2005.

21. On earlier discussions of corporate social responsibility, in general, see Ans Kolk, Rob van Tulder, and Carlijn Welters, "International Codes of Conduct and Corporate Social Responsibility: Can Transnational Corporations Regulate Themselves?" *Transnational Corporations* 8, no. 1 (1999): 143–180; Rhys Jenkins, *Corporate Codes of Conduct: Self-Regulation in a Global Economy* (Geneva: United Nations Research Institute for Social Development, 2001). For the view of employers, see International Organization of Employers, *Codes of Conduct: Position Paper of the International Organisation of Employers* (Geneva: IOE, June 11, 1999). On corporate social responsibility and labor, see European Works Councils Bulletin, "Corporate Codes of Conduct and Industrial Relations—Part One," *European Works Councils Bulletin* 27 (May/June 2000): 11–16; European Works Councils Bulletin, "Corporate

Codes of Conduct and Industrial Relations—Part Two," *European Works Councils Bulletin* 28 (July/August 2000): 7–16; ILO, Bureau for Workers' Activities, *Corporate Social Responsibility: Myth or Reality?* Labour Education 130 (Geneva: ILO, Bureau for Workers' Activities, 2003), at www-ilomirror.cornell.edu/public/english/dialogue/actrav/publ/130/index.htm (accessed June 7, 2006).

22. See Jill Murray, *Corporate Codes of Conduct and Labour Standards* (Geneva: ILO, Bureau for Workers' Activities, 1998), at www-ilo-mirror.cornell.edu/public/english/dialogue/actrav/publ/codes.htm (accessed June 7, 2006).

23. For up-to-date information as well as historical background, visit www.ilo.org/public/english/employment/multi/history.htm (accessed June 7, 2006).

24. The Organization for Economic Cooperation and Development is an organization of the most industrial countries of the world, and it is another intergovernmental organization where unions have formal representation through the Trade Union Advisory Committee. For more information, see www.tuac.org (accessed June 13, 2006).

25. On OECD, see OECD, *Guidelines for Multinational Enterprises, Revision 2000* (Paris: OECD, 2000), at www.oecd.org/dataoecd/56/36/1922428.pdf (accessed June 7, 2006); for uses by unions, see Trade Union Advisory Committee, *The OECD Guidelines for Multinational Enterprises: TUAC Internal Analysis of Treatment of Cases Raised with National Contact Points, February 2001–February 2006*, at www.tuac.org/statemen/communiq/listofcasesFeb06.pdf (accessed June 7, 2006); background interview with TUAC personnel.

26. Jenkins, *Corporate Codes of Conduct*, 5.

27. Jenkins, *Corporate Codes of Conduct*, 6–8.

28. On corporate campaigns, see Labor Research Review, "No More Business as Usual: Labor's Corporate Campaigns," thematic issue, *Labor Research Review* 21 (1993); for a hostile view, see Jarol Manheim, *The Death of a Thousand Cuts: Corporate Campaigns and the Attack on the Corporation* (Mahwah, N.J.: Lawrence Erlbaum, 2001).

29. Manheim, *Death of a Thousand Cuts*, appendixes A and B. On various kinds of union campaigns, with examples, see ICFTU, *Trade Union Guide to Globalization*, 2nd ed. (Brussels: ICFTU, 2004), chapter 11.

30. See the Global Compact website at www.unglobalcompact.org (accessed June 7, 2006). Also see Harvard's Corporate Social Responsibility Initiative at www.ksg.harvard.edu/cbg/CSRI/ (accessed June 7, 2006). The two are related through John Ruggie, currently serving as the faculty chair for the Corporate Social Responsibility Initiative, who also served as "Assistant Secretary-general and chief adviser for strategic planning to United Nations Secretary-general Kofi Annan" from 1997–2001. In that capacity he played a key role in devising the Global Compact as a strategy for re-embedding liberalism at the global level.

31. Klaus Schwab and Claude Smadja, "Davos: mondialisation et reponsabilité sociale," *Le Monde*, July 17, 1996, 10. For more information on the World Economic Forum, visit www.weforum.org (accessed June 7, 2006).

32. Ever since, the ICFTU and the GUFs have sought to actively participate in the WEF. Since the launching of the World Social Forum in 2001, scheduled to overlap

with the WEF, union leaders have had to shuttle from one to the other. For a recent statement at the World Economic Forum, see ICFTU, "Labour's Role in Achieving the Creative Imperative: Statement of Labour Leaders to the World Economic Forum (Davos, 25–29 January 2006)," at www.icftu.org/displaydocument.asp?Index= 991223330&Language=EN (accessed June 7, 2006).

33. For background and up-to-date information, visit www.unglobalcompact .org/AboutTheGC/index.html (accessed June 7, 2006).

34. See Joint UN-ICFTU Statement on Global Compact, January 20, 2000, at www.icftu.org/displaydocument.asp?Index=991209381&Language=EN (accessed June 7, 2006).

35. Many in the business world disagree with this trend, however. See Crook, "The Good Company."

36. See Ingeborg Wick, *Workers' Tool or PR Ploy? A Guide to Codes of International Labour Practice*, 4th ed. (Bonn: Friedrich-Ebert-Stiftung, 2005). Also see American Center for International Labor Solidarity/AFL-CIO, *Justice for All: A Guide to Worker Rights in the Global Economy* (Washington, D.C.: American Center for International Labor Solidarity, 2003), chapter 7.

37. See ICFTU/ITS, *Basic Code of Labour Practice*, 1997, at www/icftu.org/ www/english/tncs/tncscode98.html (accessed March 30, 2006).

38. Global union organizations are well aware of this imbalance and quite concerned about it. See, for example, International Metalworkers' Federation, *Report of the Secretariat, 31st IMF World Congress, Vienna, Austria, May 22–26, 2005* (Geneva: International Metalworkers' Federation): 40–41.

39. One of the agreements covering a U.S. company—Chiquita—applies to operations outside of the United States. The Skanska–Hochtief/Turner agreement, however, is a significant development even though it involves a subsidiary of European companies. What makes it significant is that the framework agreements of the parent companies were leveraged to produce this agreement and that it is the first one to involve U.S. employers and U.S. unions directly.

40. We have reviewed nine such agreements, but there are probably more. Two of the nine extraterritorial agreements deal with Ford and GM subsidiaries in Europe. Along with a separate agreement involving General Electric, these three agreements are considered among the strongest ones, an aspect that offers hope that European industrial relations will spill beyond Europe. For more in discussing the positive scenarios, see European Industrial Relations Review, "Global Agreements—State of Play," *European Industrial Relations Review* 381 (October 2005): 14–18.

41. See European Industrial Relations Review, "EWCs Taking on a Bargaining Role?" *European Industrial Relations Review* 332 (2002): 24–27; and European Works Councils Bulletin, "GM, Ford and GE Cases Highlight EWC's Bargaining Role," *European Works Councils Bulletin* 56 (2005): 7–13.

42. International Organisation of Employers, *Annual Report, 2003* (Geneva: International Organisation of Employers, 2004), 7; italics in original.

43. For detailed information on who represents workers in IFAs, see Euan Gibb, *International Framework Agreements: Increasing the Effectiveness of Core Labour*

Standards, at www.global-labour.org/euan_gibb.htm (accessed June 8, 2006), particularly appendix 2, "Comparative Analysis of International Framework Agreements."

44. These tensions were apparent in a fall 2006 conference that was organized by one of the global union federations to discuss the global agreement strategy and that one of the authors attended.

45. See Dimitris Stevis and Terry Boswell, "International Framework Agreements: Opportunities and Challenges for Global Unionism," in *Global Unionism: Challenging Capital through Cross-Border Campaigns*, ed. Kate Bronfenbrenner (Ithaca, N.Y.: Cornell University Press, forthcoming).

46. International Labour Office, Working Party on the Social Dimension of Globalization, *Information Note on Corporate Social Responsibility and International Labour Standards*, GB.288/WP/SDG/3, 288th session (Geneva: ILO, 2003); also see Gibb, *International Framework Agreements*, appendix 2.

47. International Labour Office, *Information Note on Corporate Social Responsibility*.

48. Thomas Greven, "Transnational 'Corporate Campaigns': A Tool for Labour Unions in the Global Economy?" *International Journal of Comparative Labour and Industrial Relations* 19, no. 4 (Winter 2003): 495–513.

49. Interviews and observation suggest that councils can be an important asset but, also, that they may be more attached to their corporations than may be desirable from the point of view of broader global union politics.

50. One rationale for global agreements was that they would help unionization in the South. Yet, as a number of unionists have told us, many countries in the North, especially the United States, are as much of a problem. On the other hand, unions in some Southern countries, such as Brazil and South Africa, are in much better shape than some of their counterparts in the North.

51. See Jane Wills, "Bargaining for the Space to Organize in the Global Economy: A Review of the Accor-IUF Trade Union Rights Agreement," *Review of International Political Economy* 9, no. 4 (November 2002): 675–700; Lone Riisgaard, *The IUF/COLSIBA-CHIQUITA Framework Agreement: A Case Study*, International Labour Office, Working Paper 94 (Geneva: ILO, 2003), at www.ilo.org/public/english/employment/multi/download/wp94.pdf (accessed June 8, 2006); Gibb, *International Framework Agreements*; International Federation of Building and Wood Workers (IFBWW), *IFBWW Experiences with Global Company Agreements* (2004) at www.ifbww.org/files/global-agreements.pdf (accessed June 7, 2006); International Metalworkers' Federation, *Background to International Framework Agreements in the IMF*, 2006, at www.imfmetal.org/main/files/06081513541679/Background_document_english-final.pdf (accessed November 11, 2006); IG Metall, *Implementing and Monitoring an International Framework Agreement* (Frankfurt: IG Metall, 2006).

52. Information for this case comes from Eironline, "International Agreement on Restructuring at Danone Biscuits," *Eironline*, November 11, 2001, at www.eiro.eurofound.ie/search/search.php (accessed June 7, 2006); and "Globalisation Blamed for Restructuring at Danone and Marks & Spencer," *Eironline*, April 28, 2001, at www.eiro.eurofound.ie/2001/04/feature/fr0104147f.html (accessed June 7, 2006).

53. Wills, "Bargaining for the Space to Organize."

54. Riisgaard, *The IUF/COLSIBA-CHIQUITA Framework Agreement*.

55. See Robert Hickey, "Preserving the Pattern: PACE's Five-year Comprehensive Campaign at Crown Central Petroleum" (manuscript, 2004), 40–41; background interviews.

56. Gibb, *International Framework Agreements*.

57. "Carrefour and Korean Commerce Union Sign Collective Agreement," March 31, 2006, at www.union-network.org/unisite/sectors/commerce/Multinationals/Carrefour_Korea_collective_agreement_signed.htm (accessed June 7, 2006).

58. A fuller discussion of this dimension appears in Stevis and Boswell, "International Framework Agreements."

59. In a recent meeting on global agreements, representatives of Japanese unions argued that they are ready to sign them but that Japanese corporations would not do so if global union organizations were also signatories. Such a development can very well lead to segmentation along national lines.

60. GM helped develop the Sullivan Principles guiding corporate actions in South Africa during the latter part of the apartheid regime. The principles are totally voluntary.

61. The few sectoral agreements that exist are generally weaker than IFAs. These include agreements on the production of soccer balls, involving several global unions; agreements on child labor in the tobacco, cocoa, and chocolate sectors, involving IUF; and an agreement between the IFBWW (now BWI) and the Confederation of International Contractors' Associations. None of them are collective bargaining or particularly strong. While there may have been some instances of international collective bargaining in the past (not including Canada and the United States, where some unions are transnational), the only case presently involves the International Transport Workers' Federation (ITF), the most suprasocietal of GUFs. This started in a 2000 collective agreement between the seafarers' section of the ITF—the only one entitled to negotiate collective agreements—and the International Maritime Employers Committee. See Nathan Lillie, "Global Collective Bargaining on Flag of Convenience Shipping," *British Journal of Industrial Relations* 42, no. 1 (March 2004): 47–67. This agreement covered about 60,000 maritime workers. It is telling that the only collective agreement is by the most suprasocietal of global unions.

62. The ICEM's experience in the context of Responsible Care, "the chemical industry's global voluntary initiative under which companies, through their national associations, work together to continuously improve their health, safety and environmental performance" (see www.responsiblecare.org, accessed March 14, 2007) is indicative. In December 1997 the ICEM publicized a report criticizing the absence of worker involvement or even awareness of the initiative. In October 1998 ICEM signed an agreement with the World Chlorine Council. In early 1999 it also entered into ILO-facilitated discussions with the International Council of Chemical Associations (ICCA), which oversees the Responsible Care program. This led to a dialogue between ICCA and ICEM and to prospects of a fairly strong sectoral agreement. In April 2001 the ICEM announced that as a result of opposition by the American Chemical Council, particularly two specific U.S. corporations, no agreement could be reached. While some contacts continue, there is no imminent breakthrough (background interview).

63. The North American Agreement on Labor Cooperation is less inspiring. Developments at the level of Mercosur are worth following, as is collaboration at the hemispheric level as expressed by the *Labor's Platform for the Americas* (at www.gpn.org/research/orit2005/labour_platform_eng_web.pdf; accessed June 7, 2006). See American Center for International Labor Solidarity/AFL-CIO, *Justice for All*, chapter 4.

64. Labor Research Review, "No More Business as Usual"; Manheim, *Death of a Thousand Cuts*.

65. See Kate Bronfenbrenner and Tom Juravich, "The Evolution of Strategic and Coordinated Bargaining Campaigns in the 1990s: The Steelworkers' Experience," in *Rekindling the Movement: Labor's Quest of Relevance in the 21st Century*, ed. Lowell Turner, Harry C. Katz, and Richard W. Hurd (Ithaca, N.Y.: Cornell University Press, 1999), 211–237.

66. Workers can participate in corporate boards in a number of European Union countries and at the level of the European Union with respect to corporations incorporated through the European Company Statute. See Norbert Kluge and Michael Stolit, eds., *The European Company—Prospects for Worker Board-Level Participation in the Enlarged EU* (Brussels: Social Development Agency and European Trade Union Institute for Research, Education and Health and Safety, 2006). There are significant limitations to that participation, however, while this kind of involvement can also bring workers closer to the corporation rather than other workers.

67. See Trade Union Advisory Committee and Committee on Workers' Capital, *Workers' Voice in Corporate Governance*. For more information, see the website of the Committee on Workers' Capital at www.workerscapital.org/. The committee has been in existence since 1999 and is a collaborative project of ICFTU (now ITUC), the GUFs, and TUAC.

Conclusion: The Challenges of the Present

1. Jeremy Brecher, Tim Costello, and Brendan Smith, *Globalization from Below: The Power of Solidarity* (Cambridge, Mass.: South End Press, 2002).

2. On the proposal for a "super union," see "First Steps towards Creation of Global Super Union," at eurofound.europa.eu/eiro/2007/02/articles/eu0702019i.html (accessed March 15, 2007). For the SEIU proposal, see Stephen Lerner, "Global Unions: A Solution to Labor's Worldwide Decline," *New Labor Forum* 16, no. 1 (Winter 2007): 23–37.

3. Craig Benjamin and Terisa Turner, "Counterplanning from the Commons: Labour, Capital and the 'New Social Movements,'" *Labour, Capital and Society* 25, no. 2 (1992): 218–248; Daniel Drache, ed., *The Market and the Public Domain: Global Governance and the Asymmetry of Power* (New York: Routledge, 2001).

4. David Harvey, *Justice, Nature and the Geography of Difference* (Oxford: Blackwell, 1996), chapter 1.

5. Boaventura de Sousa Santos, *The Rise of the Global Left: The World Social Forum and Beyond* (London: Zed Books, 2006).

6. Richard Hyman, "Imagined Solidarities: Can Trade Unions Resist Globalization?" in *Globalization and Labour Relations*, ed. Peter Leisink (Cheltenham, UK: Edward Elgar, 1999).

7. Terry Boswell and Christopher Chase-Dunn, *The Spiral of Capitalism and Socialism: Toward Global Democracy* (Boulder, Colo.: Lynne Rienner, 2000).

SELECTED BIBLIOGRAPHY

American Center for International Labor Solidarity/AFL-CIO. *Justice for All: A Guide to Worker Rights in the Global Economy*. Washington, D.C.: American Center for International Labor Solidarity, 2003.

Bairoch, Paul. *Economics and World History: Myths and Paradoxes*. Chicago: University of Chicago Press, 1993.

Barnouin, Barbara. *The European Labour Movement and European Integration*. London: Frances Pinter, 1986.

Baylis, John, and Steve Smith, eds. *The Globalization of World Politics: An Introduction to International Relations*. 3rd ed. Oxford: Oxford University Press, 2005.

Berins Collier, Ruth, and David Collier. *Shaping the Political Arena: Critical Junctures, the Labor Movement, and Regime Dynamics in Latin America*. Princeton, N.J.: Princeton University Press, 1991.

Bhagwati, Jagdish, and Robert E. Hudec, eds. *Fair Trade and Harmonization: Prerequisites for Free Trade?* 2 vols. Cambridge, Mass.: MIT Press, 1997.

Boswell, Terry, and Christopher Chase-Dunn. *The Spiral of Capitalism and Socialism: Toward Global Democracy*. Boulder, Colo.: Lynne Rienner, 2000.

Boyd, Rosalind E., Robin Cohen, and Peter C. W. Gutkind, eds. *International Labour and the Third World: The Making of a New Working Class.* Aldershot, UK: Avebury, 1987.

Braithwaite, John, and Peter Drahos. *Global Business Regulation.* Cambridge: Cambridge University Press, 2000.

Braunthal, Julius. *History of the International, Volume 1: 1864–1914.* 1961. New York: Frederick A. Praeger, 1967.

Brecher, Jeremy, Tim Costello, and Brendan Smith. *Globalization from Below: The Power of Solidarity.* Cambridge, Mass.: South End Press, 2002.

Bronfenbrenner, Kate, and Tom Juravich. "The Evolution of Strategic and Coordinated Bargaining Campaigns in the 1990s: The Steelworkers' Experience." In *Rekindling the Movement: Labor's Quest of Relevance in the 21st Century,* edited by Lowell Turner, Harry C. Katz, and Richard W. Hurd, 211–237. Ithaca, N.Y.: Cornell University Press, 1999.

Bukharin, Nikolai. *Imperialism and World Economy.* 1917. New York: Monthly Review Press, 1973.

Charnovitz, Steve. "Two Centuries of Participation: NGOs and International Governance." *Michigan Journal of International Law* 18 (Winter 1997): 183–286.

Colás, Alejandro. *International Civil Society.* Cambridge: Polity Press / Blackwell Publishers, 2002.

Crook, Clive. "The Good Company: A Survey of Corporate Social Responsibility." *The Economist,* January 22, 2005.

Cutler, A. Claire, Virginia Haufler, and Tony Porter, eds. *Private Authority and International Affairs.* Albany: State University of New York Press, 1999.

de Sousa Santos, Boaventura. *The Rise of the Global Left: The World Social Forum and Beyond.* London: Zed Books, 2006.

Esping-Andersen, Gøsta. *The Three Worlds of Welfare Capitalism.* Princeton, N.J.: Princeton University Press, 1990.

Flanagan, Robert. *Globalization and Labor Conditions: Working Conditions and Worker Rights in a Global Economy.* New York: Oxford University Press, 2006.

Friedman, Elisabeth Jay, Kathryn Hochstetler, and Ann Marie Clark. *Sovereignty, Democracy, and Civil Society: State-Society Relations at UN World Conferences.* Albany: State University of New York Press, 2005.

Gompers, Samuel. *Seventy Years of Life and Labor: An Autobiography.* 1925. New York: E. P. Dutton, 1943.

Greven, Thomas. *Social Standards in Bilateral and Regional Trade and Investment Agreements: Instruments, Enforcement, and Policy Options for Trade Unions.* Friedrich-Ebert-Stiftung Dialogue on Globalization Occasional Papers 16. Geneva: Friedrich-Ebert-Stiftung, 2005.

Greven, Thomas. "Transnational 'Corporate Campaigns': A Tool for Labour Unions in the Global Economy?" *The International Journal of Comparative Labour and Industrial Relations* 19, no. 4 (Winter 2003): 495–513.

Harrod, Jeffrey, and Robert O'Brien, eds. *Global Unions? Theory and Strategies of Organized Labour in the Global Political Economy.* London: Routledge, 2002.

Held, David, Anthony McGrew, David Goldblatt, and Jonathan Perraton. *Global Transformations*. Stanford, Calif.: Stanford University Press, 1999.

Held, David, and Anthony McGrew, eds. *The Global Transformations Reader: An Introduction to the Globalization Debate*. 2nd ed. Cambridge: Polity Press, 2003.

Hewson, Martin, and Timothy Sinclair, eds. *Approaches to Global Governance Theory*. Albany: State University of New York Press, 1999.

Hirst, Paul, and Grahame Thompson. *Globalization in Question*. 2nd ed. Cambridge: Polity Press, 1999.

Hobsbawm, Eric. *The Age of Extremes: A History of the World, 1914–1991*. New York: Vintage Books, 1996.

Holm, B. Hans-Henrik, and Georg Sorensen, eds. *Whose World Order? Uneven Globalization and the End of the Cold War*. Boulder, Colo.: Westview, 1995.

International Confederation of Free Trade Unions (ICFTU). *Fighting for Alternatives: Cases of Successful Trade Union Resistance to the Policies of the IMF and the World Bank*. Brussels: ICFTU, 2006.

International Confederation of Free Trade Unions (ICFTU). *Trade Union Guide to Globalization*. 2nd ed. Brussels: ICFTU, 2004.

Labor Research Review. "No More Business as Usual: Labor's Corporate Campaigns." Thematic issue, *Labor Research Review* 21 (1993).

Leary, Virginia, and Danier Warner, eds. *Social Issues, Globalisation and International Institutions: Labour Rights and the EU, ILO, OECD and WTO*. Leiden: Martinus Nijhoff, 2006.

Levinson, Charles. *International Trade Unionism*. London: Allen and Unwin, 1972.

Lorwin, Lewis L. *Labor and Internationalism*. New York: Macmillan, 1929.

Manheim, Jarol. *The Death of a Thousand Cuts: Corporate Campaigns and the Attack on the Corporation*. Mahwah, N.J.: Lawrence Erlbaum, 2001.

Milner, Susan. *The Dilemmas of Internationalism: French Syndicalism and the International Labour Movement, 1900–1914*. New York: Berg, 1990.

Mittelman, James, ed. *Globalization: Critical Reflections*. Boulder, Colo.: Lynne Rienner, 1996.

Munck, Ronaldo. *Globalisation and Labour: The New 'Great Transformation.'* London: Zed Books, 2002.

Munck, Ronaldo, and Barry Gills, eds. "Globalization and Democracy." *Annals of the American Academy of Political and Social Science* 581 (May 2002).

O'Brien, Robert, Anne Marie Goetz, Jan Aart Scholte, and Marc Williams. *Contesting Global Governance: Multilateral Economic Institutions and Global Social Movements*. Cambridge: Cambridge University Press, 2000.

Polanyi, Karl. *The Great Transformation: The Political and Economic Origins of Our Time*. 1944. Boston: Beacon, 1957.

Prakash, Aseem, and Jeffrey Hart, eds. *Globalization and Governance*. London: Routledge, 1999.

Reinicke, Wolfgang. *Global Public Policy: Governing Without Government?* Washington, D.C.: Brookings Institution Press, 1998.

Rieger, Elmar, and Stephan Leibfried. *Limits to Globalization*. Cambridge: Polity Press, 2003.

Sengenberger, Werner. *Globalization and Social Progress: The Role and Impact of International Labor Standards*. 2nd ed. Bonn: Friedrich-Ebert-Stiftung, 2005.

Silver, Beverly. *Forces of Labor: Workers' Movements and Globalization since 1870*. New York: Cambridge University Press, 2003.

Smith, Jackie, C. Chatfield, and Ron Pagnucco, eds. *Transnational Social Movements and Global Politics: Solidarity Beyond the State*. Syracuse, N.Y.: Syracuse University Press, 1997.

Southall, Roger, ed. *Trade Unions and the New Industrialization of the Third World*. London: Zed Books, 1988.

Steger, Manfred. *Globalism: Market Ideology Meets Terrorism*. 2nd ed. Lanham, Md.: Rowman & Littlefield, 2005.

Thorpe, Wayne. *'The Workers Themselves': Revolutionary Syndicalism and International Labour, 1913–1923*. Dordrecht: Kluwer Academic Publishers / International Institute of Social History, 1989.

Trade Union Advisory Committee and Committee on Workers' Capital. *Workers' Voice in Corporate Governance—A Trade Union Perspective*. 2005. At www.tuac.org/statemen/communiq/0512cgpaper.pdf (accessed November 7, 2006).

Tsogas, George. *Labor Regulation in a Global Economy*. Armonk, N.Y.: M.E. Sharpe, 2001.

U.S. Department of Labor. Bureau of Labor Statistics. Bulletin 268, *Historical Survey of International Action Affecting Labor*. Washington, D.C.: Government Printing Office, 1920.

van der Linden, Marcel, ed. *The International Confederation of Free Trade Unions*. Bern: Peter Lang, 2000.

van Holthoon, Frits, and Marcel van der Linden, eds. *Internationalism in the Labour Movement, 1830–1940*. Leiden: E.J. Brill, 1988.

van Roozendaal, Gerda. *Trade Unions and Global Governance: The Debate on a Social Clause*. London: Continuum, 2002.

Waterman, Peter. *Globalization, Social Movements and the New Internationalisms*. Rev. ed. London: Continuum, 2001.

Waterman, Peter, and Jane Wills, eds. "Space, Place and the New Labour Internationalisms." Thematic issue, *Antipode* 33, no. 3 (2001).

Wick, Ingeborg. *Workers' Tool or PR Ploy? A Guide to Codes of International Labour Practice*. 4th ed. Bonn: Friedrich-Ebert-Stiftung, 2005.

Wilkinson, Rorden. *Multilateralism and the World Trade Organization: The Architecture and Extension of International Trade Regulation*. London: Routledge, 2000.

Windmuller, John. *American Labor and the International Labor Movement 1940 to 1953*. Ithaca, N.Y.: Cornell University Press, 1954.

INDEX

corporate social responsibility as a form of, 110–22; in dynamic in teraction with global public governance, 114; key dates in global private labor governance, 117; limitations of democratic potential of, 139–40; multinational corporations and, 114–16; union goals and strategies toward, 5, 150–52. *See also* corporate social responsibility; global governance; IFAs; multinational corporations

global public governance, 39, 71, 79, 147–50; challenges to, 103–7; in dynamic interaction with global private governance, 114; global economic organizations and, 89–90; ILO and, 84–89; key dates in global public governance and, 81; multinational corporations' influence on, 116; union goals and strategies toward, 5, 80, 148–50. *See also* global economic organizations; global governance; global labor regulation; global private governance; ILO; state; WTO

global societal politics, 27, 30, 31–37, 147, 152; analytical scheme for, 31; characteristics of, 32–33; clarified, 164n3; effectiveness of, 31–33, 40, 42–43; global democracy and, 30, 37; global governance and, 40–43; global union politics as case of, 4, 27; from inequality to equality, 35–37; from particularism to cosmopolitanism, 35–37; political economy perspective of, 4, 30, 33–39; societal organizations and, 31–33, 164n8, 164n14, 165n10, 165n12; strategies and tactics of, 40–42; worldviews of, 33–37. *See also* global democracy; global union organizations; worldviews

global union federations, 45, 47, 49, 71, 73, 74; collaboration with ITUC, 72, 138; and content of IFAs, 125–28; and future of IFAs, 133, 136, 140; and impacts of IFAs, 128–32; and origins of IFAs, 112, 117–19, 128, 139; participation in IFAs, 125, 140; worldviews of, 74, 139. *See also* global union organizations; IFAs; ITUC

global union governance. *See* global union organizations

global union organizations: AFL and, 55, 56, 58, 61, 63, 64, 65; AFL-CIO and, 64–65, 67–70, 72, 94, 102, 118, 131, 163n59, 175n65, 176n77, 177n82; anarchism and, 52, 55, 56, 170n20; British unions and, 55, 56, 58, 64, 65, 70, 172n40, 175n65; capacities of, 50–51, 63, 69, 72, 176n80; capital and, 48, 50, 52, 56; challenges to, 21–26, 53, 76–77; Christian unionism and, 49, 63, 65, 67, 175n68; Cold War and, 62–65; communism and, 59–60, 61, 65, 75, 169n17, 173n49, 176n81; Congress of Industrial Organizations and, 58–59, 145, 172n41; constituencies and membership of, 50–51, 55–56, 60, 64–65, 69–70, 74–75, 146–47; core labor rules and, 86, 91–94, 95, 98, 100, 107–8, 120, 126, 138; corporate governance and, 138, 152; corporate social responsibility, concerns about, 122; democratization of global governance and, 3, 5, 147–52; effectiveness of, 108–9, 140–41; formation of, 50–51, 53, 55, 59, 62, 68; German unions and, 50, 54–55, 195n65; Global Compact and, 122; global economic organizations and, 89–99, 103, 108; global financial organizations and, 96–99; global

governance and, 2–3, 10, 76–77, 80,
90, 97, 103, 108–9, 143–44, 145,
150; globalization and, 71, 76; global
justice movement and, 3, 5, 152–55;
global political economy, influences
on, 50, 52–53, 57–58, 62, 66–67, 71,
76; global private governance and, 3,
5, 71, 103, 112, 138, 139–41,
150–52; global public governance, 3,
5, 71, 79–80, 107–9, 147–50; and
global union governance, 2–3, 5, 46,
49, 72–74, 76–77, 80, 102, 108, 112,
140–41, 144–47; and IFAs, 117–19,
132–36, 189n38; and ILO, 58, 84–88,
108, 182n54; International Secretariat
of National Trade Union Centers, 55;
Japanese Trade Union Confederation
and, 68; list of existing, 47;
multinational corporations and, 66,
71, 112–13, 117–19, 124–41, 150–52;
multipolarity in, 48, 67–71; need for
stronger, 69–70, 76–77, 104, 140–41,
144–46, 150; periods in history of,
48; reasons for focus on, 3–4, 46; Red
International of Labor Unions, 59,
60, 173n49; regionalism and, 38–39,
61, 64–65, 67–68, 72, 73, 105–6,
177nn82–83; social clause and,
24–26, 86, 91–94, 107–8, 178n3;
social democracy's influence on,
53–54, 58, 59, 62, 166n22, 169n17;
South and, 25–26, 60, 64–65,
175n68; Southern unions and, 68, 70,
72–74, 75; state and, 48, 52, 62, 66,
71, 79, 154–55; strategy and tactics
of, 149–50; "super unions" and,
145–46; syndicalism and, 170n20,
173n45; trade unionism and, 5, 10,
51–52, 54–57, 59, 65; unification of,
45–46, 72–77, 144, 176n79, 177n90;
World Economic Forum and, 41,
188n32; World Social Forum and, 41,
188n32; worldviews of, 51–52, 53,
56–57, 60–62, 65, 68, 70–71, 75–76,

108–9, 139, 147, 152–55; WTO and,
1, 24–26, 29, 42, 79, 90–96, 182n54.
See also First International; global
union federations; ICFTU; IFTU;
international trade secretariats; ITUC;
World Confederation of Labour;
World Federation of Trade Unions;
worldviews
global union politics. *See* global union
organizations

ICFTU (International Confederation of
Free Trade Unions), 45–46, 63–65,
67–69, 77, 86, 121–22, 138, 176n79,
188n32; and global public governance, 107–9; relations with
international trade secretariats, 49,
64; social clause and, 92–96, 100,
107, 139; unification with WCL and
others, 72–76. *See also* global union
federations; global union
organizations; global union politics;
international trade secretariats
IFAs (International Framework
Agreements), 5, 112–13, 117–23,
124, 125–32, 150–52, 190n50;
alternatives to, 191nn61–62; beyond
framework agreements, 131, 132–39;
campaigns and, 136–38; compared to
codes of conduct, 126, 140; content
of, 125–28; corporate social
responsibility and the emergence of,
5, 119–22, 187n19; coverage of, 126,
189n39; European industrial relations
and the emergence of, 122–24;
European industrial relations and the
future of, 135–36; evaluation of,
139–41, 150–51; global union
federation participation in, 112–13,
139–40; global union organization
strategies and the emergence of,
117–19; impacts of, 128–32;
institutionalization of, 127–28; list of,
112–13; and the need for public

relations with, 49, 72, 138; India and, 74; regionalism in, 73; Southern unions in, 72–73; WTO and, 182n54

Japanese Trade Union Confederation, 68

labor rights. *See* core labor rights
labor rules. *See* core labor rules
labor standards. *See* core labor standards
labor-trade linkage. *See* core labor rights; core labor rules; core labor standards; social clause

Mexican unions, 22, 101, 106, 149, 162n48
multilateralism, 165n15; U.S. approach to, 9, 158n3
multinational corporations: brief history of, 114–16; exercise of global governance by, 71, 114–16; Global Compact and, 121–22; global union organizations and, 34, 61, 65, 70, 75, 94, 150–52; ILO and, 88, 120; need of global governance for, 38, 138; Organization for Economic Cooperation and Development and, 35, 120, 138. *See also* corporate social responsibility; global private governance; IFAs
multistakeholder approach, 165n15

national governance. *See* global governance
nationalism: differences from nativism, 33–34, 164n6; particularism and, 33–34. *See also* global societal politics; global union politics; worldviews
nationalization. *See* globalization
North-South politics, 174n63; challenges of equity and, 25–26, 181n31; challenges of pace and, 21–23; class divisions and, 181n31; global economic organizations and, 7, 15–17, 89–90,

92–93, 103, 161n37, 186n3; global union politics and, 68, 69–70, 93, 96, 103; multipolarity and, 69–70

OECD (Organization for Economic Cooperation and Development), 35, 188n24
Organization for Economic Cooperation and Development (OECD), 35, 188n24

particularism, 33–34, 153. *See also* global justice movement; global societal politics; worldviews

Red International of Labor Unions (RILU), 59, 60, 173n49
regional governance. *See* global governance
regionalization. *See* globalization
RILU (Red International of Labor Unions), 59, 60, 173n49

Second International, 53–58. *See also* global union politics
social clause, 24–26, 90, 92, 95–96, 99–102, 163n59, 178n3; AFL-CIO and, 91; content of, 95–96; debates over social-clause strategy, 99–102; employers, 95–96; European Union, 92–93; evaluating the, 99–102; ILO and, 90, 92, 93, 94; Southern views on, 93, 100–101; U.S. and, 91–92, 101–2; WTO and, 24–26, 79, 90–96. *See also* core labor rights; core labor standards; global labor regulation; global union organizations
social democracy, 166n22, 169n17
socialism, 166n22, 169n17
social movement unionism, 68, 70
societal politics, effect on global governance, 40, 42–43. *See also* global democracy; global governance; global societal politics; worldviews

ABOUT THE AUTHORS

Terry Boswell (1955–2006) passed away due to complications of amyotrophic lateral sclerosis (ALS) on June 1, 2006. At the time, he was a professor in Emory University's Department of Sociology, where he had worked for twenty-two years and which he had chaired. He left behind an influential body of work in the areas of stratification and labor markets, global labor politics, revolutions, and the political economy of the world system. Throughout his life, Terry was able to collaborate productively with many people while using a breadth of methods and evidence. His *The Spiral of Capitalism and Socialism: Toward Global Democracy* (with Christopher Chase-Dunn) was a winner of the Outstanding Book Award for 2001 given by the American Sociological Association's Section on Political Economy of the World-System. Most importantly, Terry's research and life were motivated by a commitment to making a more democratic world possible.

Dimitris Stevis is professor in the Department of Political Science at Colorado State University. His areas of teaching and research are in global political economy and social regulation with emphases on global labor and environmental politics, issues that carry both theoretical and practical significance for him. He is currently researching the role of unions in regulating global capital and their attempts at integrating environmental priorities into their practice. He recently coedited *Palgrave Advances in International Environmental Politics* and has published a variety of items on global labor and environmental politics.